A Walk Across Florida

**A First Of Its Kind
A Hiking Adventure From Georgia
To Key West, Florida
By Bob Kranich**

Layout, Drawings and Photography
By Bob Kranich

Edited by Joanne Kranich

Published by: Bob Kranich
White Post, Virginia

Copyright 2015 by Bob Kranich

All rights reserved. No part of this book may be reproduced
in any form or by any means
without permission in writing from Bob Kranich.

Book design by Bob Kranich

Published by:
Bob Kranich
White Post, Va.

Printed in the United States of America

Publisher's Cataloging-in-Publication-Data
Kranich, Bob
A Walk across Florida: a first of its kind, a hiking adventure
from Georgia to Key West, Florida / by Bob Kranich
p. cm.
ISBN 978-0-9716515-9-3
1. Hiking —Florida. 2. Outdoor recreation —Florida.
3. Trails —Florida. 4. Natural history —Florida. 5. Natural areas —Florida.
6. Florida —Description and travel. I. Title.

GV199.42.F6 K73 2015
917.59 —dc23
2015911528

First Paperback Edition

*This book is dedicated to
my immediate family:
Sisters and Brothers: Denise, Jackie, David, Danny
Children: Stephanie, Richard, Matthew, Carrie, Harold
Grandchildren: Heaven, Madyson, James, Parker, Sebastian*

Table of Contents

Acknowledgements vii

Introduction ix

1 Lake City 2

2 How Did This All Get Started? 8

3 Equipment Preparation 11

4 Going North to Go South 18

5 Big Pine Country 24

6 Osceola National Forest 35

7 Oulstee Battlefield Historic State Park 48

8 Camp Blanding
    and Mike Roess Gold Head Branch State Park 54

9 Cross-Florida Barge Canal 72

10 Ocala National Forest 84

11 Bypassing Orlando 104

12 Kissimmee Cooperative Bald Eagle Sanctuary 118

13 Okeechobee, City and Lake 148

14 Brighton Seminole Indian Reservation 158

15 Hoover Dike and Clewiston Sugar 172

16 Devils Garden and Seminole Country 192

17 Big Cypress Swamp and the Everglades 200

18 Tamiami Trail 214

Table of Contents, Continued

19 Homestead and Florida City..................................234

20 The Hike That Went To Sea....................................242

21 Keys At Last!..248

22 Flagler's Monumental Bridges............................270

23 Key West On My Horizon......................................284

Acknowledgements

I am greatly indebted to my Uncle Norman and Aunt Dolores. They were my final destination in my hike across Florida. They welcomed me into their home for an entire month. They were so pleasant and helpful as I explored Key West with the bicycle they had rented for me. My uncle was always concerned for all his nieces and nephews. He always had some very excellent advice for all of us children. My aunt was a sincerely enthusiastic person to be around. She had that slight German accent and I can't forget ….she was a fantastic cook!

I have to thank Boy Scout troops in both Wisconsin and Florida for my camping and hiking experience. I can only remember the scoutmaster of my last troop in Drew Park, Tampa, Florida. Thank you Mr. George Winton. He was a volunteer who was dedicated to youth.

Then there is the book that really got me fired up, Colin Fletcher's *The Thousand Mile Summer*. In his book he tells about his walk in 1958 through California along the east side of the High Sierra mountains from the Mexican border to Oregon. I also read his second book *The Complete Walker*. It came out in 1968.

The U.S. Army deserves some credit. They drafted me in January of 1966. After training me, they sent me to South Korea. There I met my friend and army buddy, Ed. We would hike the hills of Korea following the dirt pathways and trails. Many nights after we missed the Army bus we would walk the 10 miles back to our base. It was only a one lane dirt road between the dark high looming mountain shadows on one side and a river valley on the other. All these adventures helped to whet my appetite for hiking.

Of special note, I would like to thank Charlotte and Ed Osterman for their final review. Charlotte lent her PHD in English to this endeavor. Their comments were rewarding and helpful.

Lastly, I would like to thank my wife and my editor. She never tired of encouraging me and telling me how excited she was that I was telling this story. Thanks Joanne! I love you!

Bob

Introduction

It was a strange circumstance that finally sent me off on telling the story of my hike across Florida. I was working on a project and it came to a screeching halt. I was trying to figure out what I would start next and then I remembered, hey it's about time that I tell the story of my Florida hike! My kids, family and grandchildren would hopefully enjoy it.

I rummaged around the basement and found a battered briefcase wrapped up in a sealed plastic bag. I pried opened the case and there it was...all the materials that I had saved from 1969! My diary (a spiral stenographer's pad) written on front and back, six rolls of developed and printed film (two color and 4 black and white), the U. S. Geological Survey full-color topographic maps that I had cut down to fit both my route and a plastic waterproof tube, and my two sketch pads. There were also a bunch of brochures and various hike–related keepsakes.

The prints of the film were faded. I wondered if anyone still made prints from film? I started calling around. Now I live near a somewhat small town near Winchester, Virginia and there were, as to be expected, no custom photo labs. So I thought, let's give it a try. I dialed the photo department of my local Stephens City Walgreen's drug store. "We sure do," a clerk said. They reprinted my rolls of 2 color and 4 black and white film. They looked good! Now I was in business and the rest of the story is this book!

Bob

As an afterthought, as I have written this book and relived my travel and adventures, I am very impressed by the many people who befriended me... from the many rides that were offered and had to be turned down, to the people who gave me water, food and in so many cases just talk. Isn't the human spirit grand!

I also must say that I didn't know it then, but I know now, the Lord had His angels watching over me during the entire journey. I wish to deeply thank Him for it!

Map compiled by the U.S. Geological Survey 2001, printed 2002
From: Perry-Castaneda Library Map Collection.
"Courtesy of the University of Texas Libraries,
The University of Texas at Austin"
www.lib.utexas.edu/maps/florida.html

1
Lake City

"Lake City, we'll be there in ten minutes."

I was jarred awake by the bus driver's announcement.

We took the ramp off Interstate 75, stopped, and turned right...taking off with a roar. I looked around. It was dark inside except for the faint glow from a few instrument lights on the driver's dash board. A couple of passengers were starting to stir. I could hear the rustle of packages. Not many had got on board back at Tampa. Looking out the window, Lake City, Florida was very dark, only an occasional dim street light. We pulled into a small station and parked. There was that sudden sound...ssswiisshh, the air brakes make as the driver shut it down.

I followed a couple of people down the aisle and then the steps. I immediately noticed the dampness in the air. The fog was being cut by the yellow light of two downward facing street lamps over the combination waiting room, snack bar and ticket counter. There were bugs flying around buzzing and bumping into the two lights in an attraction craze. It appeared that three busses had converged here simultaneously. Because of that there were a few more customers here than at the Tampa station. I had left at 12 AM. I glanced up at a clock over the door. It was 4:05 AM. We had made very good time. My driver unloaded a few pieces of luggage and some newspapers, and before I could get his attention, he went inside.

Where is my pack? The bus was not going to leave until I got it! I could see through the window, while I guarded the bus, that my driver was talking to his fellow drivers, leaning on the food counter and drinking a cup of coffee. In a few minutes he came out and stood by the door of his bus. I made my move, armed with my baggage claim check.

He was surprised, "They didn't say anything about it in

I looked fresh with my clean clothes, new pack and equipment back home in Tampa. There would be a lot to learn on the trail ahead!

Tampa!" he exclaimed.

We went over to the outside center of the bus. He reached down and turned a handle which opened the compartment. He pulled the door up. I could see in.

"There!" I proclaimed, as I pointed to my new red pack.

He pulled it out, set it on the sidewalk, and took my claim check.

To the amazement of all, I slipped it on, and headed down the street towards the bus line's competitor, a few blocks away. I noticed that there was only one other business open at this time of night. A gas station on the corner was all lit up but no one seemed to be moving about.

The dampness was now turning into a misty fog and it floated down and reflected in the occasional street lights. It was pretty in an eerie sort of way. I shivered. It was getting real cool!

There it was. The small bus station had only one night light and an old baggage cart out front. Faded, chipped paint, iron wheels...even so, I knew that the cart's wooden bottom would be easier and somewhat softer to sit on than the concrete curb. It wasn't long before just sitting there, inactive, brought a chill clear through to my bones. Shivering, I zipped open the bottom flap of my pack, dug into the clothing part, and brought out my hooded cotton sweatshirt.

Still sitting there, I now started to process my situation. Lake City was 32 miles south of the Georgia border. I had ridden up here mostly on I-75 from Tampa. Occasionally the bus would go over to 441/41 which sometimes paralleled I-75 to stop at a town. From here the Greyhound I had been on would resume its travels, but instead of going north, it would change direction and take highway 41 northwest to Valdosta, Georgia. I needed to go north on 441 to the Georgia border, which brings me to what I was doing at this Trailways bus station. This system had a bus that went straight up 441 north. This was the way I needed to go to get to the border.

So here I sat, 5 AM and nothing happening.

The bus station wasn't even open!

I wandered over to the lit-up gas station. An attendant was inside at the desk, head on his hands.

"Sir, what time does the bus station across the street open?"

"Not until 6 o'clock this morning," he said, looking up sleepy-eyed.

I went back to the Trailways station, sat down on the

Lake City, Fla.
Bus Station
April 1969   Bob Kranich

Lake City Greyhound Bus Station. Early morning April 1st, 1969.

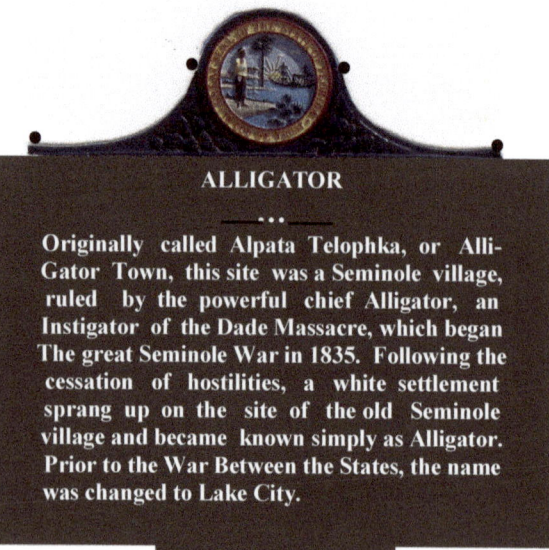

ALIGATOR

Originally called Alpata Telophka, or Alli-Gator Town, this site was a Seminole village, ruled by the powerful chief Alligator, an Instigator of the Dade Massacre, which began The great Seminole War in 1835. Following the cessation of hostilities, a white settlement sprang up on the site of the old Seminole village and became known simply as Alligator. Prior to the War Between the States, the name was changed to Lake City.

Florida Board of Parks and Historical Memorials. Park on north side of Lake City.

cart, took a snack from my pack, ate it and then laid down. I'm sure I looked like an old tramp sleeping there on that cart.

I drifted off. (I had hoped no one would come by and hit me over the head!)

I was awakened by a car's headlights and the crunchy sound of the gravel in the drive. As I sat up and rubbed the sleep from my eyes, I noticed that there was no let-up in the fog. In fact it had become worse!

"I'm sorry sir," the newly arrived attendant said, "the next bus won't be until 2 o' clock this afternoon! How about a cup of coffee?"

"No thank you ma'am, I guess I had better be going."

I had been here long enough. I'm not going to wait another 8 hours! I would try to use the educated thumb as I headed north through the town. It sure was deserted. There were only ghostly outlines of the buildings. They loomed up on either side of me as the fog drifted about.

I soon came to a quaint city park and decided I needed to take a break. I sat down on a park bench and while resting I saw one of those historic markers, (you know, the cast aluminum ones). It stated: "Lake City was the site of a Seminole village named *Alpata Telophka,* meaning *Alligator Town*. It was named after and ruled by the powerful Chief Alligator. By 1830, a Euro-American town called Alligator was established, adjacent to the Seminole town. In 1859 the town was incorporated and the name was changed to Lake City."

I continued north up highway 441. I tried my thumb, but was turned down by the occasional speeding vehicle. I had been walking for a little more than an hour now. It was getting a bit lighter but the fog was still thick. Ghostly outlines of the trees with Spanish moss hanging down from their limbs made it kind of spooky!

I started thinking, here I am going north so I can go south! And think about it.....it's April first. Maybe I was the April fool! As I walked along I started reviewing all the events of the last month.

Just how did this all get started?

11 MAR. 69

GENTLEMEN,

 I AM INTERESTED IN OBTAINING INFORMATION ON THE FLORIDA TRAIL. I WOULD NEED AVAILABLE CONDENSED MAP SUITABLE TO CARRY ON A HIKE THE ENTIRE LENGTH, IF SUCH IS AVAILABLE, OR ANY OTHER INFORMATION YOU WOULD FEEL THAT WOULD BE HELPFUL TO ME IN THIS VENTURE.
 MAPS AND INFORMATION MAY BE SENT "COD".

    THANK YOU,

    Robert E. Kranich
    ROBERT E. KRANICH
    4702 N. LOIS AVE.
    TAMPA, FLORIDA
      33614

Bob's letter to the Florida Trail Association. As you can see by the date, 11 March 69, that April first, which was the date Bob was going to start on his hike was fast approaching.

2
How Did This All This Get Started?

That sure was an interesting adventure, I thought to myself. I had just finished reading Colin Fletcher's book* *The Thousand Mile Summer*. In it he tells of his 6 month backpack trip across the entire state of California, from the Mexican border to Oregon along the east side of the High Sierra.

Imagine what it would be like to go on a hike like that! The names Colorado River, Death Valley and the High Sierra brought excitement to my thoughts.

I had just started some serious backpacking myself last fall with two different hikes. One was a week in the Smoky Mountains National Park, from Deep Creek campground, North Carolina, up to Clingman's Dome and Silars Bald, both on the Appalachian Trail, and then return (40+ miles). The other was another week's hike from the Appalachian Trail in the Shenandoah National Park, Virginia, down through the Shenandoah Valley over Massanutten mountain on 675. It took me up through the Shenandoah valley along the North Fork of the Shenandoah river and Highway 11, around Strasburg and back up the Appalachian Trail at Front Royal to where I had started (80+ miles).

My training and interest were gleaned from two sources. The earliest was from the Boy Scouting skills I learned by camping and hiking in my teen years. The most recent experience was in 1967. It was the second year after I was drafted into the U. S. Army that I spent in South Korea. There were few paved roads and mostly paths and trails going over the low mountains from village to village. On weekends my army buddy Ed and I used to spend hours hiking these trails exploring. The experience was extremely rewarding and aroused my interest in formal hiking.

Then, as if it was destined to be, the very next Sunday, the Tampa Tribune featured an article in its magazine section

FLORIDA TRAIL ASSOCIATION, INC.
33 S. W. 18th Terrace • Miami, Florida 33129

Mr. Robert E. Kranich
4702 N. Lois Ave.
Tampa, Fla. 33614

When Bob got home this letter was waiting for him (check date on envelope, 12 June, 1969) Later he came across the Florida Trail twice during the hike and made use of it, (mostly in Ocala National Forest). Apologies accepted. (Florida Trail info in reference section)

FLORIDA TRAIL ASSOCIATION, INC.

33 S. W. 18th Terrace   Miami, Florida 33129

JAMES A. KERN
President

Dear Mr. Kranich:

    Your note, which I am enclosing, was just discovered among some things to be filed. I wonder if we ever replied to you.

    If not, the enclosures may be helpful including the letter we send to our new members.

    If apologies are in order, please accept them.

Sincerely yours,

James A. Kern

entitled: *The Florida Trail.* The story said that in years to come, this trail association would have a foot path from Everglades City north through the center of the state and around the panhandle to Panama City. The trail would traverse the three National forests: Ocala, Osceola and Appalachicola.

This trail could some day link up with the Appalachian Trail, if Georgia were to provide the missing link.

Years to come! I had better get a letter off, right now, to see how much is completed! The more I thought about it, the more I wanted to be the first to hike across my state, from Georgia to Key West!

I got the letter written and mailed. I had to get started because I had a lot to do to get ready.

I was between jobs and had not received a call or reply to the resumes I had sent out. My occupation was contract drafting and design. I worked temporary jobs around the country helping employers out of a jam when they had a deadline to meet.

I made myself a promise. I would get my hiking equipment ready and if I didn't get any job offer, I would backpack across Florida.

3
Equipment Preparation

I needed to upgrade most of my backpacking gear, or at least the major items. The pack I had was an old army surplus ski pack I had bought from a buddy. Its frame bent snuggly around the waist and there were no provisions for a hip belt to transfer the load to hips and legs. I'm sure these were designed to keep the load low for balance. My sleeping bag was cheap and inefficient.

As luck would have it, the very next day I found out that an outfitter in St. Petersburg, Florida, "Bill Jackson's," was having a sale. I started up my trusty 1958 Ford Ranchero pickup and went around Tampa Bay and over to St. Pete.

The red nylon Camp Trails pack complete with hip pad and belt was four dollars cheaper than catalog price! He also had down sleeping bags in stock and for 50 dollars more I was the proud owner of a very nice down bag. I must have spent most of the day in there but only bought a few choice items. It always has taken me quite a while to decide, going back and forth between brands, balancing their advantages and disadvantages. I couldn't forget to consider weight as an important factor. I was fortunate that a few of my original accessories had worked out favorably on my two prior hikes in the Smokies and the Shenandoah Parks.

When I got home, I thought the red nylon pack sure looked good on the frame. I was like a kid with a brand new toy trying the sleeping bag out on the living room floor. My parents were humoring me in the background.

My shelter was next. On my other hikes I had shied away from those expensive nylon super-tents. I liked the feel of being outside to enjoy my surroundings. I had used a 6' x 8' black plastic tarp. This together with added grommets and 1/8" x 500 lb. test nylon cord was an inexpensive method to work as a lightweight lean-to. If it rains and you choose a good drained site, you just drop the roof to keep dry.

But I had a different problem. I was going to hike across Florida. I had never seen an alligator or cotton-mouthed moccasin snake and I contemplated sleeping on the ground with them. No, I didn't think so! I went to a local Tampa army surplus store to look around. There I found just what I was looking for; a lightweight, cheap (only 4 dollars) cotton-canvas small hammock. This would be a new camping experience for me. It would be an experiment that only time and use would successfully prove out.

I bought one more item there, a one quart steel army-surplus canteen. This kind fits into a big metal cup with a folding handle and then into a canvas cover and holder. It had the date 1945 stamped on it. I felt that the steel, even though it might be a little heavier, would keep liquid cooler longer. The steel folding cup can also be put right on the burner. One could then heat one large cup of liquid for hot chocolate for example. For me this was a very useful item. I now would have two identical canteens for my trip.

I had all of my equipment ready, except a week's supply of food. I decided that I would not use caches (hidden food supplies) but would resupply by buying provisions once a week. Some hikers use the expensive trail foods, which are freeze dried and dehydrated. Myself, partly because of my limited budget, I liked to find good substitutes for these in neighborhood supermarkets.

Some of the items I used on my two previous hikes and would use now were: powdered soup which contains vegetables and meats (add a little instant rice to this for a wholesome and filling meal), oatmeal, raisins, powdered milk, Poptarts, Kool-Aid, crackers, peanut butter, instant puddings and M & M candies (peanut or regular) that don't melt in the pack. I found it very interesting to just wander around the store to see what I could find.

By now it had been a couple of weeks, and *no answer* from the Florida Trail. Also no job calls. (In a way I was secretly

U.S. Geological Survey Maps, Scale: 1:250,000, 1/4" = 1 mile. They are spread out in order across my living room. These are excellent maps that show elevation contours, vegetation, small roads, railroads, etc. The plastic tube for the rolled maps can be seen upper left.

hoping that I would not hear from them). I was beginning to get impatient, and found myself trying on my pack more and more. By now it was ready. Heavy, but not unmanageable. A good frame sure does distribute the weight. I can remember the first pack that I had mentioned earlier, the Army ski pack. Because of the nature of its construction, it had me leaning forward looking down at my feet to counterbalance the load. This had been really bad on my shoulders. Then after a couple of days on the trail my cheap boots had disintegrated leaving me with sore back, shoulders and feet. That is why I was taking so much time choosing equipment.

I have found out from past misgivings and experience that the cheapest way to go in the long run is first-class. Save up and get exactly what you want and need. Don't settle for second best.

I then realized that I was missing one thing...maps! I tried the local library—only highway type. I needed to find contour maps. I thought of the unknown: forests, swamps and grasslands. How was I going to make it? Especially after friends and family started telling me that the snakes, alligators, panthers and swamp lands would bring me to a quick end! I had to find those maps... and find them fast! I needed to start backpacking soon because this was May and if I didn't start, I wouldn't have to hike, the mosquitoes would carry me!

I had an idea. The marine suppliers usually had maps of the water areas for fishermen. Since Florida had a lot of lakes, I would see if a local shop had maps of the entire state. Sure enough they did. I now had, for a dollar apiece, eleven U.S. Geological Survey maps of the 1:250,000, 1/4" equals one mile scale. These maps covered Florida from Georgia to Key West, plus a lot of water on the side. Each one was 13" by 21", so you can imagine when I laid these out on the living room floor just how much room they took up! Wall to wall maps! It was then that my folks began to think I was really serious or else seriously crazy!

"Yep," I said, "from here to there." But when I saw the

panicked look on my mom's face, I said, "Well, I probably won't go all the way, just a couple of weeks through the two national forests. After all I always wanted to visit them." But deep down inside I knew that I would need all of these maps!

I laid out my route on the maps and then gave myself 6 1/2" on either side which made my maps 13" by 21". I then folded the maps in half, 10 1/2" by 13" and slipped them into flat plastic bags. I sealed the ends with clear plastic tape and now had water-proof maps. I put them in order, rolled them and placed them into a plastic tube with a sliding end. This fit neatly into the top–side pocket of my pack.

As far as additional equipment was concerned, I had learned from the previous hikes that I should carry a larger first aid kit. This is primarily because I always travel by myself. Why alone? I have tried, but it seems that it is hard to find a person who is *bold* enough go along with me on my adventures. Honestly, I have really tried! I even made a last minute call to one of my army buddies in Michigan, but his mom put the skids on to any participation on his part.

Getting back to the equipment, I would never be without a good compass. I even found myself using it on highways. It's invaluable in orientating maps. I also took a snake bite kit. Florida especially! Keep in mind this is only for <u>last chance</u> use. I believe a little common sense and keeping your eyes open is 99% of the battle. *Keep your feet and legs where you can see them.*

I was ready! I had no job calls and only had to make the decision to get started. I did have one last problem. How did I get to the Georgia border? I called the Greyhound Bus Company in Tampa, Florida. They had one leaving at 12:00 AM that night.

It now was Monday evening. My dad was at his usual place, watching TV. He usually called it a finished day around 11:00 PM, and with my bus leaving at 12 midnight it would be perfect.

I asked him to drop me off at the bus station downtown.

This was an unusual request, but he consented. I could detect a feeling in the air—maybe my folks *did* think that I had finally lost my mind! I again reassured them that I probably would just hike through the two national forests.

I shook hands with my dad, shouldered my pack, and headed into the bus station. I got a few puzzled looks as I carried my odd luggage in. I was wearing well-used army boots. I went up to the counter and bought my ticket to Lake City.

Bus stations were interesting. People watching people, the ticket agent busy with his paper work, baggage men searching through their maze of freight. You could always hear a pinball machine ring, or go into the restaurant for a coffee, coke or look at magazines. Then sooner or later the announcement: "Scenic cruiser now boarding at gate number 4, for Brooksville, Leesburg, Ocala, Gainesville and Lake City. All board!"

The bus moved out onto the brick paved street, rumbling as it went. Tampa was quiet, only a person or two standing around the station. Soon we were up the ramp and onto Interstate 75. I closed my eyes, opening them in a half daze whenever the movement of the bus varied too much. It usually was a stop in a local station, and I would, still in a half daze, try to guess where I was, and then close my eyes again. I was jarred awake by the bus driver's announcement, "Lake City, we'll be there in 10 minutes."

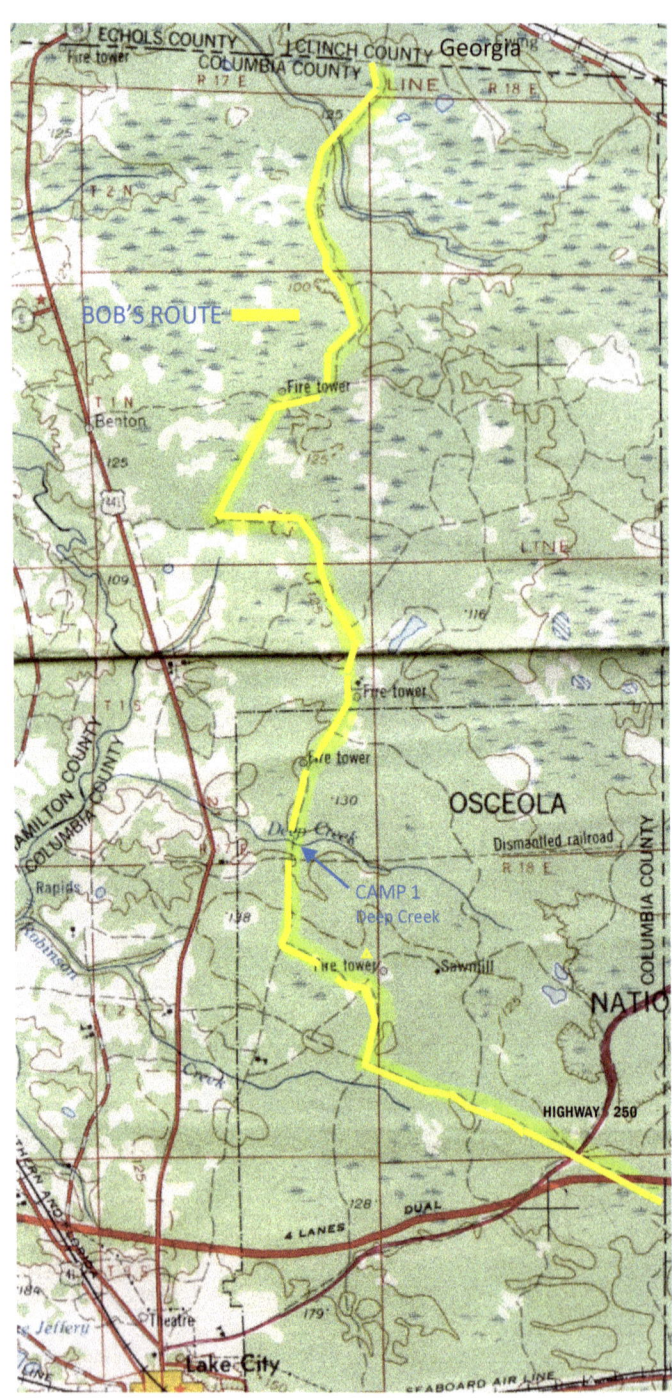

17   A Walk Across Florida

4
Going North to Go South

I guess I must have been daydreaming as I walked along.

Had it been an hour or two since I left the Alligator roadside? There's the junction 41 heading northwest and the 441 due north, the one I wanted. I headed to the right and started up the highway. Hey! That pickup's stopping up ahead. I started to run, Ever try to run with 60 pounds extra on your back and just flopping around from side-to-side? It just doesn't work very well.

I tossed my pack in the rear and climbed aboard. We bounced back on to the highway.

"Where you heading son?" He said.

Not wanting to brag about cross-state. "I'm going to start at the Georgia border and hike down through Osceola."

"Shucks son, ain't nothing here to see 'cept old pine trees."

I had heard this kind of attitude before from locals on my hike across the Shenendoah Valley, and I had my reply ready.

"Yes sir, but you see I'm from Tampa and we don't have any forests like this in the city, nor any logging operations." (It seems that most of us are not aware of the beauty around us. We just take it for granted.)

He looked up, "As a matter-of-fact, I'm cutting a bunch of them now. I've got a logging operation go'n on now, right off this highway. If you want, I can take you back in and show you what I'm doing."

"That would be great, sir!" and I really meant it.

"You'll be right on the Georgia border but there won't be any highway sign, only forest."

I thought of not getting a picture of a border highway sign, but I didn't want to miss this. We bounced off the highway and headed into the forest on a graded sand road, tall pine trees on either side. There was a glow of light in the sky overhead. Those pine trees had some color on their very tops.

"There's Benton Tower," he said.

I could see its base through the trees on the left. Sure enough, my map had shown a state fire tower in this area. I had been studying the northernmost map quite a lot the last few days at home. We turned a sharp left and best I could make out was that we were heading north. He started to slow down for an old wood timber bridge over a small stream.

"Might see some otter here son. They play around a lot near this bridge." We approached slow and quiet, but I was to be disappointed. I made a mental note, he *was conscious of nature around him.*

"How about the water in this area?" I questioned.

"No worry," he spoke up. "don't mind the clear brown color, it's from the tannic acid in the trees. Just as long as it's movin', I've drank it all my life."

I could hear the sharp whine of a chain saw now, as well as the running of a powerful engine.

"There's my operation now," he said, "and we're right near the Georgia border."

The truck bounced up off the sand road and into the clearing. We got out. He headed over and spoke to one of the men driving a huge tractor-type vehicle with large wheels (a skidder). I looked around. All that remained in the clearing was a few saplings, a lot of stumps and lots of broken branches. They sure cleared it out, I thought. In the back near the tall trees, two men were cutting away with chain saws. I had never seen this kind of saw before. It had a big 360 degree circular track for the blade instead of the usual long thin rectangular type.

There was also a tractor-trailer half full of logs and a truck with a boom for loading what the skidder pulled over to it.

The logger came back, "How about it?" he said.

"Real interesting sir."

"Well I got'ta go, lot of trees to cut. Take it easy son."

I shouldered my pack and headed back the way we had come in. Walking down the road I could hear the high pitched whine of the chain saws chewing up pine trees in the background.

Since my hike these strange chainsaws have always intrigued me, so I recently did some research. I couldn't find any modern day chainsaws that looked like what I had observed. Then, an idea...I would look up logging businesses in Florida, in particular in Lake City. This produced results. I found three companies that buy logs. I settled on "Levings Forest Products Inc."* I called on a Saturday and got the company voice mail which included a cell phone number. I left a message at the company and then dialed the cell number.

A female voice answered, "Hello."

"Hello ma'm, I'm calling for Mr. Levings. I'm writing a book and would like to ask him a couple of questions about logging in his area."

"Just a sec," and she left the phone.

"Al Levings," the voice said.

"Mr. Levings, I don't mean to bother you, but I'm writing a book about my hike across Florida in 1969 from Georgia to Key West, and it started in the Lake City area. I would like to ask you a few questions about logging."

" Not right now, I have to go out. But you call me Monday morning and we'll talk then."

"Thank you sir, should I use your company phone number?"

"Just call me on the cell."

"Thank you sir, goodbye."

Monday came. I made a call at 9:30 AM and got the voice mail message. Tuesday came. This time I said to myself let's try earlier. No luck, voice mail again. "Mr. Levings, I'm sorry I missed you. According to your phone message it seems that you are real busy, so if I don't hear from you by today I will just move on. Thanks so much."

That message did it. A couple of hours later, my cell phone rang.

"This is Al Levings, is Bob Kranich there?"

"Yes sir, it's me. I really appreciate you returning the call. By your phone message it seems that you are really busy."

"Well Bob I seem to run around a lot but I'm not making much money...Hey Bob, tell you what, just call me "Gator". everyone around here calls me by that handle."

"OK. I know exactly what you are saying about not making much money...Gator. How am I doing with the handle?'

"Real fine Bob, that'll do."

"To start with, I just wanted to ask you a few questions about logging. I've been in the woods a lot, but don't know much about logging. I'm writing a book about a hike I took in 1969 that started on the Georgia border just above Lake City in your area. I was picked up by a logger who had a logging operation in process next to the border."

"Do you know his name?" Gator asked.

"No sir, I wish I did. Well he had some men cutting up fallen trees with a strange kind of chain saw. They had a 360 degree blade guide. Do you know what kind of chain saws they were?"

"They were bow saws," he said without any hesitation.

"I couldn't find any information about that type of saw when I did on-line research."

"Try Huskey-Varner, Homelite or Poulan. Originally they all made them but I think Homelite made some of the first ones."

"Why don't we see these any more?" I questioned.

"I think they went out because of insurance. They would cut the logs up real fast but were very dangerous."

"What kind of trees are you cutting mostly now?"

"On private land, we are cutting mostly Slash and Loblolly Pine. If the National Forest lets some trees to be cut, some could be Long Leaf Pine."

"I have a question about land I went through on the sand road south of Benton tower. There was a gate across the road and it said Rainier Logging and Pulp Company.** (See page 23

Do they still own that land?"

"Yes, they still own that land...in fact, Rayonier owns a lot on land in this area."

"One last question Gator, is there anything else you would like to say about logging?"

"I think that the people that don't want trees cut should do their research. You know that a forest is a renewable resource if it is taken care of. Pine trees are used in a lot of different ways--many ways people don't even imagine. Besides the lumber and paper we all know about, pine trees are used in food and medicines. The pulp is cooked down and the solid is cellulose which can be used in insulation and fibers. Then the liquid that is left in the cooking pot is used in medicines and even ice cream! They call this liquid *pot liqueur*. It's like when you boil a pot of greens to cook, the green liquid that is left over after you take out the greens."

"Gator, I really want to thank you for the interview and the information. I would like to reference you and your company in the back of my book, is that OK?

"It's OK with me."

"Bye now," I said.

I immediately went online to research *Bow Chainsaws.* * I found a very interesting history of Bow Chainsaws on an internet site. The history was written by Tom Hawkins and Sons. They said that Bow Chainsaws are used mostly for cutting small diameter logs into 4 foot lengths. This pulpwood is made into paper.

The Poulan Company made the Bow Chainsaw in the USA during the Second World War. They made the cutter bar with a bow or spike that pointed down. That way the point was on the bottom of the log while cutting. By 1950 many North American companies started producing Bow Chainsaws. A company called Mall was one of the first to produce the full circle saw. In 1955 Homelite offered a new teardrop shape and a full circle type with a lightweight frame.

The Bow Chainsaw is used to cut logs that are lying on the

ground. An advantage is that it has a greater cutting area, much larger than that of the straight bar saw. This is good and bad. Because it can cut through a log faster, it also has a greater possibility of kickback. (It appears that Mr. Al "Gator" Levings was right-on.)

Bow Chainsaw designed for cutting logs lying on the ground into 4 foot long lengths for pulpwood (to make paper). They are much more dangerous than the now used straight guide bar chainsaws. This Bow has a full 360 cutter bar. Note the spikes on the top and bottom to stick into the wood during the cut.

**Note: Today's "Rayonier" was started as "Rainier Pulp and Paper Company." (see page 25) In writing this book, I'm referring to my original hiking diary notes. I got the spelling off of a woodland gate sign. Those signs may still have had the old name "Rainier" on them.

5
Big Pine Country

I have done some research on the forests in Florida. The large pine trees in north central Florida are mostly Longleaf and Slash Pine. It is now all second growth. The last of the great virgin pine forest was all but cut down by the late 1940's. Along with the forest went the once thriving company logging towns and the company culture that they spawned.

Florida was the first state in the southeast to have a National Forest. This was because it was the only southern state east of the Mississippi river that had any large tracts of land owned by the United States. In 1908 President Roosevelt and then in 1911 President Taft designated Florida National Forest areas. Even though these lands had been public land they had been misused by over-cutting and burning.

In 1924 conservationists helped to get the Clarke-McNary Act passed. This act allowed the Forest Service to buy depleted land, rejuvenate it, and grow trees

A demonstration forest was needed in the southeastern United States. In 1929 a unit was started in northeast Florida, and in 1931 President Hoover named it Osceola National Forest. There are now four National Forests in Florida for a total of 1,600,000 acres. The other three are Ocala, Apalachicola and Choctawhatchee.

The National Forests belong to the people of the United States. It is the Forest Service's responsibility to protect and manage these resources and to plan their uses. Good forestry practice on both public and private lands should be managed correctly. Mature timber should be cut at the correct time. Just remember pulpwood and timber take much longer to grow than farm crops.

A good forestry operation will manage the land so the timber is not depleted. This involves protecting the forest from fire and not using the old *"cut-out and get-out"* method. This method has destroyed much if not most of the original forest. Today we have only a small amount of what once was, and much of the land is now second rate.

In addition loggers should use methods of cutting that will leave some small trees and larger trees to reseed the area naturally. Planting should also be done on an as-needed basis.

By using this "Sustained Yield management"* method, forests are like "money in the bank." When the forest growth is no less than what is cut, the forest will be perpetuated.

When I got to Benton tower a road headed south. There was a gate, but a sign stated:

> PLEASE KEEP GATE CLOSED
> RAINIER LOGGING & PULP CO.

Rayonier Inc.* is now an international company. Its products are produced from timber. It is located in at least 70 different countries. It owns or operates over 2 million acres of forestry land in United States and New Zealand. In the United States, it has two paper pulp and three lumber mills. In New Zealand it has a fiber-board facility.

Over two-thirds of Rayonier's business is from timber and wood products. Other income is from sales of specialty wood pulp products, fibers and cellulose. Many of these uses for wood are not known very well by most people. These include ingredients in hair shampoo, cream rinse, toothpaste, ice cream, photographic film, cellophane, paint, cement, printing ink, explosives, diapers, filter and specialty printing, writing papers and textile fibers. This list of what wood products are used in goes on and on.

Rayonier was founded in 1926 as the Rainier Pulp and Paper Company in San Francisco, California. Its first mill was in Shelton, Washington and the second on the Olympic Peninsula. They were using western hemlock trees to produce high-quality bleached paper pulp. In 1931 they began working with the Du Pont chemical company to produce rayon from the hemlock pulp.

In 1937 the name was changed to Rayonier, a mix of the words, rayon and Rainier. In 1944 the company moved its offices to New York City and in 1978 to Stamford, Connecticut. In 1999 Rayonier purchased almost one million acres of forest land in Florida, Georgia and Alabama. They saw the potential in the southeastern woodlands and relocated its corporate office to Jacksonville, Florida, where it is today.

Timber in the southeastern United States will grow much faster than in the northwest. The softwoods such as Southern pine will mature in only 20-25 years compared to northwestern Douglas fir and hemlock's 45-50 years. This why the southeastern United States' softwoods have become so important to the Rayonier company.

As with any large company whose products come from the environment, Rayonier has had its share of environmental problems. Rayonier has to observe so many state and federal environmental laws and regulations. Its air emissions, water discharge and waste disposal operations have been controlled by federal laws governing the cutting of timber, particularly the Endangered Species Act. In Washington State their forest holdings include many endangered species, such as the northern spotted owl, the marbled murrelet, and some species of salmon. Consequently they have had many ongoing negotiations which included different state agencies, environmental organizations and the Environmental Protection Agency (EPA).

One of their largest civic programs is hunting. They lease out parcels of land for a total of approximately 95% of all their holdings to hunters. They say it's a great partnership, because the hunt clubs are concerned and take care of the land. If the hunters see anything wrong or have a problem they will immediately inform Rayonier.

I opened the gate, went through and closed it very carefully, making sure the latch was fastened. This was a fair way to operate. It was ok to go through, if I just closed the gate behind me. By this time, the fog had long since evaporated. Only I didn't remember it happening.

I started down the sand road but was suddenly startled by a rooting and grunting noise...I looked up just in time to see a scrawny but wiry little hog running off into the brush. Well, my first wild animal sighting. I was relieved it ran the other way. I had read something about Florida wild hogs and it said to steer clear of them.

A little farther along and I saw an animal I would not stop seeing until much farther south: a thin wiry-looking "Florida scrub beefer." These cattle, when they first see you, get that *wild eye look* and then they scat.

By now the Florida sun was really getting warm! I had long since shed my hooded sweatshirt. A fast stop in the shade for a snack. It was then that I realized I should have filled my canteens at Benton Tower. The sand road suddenly emerged from the big pines into a great cleared area. Yes the chain saws had recently been busy. Boy, it sure looked desolate! There were just piles of branches and barren land. Here I had to make my first direction decision. The road T'ed and I could go either way, east or west. I started a precedent which I was to continue until I reached the causeway to the Florida Keys: a southeast direction always. If you check on a map you can see that Florida drops to the southeast.

Along this road the land was fully timbered, with huge straight long-needled pines on both sides, cool and shady. As a matter of fact, I soon found out, too cool. The nearby swamp had seeped up and onto the road. In fact, in some places it was boot deep! Not to be discouraged I sloshed on and it soon dried out. This little used, grass-grown-over pathway was twisting in all directions. But I soon came out onto what seemed to be a thoroughfare judging by the vehicle tracks in the sand. I was still heading south and in the distance I could hear the whine and crashing sounds of logging activity. I finished the last of my warm water.

Whew, I was really starting to perspire! I dug my large red

bandanna out of my pack, mopped my brow and tied it onto the top of my pack so I could use it while I hiked. Back on with the pack and down the road. The Florida sand gets powdery, dusty and dry.

The road T'ed again and a logging operation was before my eyes. I set my pack down and watched. This was a much larger operation than I had seen this morning. Two skidding tractors were running back and forth. All kinds of chain saws were in operation. The workers were cutting the logs into 10 foot sections. They were being piled into staked containers and then the containers were being loaded on a 10 wheeler* logging truck.

I noticed a huge ice cooler sitting on a truck and my parched mouth sure wanted some! But my hiker's pride wouldn't let me ask. I wandered over and asked the driver of the 10 wheeler (who was busy winching one of the log-filled containers up on to the back of his truck with a hand-held electronic control box) which way to Osceola National Forest. His directions were sketchy, but as I should have guessed, east and then south.

So east I went and for the first time I noticed smoke off in the far distance. You can imagine the questions this brought to my mind. Nevertheless I was needing water. It's funny what you'll notice when you are thirsty. I stopped a moment to look at a large pond of stagnant smelly water. No, I wasn't that thirsty, not yet! I trudged onward toward the ever increasing smoke clouds ahead. As I rounded a turn in the road I saw huge piles of branches smoking and crackling. This fire was in a large field next to an old ranch type house. A truck nearby had a small caterpillar tractor on it and a few men standing around it. I ambled over, noticing that the trucks bore the Rainier Logging and Pulp Co. markings on their sides.

"Hi, I was wondering if you-all owned that house, because I'm needing some water," I questioned.

"Nope, but I'm sure if you ask they'll give it to you," the biggest gentleman said.

Comparison of a logged over area above and a good stand of pole and pulp trees below not yet touched. The few trees left standing above may be the seed trees. The brush and limbs appear to be still smoking from the gasoline torching. Keep in mind that this is private forest land and it is in their commercial interest to use sustained yield and to replant and or reseed.

"How come the big fire?" I questioned. They had gasoline torches and one man was filling his.

"It's the way we clear after the logging crew gets done. We burn the slash and then we come right along and replant."

"Why the pack son?" the same one asked. I proceeded to explain my hiking kick.

"Great idea, it sure is the way to live," they all agreed.

"Well, I'm sure dry, so I'd better fill these canteens," I said, heading towards the house.

The gate was closed so I called in because a few hound dogs were nearby. A young girl in her teens came to the door.

"Excuse me ma'm, but could I have some water?"

"Shore enough, spicket's round back," she said and closed the door.

Dogs or no dogs, I proceeded to fill both myself and the canteens. The water had a strong iron taste but I didn't care.

Back on with the pack. I stopped once more at the truck. The two men were still there. I inquired how to get to Osceola National Forest, I got the same directions, south and east, and down that same road.

"Let's go Joe, we got some backfirin' to do," the big fella said as he grabbed his gasoline torch.

"Good luck on your hike," the other one said.

I thanked him and then I was back on the sand road.

As I rounded the bend, I looked back across the field and could just barely see the men in the dense smoke, torches a-blazing. Whew! It's hot enough just with the sun!

This was the first clear-cut I had ever seen. I noted that when they finished the replanting it would be a pine plantation. I have recently just read a book, *A Year in the Maine Woods** by Bernd Heinrich where he made a personal physical comparison of two sites after about 7 years. One was a clear-cut and the other a selective cut. He said that seven years ago he was sure that the clear-cut site looked like 'hell.' But now he could see that nature was restoring the woods. It was an area of fast growing trees in competition for the sun.

The slash (tree debris left over from a logging operation) and old broken trees make the soil rich and provided homes for many types of rodents, small animals and birds. The open areas provided grazing for larger animals. This area was returning but it would not be as diverse as the original forest.

In the selective cut the loggers had removed only the largest trees and left the rest standing. The light let in was used by the young trees waiting on the forest floor to start growing. The open habitat grew different types of brush and grasses which then supported a variety of forest life. He thought that sometime in the future a person would not be able to tell the difference between the selective cut forest and the original. From what he said, and I agree with him, this selective cutting may be a great way for our national forest to harvest trees. I realize that private property will be planting the tree plantations for maximum return on their investment, but they still should use the sustained yield method to replace the trees.

The road was heading due south now. The trees were a little thinner, but up ahead they were tall and dark green. I came to a fence line on either side of the road and there were railroad rails across the road. They were set perpendicular to the road with about 3 to 4 inches between them. There were 6 of them probably on a base of concrete. I know that cattle don't like to cross this sort of arrangement. A small metal tag on a nearby tree proclaimed that this was now National Forest land. These rails were to keep the cattle out of the National Forest. The sun was getting low in the sky and I was beginning to run down. This had been a long day. I carefully crossed the cattle guard rails and continued on.

Soon I was overtaken by a ranger driving a pickup truck. He waved and went on. I watched him as he drove onto the right fork in the road and out of sight. When I reached the fork I walked the same way he had gone, due west without having thought which way to go. About a mile of walking and thinking brought me to realize that I should have been walking south and east. I back-tracked and headed south. As far as

I could see it was a long graded sand road with tall pines lining both sides.

My thoughts turned toward stopping for the night. I longed for a perfect camp site near a stream with cool fresh drinking water and a friendly breeze. Of course this was just the picture I had of myself on my first night out on this venture. I had enough water for the evening meal and other incidentals but some how I kept walking…..and walking. I sat down against a tree for a moment. I reassured myself that after a minute of rest and a sip of water I'd continue for a while in hopes of finding a suitable campsite for the night.

As I walked along I continued to scan the area ahead. Suddenly a small rise appeared in the distance. It looked different somehow, and this I had to see. The closer I got the more enthusiastic I became. As I reached the small crest I could see that the road actually sloped down to a beautiful creek. What a find! This was much more than I'd dared to hope for. The road forded here. No wonder all those tire tracks and the ranger had gone to the right back there!

Imagine an oasis in the middle of a pine forest. On the other side of the stream, I could make out, in the fast disappearing light, a nice camp site.

I had to ford now. The realization set in. I never before had to ford a creek. But being very warm and in need of a bath, I guessed it couldn't hurt anything. I exchanged my boots for my camp moccasins. I picked up a nearby stout stick and probed the stream bottom. The stream was an average of 8 feet wide and had widened out to about 15 feet here at the ford. The good news…..the wider section was shallower.

I plunged in, and it sure was refreshing. I had momentary fears of water snakes and alligators but nothing happened except it felt real cool. It was only about hip deep but the current was still swift.

Now it was dark. I set my pack down against a picnic table which was snuggled in between the tall trees in this campsite area. It must be a National Forest remote campsite. I was

Deep Creek ford and the first nights camp area near the Deep Creek recreation area, Osceola National Forest.

somewhat refreshed from my crossing. I dipped into the stream and got a pot of water and placed it on my one-burner Coleman white gas stove. I plumped up the stove and lit it. I now had the water for my supper warming. I got out a wash rag, soaped it up and washed myself. Then I took a canteen of water and rinsed off standing in the sand some distance from the stream. A good backpacker does not put soapsuds in a clear stream. I dried off and got into a change of clothes and my hooded sweatshirt. By this time the water had boiled. Between chores of setting up camp, I added the powdered soup and a few potato flakes to thicken the brew.

I guess it is hard for someone sitting at home at the supper table to think this would taste so refreshing. I have found that after an exhausting day of hiking just about anything tastes like a feast! Now I could get down to setting up my canvas hammock. Two nearby average size pine trees served nicely. I tied and stretched a small 1/8 inch nylon 500 pound test cord between the same trees about 3 feet above the hammock. This would support my lightweight black plastic tarp which I had reinforced along the edges with silver duct tape and added grommets.

Getting into this for the first time was a little difficult. Being so small it was very tipsy. But once I slipped in, I could tell that it was going to work out and be a comfortable sleep (if I don't fall out!). Only once that night did I wake up, and looking towards the stream I was awed by the magical reflection of a full moon shining through the canopy above. I was soon lulled back to sleep by the melody of the night wood sounds and the gentle swaying of the hammock.

6
Osceola National Forest

Hey, it's light! I awakened to what seemed to be another world. I had set up camp in the dark and never really saw what was around me. A thick woods of tall, rough bark pine trees with bushes of all sizes interspersed between surrounded me. I could hear the early morning woods activity as I lay there. Birds chirping and singing, a squirrel jumping amidst rustling leaves and pine needles and the constant gurgling of the stream. I turned over on my side and looked over the edge of my hammock. A small brown, orange and white robin was hopping all around looking for his breakfast. (The early bird, I guess.)

Here I was, in Osceola National Forest.* This National Forest of approximately 162,000 acres was established in 1931. It was named for Osceola, a Seminole chief. The details of his capture and subsequent imprisonment at Fort Marion, St. Augustine are not very complimentary to Florida's history. This forest was to be an experimental area for the growing of pine trees for naval stores. Just what are *naval stores*?* It is resinous gum that the tree extrudes when it is scarred. In the old days of sailing, raw gum, turpentine and rosin were in great need for use by sailing ships. These products are made by distilling the pine gum. There is a need to preserve and perpetuate the source of these pine tree products because 85% used in this country come from this southeast USA area.

There are some forest management, research and demonstration areas in this National Forest. One is a naval stores branch of the Southern Forest Experimental Station. It is the naval stores laboratory of the Bureau of Chemistry and Soils. It has a complete modern seed facility which furnishes pine seed for National Forest nurseries throughout the USA.

The forest land is primarily flat and has many small ponds and swamps where the soil is covered with water from a few inches to several feet. Slash pine and cypress grow in the shallow swamps, with hardwood and cypress in the swamps which have much more water. In the larger swamps there are some virgin stands of cypress. Long leaf and slash pine grow in areas which are at a higher elevation.

On a sustained-yield basis the production of the forest products are: turpentine, saw timber, pulp wood, poles and turpentine butts as fuel wood. The cypress wood is cut as saw timber and cross ties.

Lastly for recreation there is Ocean Pond, a lake of open water, 1 1/2 miles in diameter, which is used for fishing, boating and swimming.

Woodpeckers were pounding away in nearby trees. The sun was penetrating among the big pines and oaks. It was truly a paradise. This brought back the conversation I had when I had called my Michigan buddie's mom and was trying to get him to come with me on this trip.

"I don't envy you!" she had proclaimed.

I guess everyone has his or her own dreams, and this was mine. I stretched and slowly swung up and out of my hammock. Ouch! I was refreshed but sure had some aches. That was part of the first few days of carrying a pack on any trail.

I slipped down to the creek and dipped a pot of the clear brown water. I remembered what the logger had told me yesterday morning, it's from the Tannic acid in the trees, just as long as it's movin'. Also, this water was going to get boiled.

I was soon enjoying my morning oatmeal. While sitting at the table I noticed a movement on the far side. A Florida black scorpion was coming to visit me while I ate my breakfast! It was about 2 inches long and had a long pointed tail arching up and over the top of its back. I must have scared it, for he scampered off the table top, down the side, and fast disappeared into the underbrush and old leaves. Definitely an unexpected and unwelcome visitor. I cleaned up my equipment and packed it away.

Every now and then I get the urge to sketch and I could feel it coming on. I grabbed my pad and pencils and headed over to the road where it came out of the stream. There on a small rise I sat down and started to draw. I was trying to capture the serene scene before me and then, as if by magic, out of the sky, a pair of Mallard ducks set down, plop, plop! causing ripples to form on the top of the steady, slow moving water. They must have looked around and suddenly realized that the strange shape on the bank was a possible threat and that was all they needed…..they were off with a loud beating of wings and a few squawks, as fast as they had come. This had surely been a special moment.

I finished my sketch...tall pines with the sandy road, thick palmettos and brush along the banks, oak trees all casting their reflections in the ever so busy stream. This stream was doing its small part, adding to the Suwanee river a couple of miles downstream to the west. The spell was broken by the *meow* sound of a cat bird somewhere in the thick brush.

The sun was up fairly high, so I guessed I should continue on. My pack was ready. Everything ok, I thought, looking around as I slipped my drawing materials back into the pack. I always make it a habit of looking around the campsite before I leave. It is so easy to forget equipment and you also want to *leave nothing but footprints.*

I soon found myself hiking along and singing my favorite camping and hiking tunes. It was a good thing no one could hear me. When the trail is flat or gradual downhill it's a nice way to pass the miles and time away. I noticed that the pines along here were a good height, about 50-60 feet as an average. Every now and then I would come upon a small thinned out area, about an acre or two. I wondered about this, and I found out later that these thinned out areas serve more than one purpose. First a national forest actually harvests and replants the timber. Second is the fact that thinned out areas produce brush and plants that wild game feed on.

I also could see that on occasion there were all sorts of colored ribbons or flagging on the trees in certain areas. I also found out about this by calling a forest ranger near Tampa some time later. He explained the colored ribbons to me. When an area is to be harvested, it is marked by these colored ribbons or paint. The 5 1/2 to 9 inch diameter trees are designated for pulp wood and 9 1/2 inch or larger would be saw timber. Other markers could designate boundary trees of the area to be harvested. If a whole area were to be scrubbed out ,they would mark the largest and most healthy trees to be saved for seed trees. The color code would be peculiar to each individual National or State Forest.

It was in one of these cleared brushy areas that I was suddenly startled by two small Florida white-tail deer. They took one look at me and the next thing I saw was the two tails bobbing up and down amongst the palmettos. Wow, they sure could move! I was surprised by the small size of them, only about 4 feet high.

It was beginning to be impressed by the extent of the pine forest in north Florida. Here I had been walking for a day and a half already and except for a few logged areas, it was all pine trees. About a mile farther as I was looking down I suddenly saw some very large tracks in the damp, sandy road. They looked, (and I didn't want to think it), like large cat tracks. They were heading along the road in the same direction I was going. I set my pack down and traced the approximate outline onto my notepad. It may have been a panther.

Florida panthers* can weigh up to 150 pounds and can measure up to 8 feet long from the nose to the tip of the tail. They can be found in pine forest and hardwood hammocks. They may also be found in swampy areas. Their range is from 70 to as much as 270 square miles. They are nocturnal, will sleep in the day and hunt at night, dusk and dawn. Their hunting takes them in zig-zag pattern. They can swim and also cross rivers or lakes. Panthers have a very good sense of smell, their vision encompasses 130 degrees, and they have excellent sight. They can run in a sprint, (a few hundred yards) up to 35 miles per hour, but prefer to stalk their prey

Animal tracks found in the sandy road traced on Bob's notepad. They are full size. I since have checked animal prints * and they say that all cats prints do not show claws. I can't remember if claws were in the prints in the sand or not. Without claws it does resemble panther tracks, with claws it could have been a large dog. See below left.

Panther tracks *
Front and rear tracks maximum 4 inches long, claws seldom show in tracks

Black Bear tracks *
Resemble human footprints

39   A Walk Across Florida

which is primarily deer and wild hogs.

As I was concentrating on this find, a car suddenly approached. As it drew abreast of me, we all waved. A ranger was driving and a couple of persons were with him. I thought to myself, there go my panther prints. Sure enough, most of them were gone, tire tracks now in their place. It was a good thing that I had just finished the tracing.

It wasn't much longer before I came to a sand road intersection, complete with a sign:

> West Tower – 2 1/2 Miles

The road headed southeast. Off to my right I could see a few old logging trucks parked in the trees, stark and silent. The two miles passed by quickly, and I soon came to another junction. Off to the north I could see the bright orange and white striping paint on a forest tower. I was curious to see what all this area looked like from up above, so I headed for the tower. As I drew near I could see that the brush was cut from around it and a ranger's truck with Osceola National Forest markings was parked near a small house. It sure felt good to sit down on the tower steps, as I leaned my pack against a metal support.

"Boy, you sure got a load there!" a voice boomed down.

"Come on up and visit a spell," the ranger invited.

"Yes sir, I just need to rest a minute." With each flight of steps, I could see farther, until soon I had the same view I'm sure as the velvet black crow off in the distance. If I had thought before that there were a lot of pine trees, now I was convinced! A sea of green stretched out before me, as far as I could see. The trap door in the floor above me opened up.

"Come on in."

"Thanks sir, you sure have a great view."

"Yep, a lot of pines," he said.

We talked a lot about Osceola National Forest. He gave me an excellent map of the forest, a regular brochure put out by

West Tower Osceola National Forest

the Department of Agriculture. If I had obtained it earlier, I would have known that last night I had camped in the Deep Creek rustic recreation area. Also I was able to determine that the first day of my hike I had covered 22 miles. No wonder I was so tired last night! In the flat country you can cover some ground. I know that in the Shenandoah mountains and the Smokies I thought that I was fortunate if I was able to hike at least 10 miles a day. I could also tell by the map that I had about 10 miles to go because I wanted to reach Ocean Pond campsite by nightfall.

I had to cut my visit short because the sun was already way on the afternoon side of overhead. I thanked my West tower ranger friend and went down. By the time this hike was over I was to lose any fear I previously had concerning the climbing of fire towers. It seems that in Florida, if you want to see what you've covered, you have to climb one. There are no convenient mountains to use as look-out vantage points.

I headed out on a trail that the ranger told me was an old logging railroad roadbed. My logging roadbed soon turned out to resemble a canal, with all the water in it. I backtracked and took a trail which headed towards the main sand road. I had been on this trail a short distance when I saw bear signs.

The torn-apart rotten log had aroused my suspicions and sure enough a few steps farther the tracks and droppings confirmed them. The tracks disappeared when I got back onto the main sand road. The vehicle traffic in this area was enough to have obliterated them.

The Florida black bear* is the state's largest native land mammal. The black bear's footprint is unusual for an animal because it resembles a human footprint. This is because they walk on the entire foot like a human does, from heel to toe. In comparison, cats and dogs walk on their toes. If you meet a full grown bear you will be looking at an animal weighing between 200 to 350 pounds. They can run fast and climb trees. One can't outrun or outclimb them. They also have good hearing, eyesight and sense of smell. They eat any type of plants including berries, acorns, grasses, seeds and tender parts of the palmetto. They will eat insects such as honeybees, yellow jackets and even ants and termites. If they can get them, they will eat some animals, among them deer, raccoon, wild pigs, armadillos and carrion.

The Florida black bears can be found in many different locations throughout Florida. This includes hardwood hammocks, cabbage palm and pine woodlands and various swampy areas. They wander around an area looking for food and use their very good senses to locate it. They are not bothered if another bear wanders into their territory meaning that they will usually not fight for it.

I was sure of my route now, and I proceeded on the sand road. I could see by the fence posts and a house in the pines that a small tract of the forest here was privately owned. When one travels in National Forest land, one must be respectful of both private and public land.

About a mile farther and I came to the junction of Forest road No. 263. This one would lead me to my evening's campsite at Ocean Pond. Only 8 more miles to go. Then I saw big cat tracks just like I had seen earlier. I guess that they must like to travel along the sand roads.

After about 3 miles I came to a highway which cut Osceola National Forest diagonally in half, State Highway 250. I could see that it wasn't very busy. I sat down and leaned my pack against a fence post. It was time to rest and eat. I just stayed there watching as an occasional car roared by, the people unaware of me sitting and watching them.

I had best get moving, for it was approaching evening. Across the highway and a couple of miles farther I was greeted by a small group of range cattle. The older ones ran off but one young calf stayed on looking at me with its big eyes. I started slowly approaching. He was sure curious. I was really close when I suddenly became conscious of an automobile heading our way. Looking up I could see a cloud of dust bearing down on us. Both cow and I got off into the brush as the car sped by. Good grief, some people! My cow friend was long gone and I proceeded to get moving as well.

I came to an overpass, which to my surprise passed over an expressway, U. S. No. 10, which sliced across the southern one fourth of Osceola National Forest. It's interesting--we set aside areas of forest land and then proceed to slice it up with ribbons of concrete! Real good conservation practices, I thought, as I stood on top watching and listening to the continuous flow of on-rushing roaring traffic.

I didn't need any coaxing to leave that mad house. Down the other side I went. The road on this side was paved and I soon could make out in the fast disappearing daylight a sign proclaiming:

OCEAN POND RECREATION AREA

As I headed down the road and into the tall pine and cypress trees I could feel myself tiring out, in fact dragging! I was now at my evening's destination and was thankful for it. I used the steps which went up and over the fence. I found myself in the camping area. Small dots of light flickered around in the background. A lot of campers were using this area. I found a site and set my pack down against the table. It was sure great to be setting my pack down for the last time today.

While my water was working on boiling, I got my hammock set up on a couple of convenient oak trees. It was now very dark and I guess the people in the next campsite felt sorry for me. Two little boys came over and said that their Dad had a lantern that I could use. It was a real nice offer, but I declined it and showed the two boys how my candle lantern worked. They lingered a while asking various questions as all children are inclined to do and then, at their mother's call, unwillingly departed. After finishing eating, I went down to the dark lake and got wet before turning in. It sure felt good. I slipped into my cozy, warm sleeping bag, swinging in the hammock.

It was morning. I had slid down to the center of my hammock during the night. I slowly peeked out of the opening in my sleeping bag. I could see out through the trees and to the lake. My two little friends from the night before were on the nearby pier with their fishing poles. The rest of the camp was quiet. I slid back my black plastic tarp, reached behind me grasping the hammock rope and pulled myself back up out of

Camp site at Ocean Pond, Osceola National Park.

the center of the hammock. The main rope must have loosened and the hammock sagged. I just sat there and looked around.

It was warm enough so I decided to take another swim. On the way back I filled up both of my canteens at a faucet. As I was eating breakfast, my camper friends came over with their two boys. They said that all their boys had talked about was my hiking, my camp and the candle lantern that I had showed them last night. It seems that the boys wanted a picture of them with me so they could show it to their teacher and classmates at school. We took the pictures and said our goodbyes.

A cypress tree growing in the water along the shore of Ocean Pond. Top: Colored pencil, Bottom: ink pen.

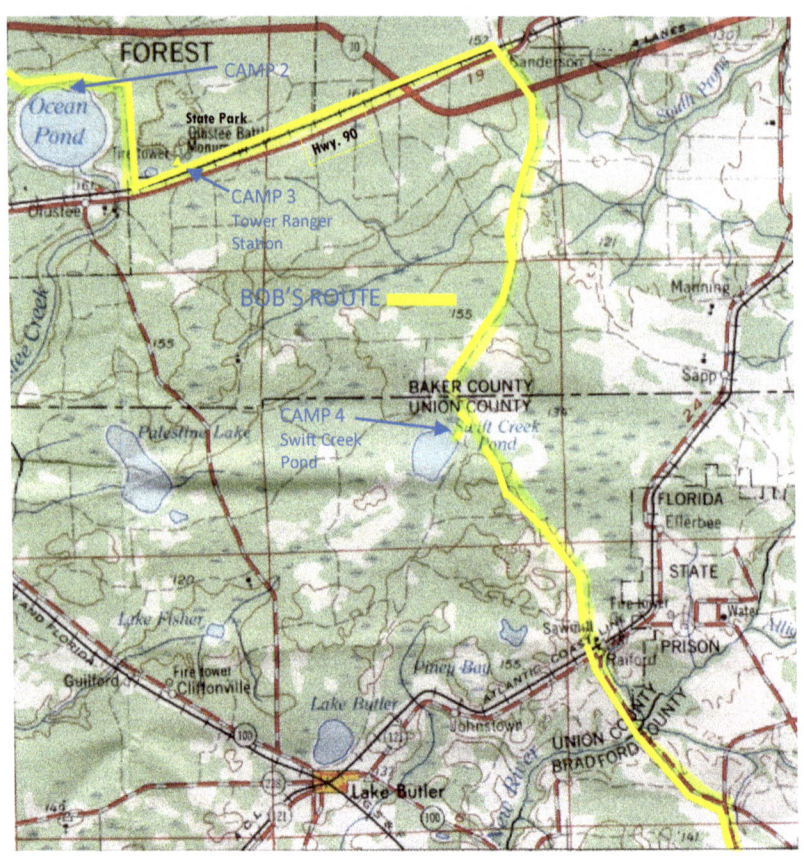

7
Olustee Battlefield Historic State Park

I packed up and headed through the park. I waved to a man I had met yesterday when I was swimming. He had told me that he was down here from Massachusetts. At the end of the campground the gate was closed and locked so I had to put my pack under the fence and climb over. There was a dirt road that took me south about four miles to the paved road. When I got to the paved road U S highway 90, which was the southern boundary of the park, I headed towards the east and walked on the side of the road which was next to the railroad tracks. I could see the Olustee fire tower with its bright orange markings in the distance. That's where the museum and battlefield were.

In 1909 three acres were donated by two parties to the State of Florida. This was to erect a monument in commemoration of the Civil War Battle of Olustee. The monument was completed in 1912 and was administered by the Daughters of the Confederacy until it was taken over by the Florida Board of Parks and Historic Memorials in 1949. In 1994 Florida entered into a agreement with the U.S. Department of Agriculture's Forest Service. This agreement allowed them to manage 688 acres of the Osceola National Forest Service property as part of the Oulstee Battlefield Historic State Park.*

Today visitors can visit the Monument, go through a visitor center museum, and walk interpretive battlefield trails. This battle took place on February 20, 1864 between Union troops advancing from Jacksonville and Confederate forces from Florida and Georgia. The battle included more than 10,000 cavalry, infantry and artillery troops and was the largest battle fought in Florida. The fighting first started near the railroad at Olustee Station. The Confederates then dropped back, and the fighting took place in the Ocean Pond area. The Union attacked and the battle took place in open pine woods. The Union was repulsed and by the end of the day had to withdraw. The Union retreat was protected by both the famous 54th Massachusetts Volunteer Infantry and the 35th United States Colored Troops.

Two national forest trucks at the Olustee fire tower and work center. The big Ford 10-wheeler flat-bed has a caterpillar tractor pulling a disk/plough to cut fire breaks.

Looking down at the Osceola national park work center from the Oulstee fire tower. You can see just how far a ranger can see from the fire tower high above the trees.

When I got to the fire tower I saw that it was part of a National Forest work center. There were some shop buildings, parking areas, and what appeared to be an office off to one side. Parked in the center of the lot were two National Forest trucks, a pickup and a ten-wheeler. The ten-wheeler was a flatbed loaded with a small caterpillar tractor which had what appeared to be an apparatus to cut fire breaks attached to it.

"How you doing young feller?" I turned around and there was a man wearing an aluminum hat just stepping down from the fire tower. He was carrying his lunch box.

"Hello sir, fine, thank you? I just came from Ocean Pond campground, I was hoping to visit the museum and see the Olustee monument."

"Well you can look at the monument, but I'm afraid that the museum is closed today. You can see it tomorrow, it'll be open."

"Would it be ok if I did two things? I would like to camp here so I can see the museum tomorrow and I would like to go up the fire tower and take a picture of the area."

"Make yourself at home, it's quite all right."

"Thanks a lot, I really appreciate it."

He headed towards his car and drove off. I set up my camp right next to the fire tower. I decided not to put up the hammock and just sleep on the ground. That way I could pack up fast in the morning and not make such a sight with the hammock hanging between some posts. I climbed the tower as far as I could go, to right under the trap door.

The sight was really great. Tall pines as far as I could see in all directions. I stayed up there and watched the sun set into a sea of pine tree tops. I went down, crawled into my sleeping bag, and was serenaded by a chorus of crickets and tree frogs.

I woke up with the rising sun. It was all quiet at the work camp. I ate some pop tarts and chocolate and packed up. The museum was just a short distance away between the fire tower and the monument. The monument is made of decorative cut stone about 25 feet high and guarded by two Civil War cannons. I was investigating the monument when I saw that the museum had just opened. I went in there and looked around. It was small but had enough information to explain the battle. Today the park is much larger than the original 3 acres, 688 to be exact, and has much more to it. The museum is larger, and every year during the second week of February there is a huge reenactment.

When I came out I could see that the fire tower was occupied. I climbed up. As the trap door opened, I was surprised to see a lady tower ranger. She invited me up into the tower and we had a nice talk. Her name was Gertrude. She had lived there all of her life. Her husband had been the head of this Osceola National Forest until he retired 3 weeks earlier. He did 40 years of service in the National Forest. They had two boys, both in the United States military. One was in the medical

Looking out towards the west from under the Olustee fire tower trap door. One can see Highway 90, the Seaboard Air Line Railroad and a dirt road going along the railroad. The forest on the right is the Osceola national forest and the trees across the highway on the left are private woodlands.

corps in South Korea and the other was in the Navy and had just finished a tour in Vietnam. It sounded like an all American family. I thanked Gertrude and climbed down from the tower.

The old Sanderson freight station. Nice 57 Ford parked alongside!

Swift Creek Pond. A pickup can be seen on the left near the lake.

8
Camp Blanding and Mike Roess Gold Head Branch State Park

I shouldered my pack and started hiking down the dirty sand work-road that paralleled the railroad tracks. This time I was heading east-north-east. About four dusty miles further and I came to that infernal noisy and busy Interstate 10...again. This time Highway 90 and I went under it. The freeway and I had left the national park about 2 miles back. A couple of miles farther and I came to Sanderson. It's a small community at the intersection of a couple of secondary roads and Highway 90. The railroad's mainline shoots straight through but it does leave one siding for the town....a sign of past and better times.

I stopped at a small gas station to fill up my canteens. As I was doing this, at a faucet near the pumps, a young man about my age approached me. He was wiping his hands on a greasy mechanics rag.

"Hey I saw you hiking up the road. What you do'n?"

"I just finished hiking and camping though Osceola and now I'm heading towards Ocala," I answered as I tightened the caps on my two canteens.

"I had my share of hiking in Vietnam with the Marines, I got all shot up. I'm doing ok now," he said.

"I'm sorry about that. I was in Korea and got hooked on hiking there. An army buddy and I used to explore the back-country, villages and mountains on our times off," I answered. "This hiking is a lot safer than what you had to do, no one has shot at me. At least not yet."

"Well I got to get back to work. You take care, y'all-hear? He headed back towards the station's auto repair area.

I saw that there was an old dilapidated railroad freight station along the tracks. Even though its condition was

Raiford's freight station doesn't look much different from Sanderson's. However, they do belong to two different railroads.

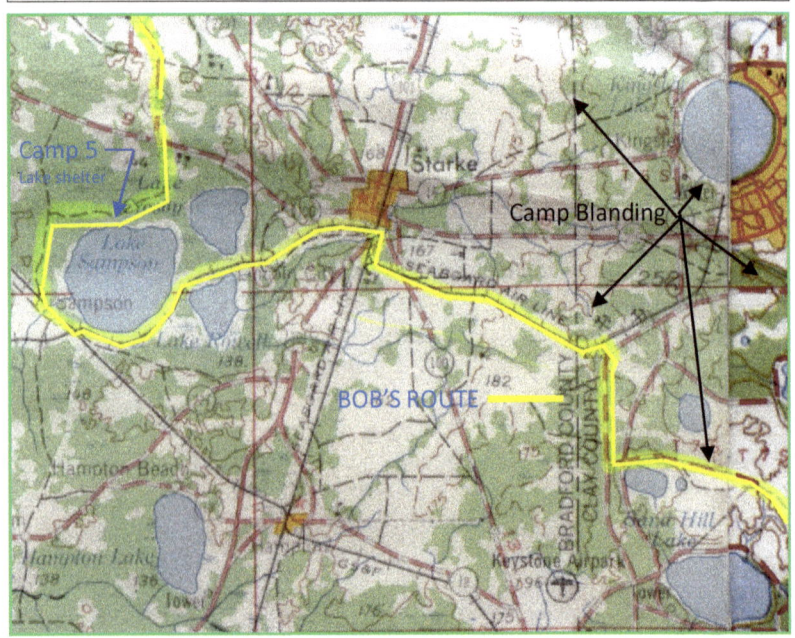

questionable, it appeared that it was still being used for something. It had an electric meter on the wall and drums and tanks on its deck. There was a semaphore in front of it that at one time was probably controlled by the station master. Now, it was actuated automatically. I couldn't help admiring the '57 Ford parked nearby. It reminded me of my old Ford Ranchero. I took a photo, I just couldn't resist it. I admire old railroad structures. They show such a interesting passage of time.

On my way out of Sanderson I started down a two lane paved road, Secondary 238. A mile or so and the road crossed over US No. 10.

"That's the third time I have crossed this interstate," I said out loud, "I hope that it's the last!"

As I was walking down this road, I had two offers of a ride. One was a well-to-do looking man driving a new Ford Ranchero, and the other was a boy in a Triumph sports car. This just shows how times have changed; today I'm sure they wouldn't have given me a second glance!

There was a lot of cleared land for farms along this road. The houses were small and far between and I got some strange looks. One lady called her kids inside when she saw me coming down the road and continued to watch out her window as I walked by. One old greying man got into his Chevy with his hound dog and drove by me real slow. Just looking, I guess.

About 8 miles down this road I came to what is called Swift Creek Pond. I left the two-lane and walked over to the shore. Tall but thin pine trees surrounded the pond, which was in my opinion large enough to be a small lake. There were a few pickup trucks here amongst the trees and some people fishing, some from the shore and some out on the water with small boats. I dropped my pack. As I was looking around, a man who had just come in from fishing, asked me if I would help him load his aluminum skiff. I was rewarded as he gave me the water from his ice chest.

I was thankful for it, because I wasn't going to drink that

lake water! I remembered what the logger had told me, "As long as it is mov'n." This was just a body of water, no campgrounds. I set up camp, then got wet in the water and hand washed some clothes. The lake was brown (tannic acid) with cypress leaves and pine needles floating around in it.

I can remember a few things from that night, starting with a whip-poor-will's serenade lulling me to sleep. Then in the middle of the night, two fishermen returned and noisily loaded their boat. The unwanted pesky mosquitoes appeared early in the morning.

The morning broke with technicolor sunlight. I was just sitting in my hammock looking out at some faint mist rising off the lake, when a man came up and unloaded his boat. He said that he was going fly fishing. He had a 9 HP outboard motor and aluminum skiff. It seems that his was the boat of choice for this water. As he was getting in his boat he looked over his shoulder and said,

"That sure is the life! Call me when breakfast is ready." He started his motor and purr-put-putted out into the lake leaving a faint wake behind and a little bit of oil exhaust smoke blending in with the mist.

I couldn't wait for him and he wouldn't have liked my breakfast of poptarts. So I continued down the road I was on yesterday but it wasn't more than a mile before I came to a fence across the road, barring my way.

Road Closed
No Thru Traffic
Cattlemen's Association
No Rustling

I had to make a decision. I could see by the map that this road would take me to Raiford. It was the next destination on my route, so over I went. For sure I wasn't going to do any rustling. As my army buddy and great friend from Chicago used to say; "Sometimes you just have to have a healthy disrespect for the rules!"

As I walking along I was surprised when a boy and girl in an old 50 Ford stopped and said that they could take me to Raiford. I declined, thanked them and asked,

"How far?"

"About a mile," they said.

I wondered where they came from? I never did see a house, side road or even hear them coming.

Raiford had 4 corners, a store and another old railroad freight station. It was not much different from Sanderson, but it had a different addition. There was an old railroad man standing next to this weather-beaten station.

He wanted to talk and exclaimed, "It's something else you're-a-doin, folks now-a-days wouldn't go across the street without drivin."

I had a good laugh. He said that he was waiting for a wayside freight to meet him here and receive the goods for the station. He was curious about my route. We talked for a few minutes and I bade him good-bye. I crossed the Atlantic Coast Line tracks, Highway 121, and then said good-bye to Raiford as I took the secondary paved road 229 to the southeast.

I have done some modern day Googling and found out that both the Sanderson and Raiford freight stations are now gone. In fact the Atlantic Coast Line railroad is no longer there in Raiford! I looked very hard from a distance on Google Earth and you can see the faint remains of where the track ran from Lake Butler up to the northeast. I guess that my photos are now historic.

I had to turn down another ride and came to highway 100. I crossed it and took the sand road with a sign indicating a boat ramp 3 miles ahead at Lake Sampson. It was dark when I got there. I found a shelter that was under construction for the lake frontage. I set up under there. It was a good find because there were a few drops of rain and wind. I ate a cold supper, went right to sleep, got up early, had a cold breakfast and

The Seaboard Air Line branch heading east-south-east from the "Y" at Starke.. It was easy hiking along this track. See the weed overgrown ties.

Pine trees with "V" slashes, collectors and flower pot shaped pails collecting pine resin for making turpentine. In the grass on the right can be seen some fire scars where the resin was heated to flow into shipping containers.

started out. It was chilly and damp from the weather the previous night. I needed some water because there had been nothing but uninviting muddy lake water back there.

The road continued around the west side of the lake. I came to the intersection of the Georgia Southern and Florida, and the Seaboard Air Line Railroad. I took the Seaboard Air Line around the southern part of Lake Sampson towards Starke. I was really enjoying being a hobo. The railroad tracks I was using were scenic and lonely, with lots of natural habitat along them and I still hadn't seen a train, almost as good as having my very own trail!

Both of these railroads appeared to be old railroad grades. They were weedy, overgrown and easy to hike because between the ties they were filled in with soil. At the outskirts of Starke I got my canteens filled at a gas station that was on a road that started running along the railroad track. My map showed me that there was a "Y" just south of Starke on the main Seaboard Air Line track heading towards Gainesville. This would take me towards the east a couple of miles. To explain a railroad track "Y", the tops of a "Y" come off another track. It is a place where an engine can travel all parts of the "Y" and in the process turn around and head back the other way and not have to use a turntable.

I headed down the line and sure enough, there was the "Y" and the Seaboard Air Line branch line heading east. There was a railroad freight station almost at the "Y". A station attendant hollered in a friendly way to me as I walked by,

"I bet when you get to a stream you'll take a swim!" I laughed and shook my head yes.

It was nice hiking this old track. It was also overgrown like the two other tracks I had been on. The ties were sunk in the dirt, consequently there were no bumps. It was very much like hiking a woodland trail. Soon I started seeing that every large pine tree was slashed with "V"s to collect pine resin.* There were small metal pieces attached to the trees under the slashed "V"s aiming down at flower pot shaped collection cups.

Every so often I would see fire sites where I guessed the resin was melted so it could be poured into pails for shipment. It was easy for the pine resin collectors to just walk down the railroad tracks to tap these pine trees.

When Slash and Longleaf pine are cut through the bark they extrude a resinous gum which seals the tree against insect invasion. To harvest this resinous gum commercially the trees are chipped or cut with a "V" shape. This "V" is about one half inch wide and deep. They renew this cut about every week, except during the winter months. This "V" is cut above the old scarred area. This area is about one-third of the distance around the tree. Every couple of weeks the gum which has been collected in the flower pot shape container is taken to a turpentine still. At the still the rosin and turpentine are extracted from the gum by a distillation process. Turpentine is used for the making of many products, such as: paints, varnishes, shoe polish, leather dressing, oils, greases, linoleum, and roofing. Rosin is used in the manufacturer of paper, soap, paint, varnishes, chemicals, matches and pharmaceuticals.

In the days of the sailing ship, the resinous gum was cooked into pitch and used in the building and repair of these ships. The longleaf and slash pines can be used for many purposes. After the resinous gun is mostly depleted, the pine trees may be cut unto saw logs, poles and pulpwood. In north Florida many towns will have turpentine orchards and a still.

There was a dark oil stain down the center of the tracks. I guessed that the diesel switcher that made this run must be a very old veteran. According to my map the railroad curved to the northeast and that was when I should find a road on the right heading south. The track made its turn to the northeast. There then appeared on the left side of the tracks signs on some pine trees:

Posted
No Hunting
Keep Out
Du Pont Industries

My map had the crossed picks on it which stood for a mining operation. A small one-lane paved road came in from the left; it had a cattle guard across it. This road crossed the tracks so I took it to the right. I didn't see any signs there. As I came out of the extreme dense vegetation along the railroad right-of-way, I was surprised. I was now in what had the appearance

The desolate desert looking area left over after the mining of the heavy minerals on the western part of Camp Blanding. The top soil has been taken off, the ore removed and the sand left. My research has informed me that reclamation is supposed to take place and the topsoil is to be replaced after the minerals have been removed.

of desert-drifting sand dunes with occasional clumps of grass and low bushes hanging on precariously. It was really a mined over area. They had removed all of the top soil, took what they were looking for and left just sand. It seems that this mining operation was very large, for as far as I could see there was just sand and scrub vegetation.

I have since done some research on this Du Pont mining. The area is called the Trail Ridge Deposit*. It was discovered by Du Pont geologists in 1947. In it were heavy titanium minerals such as ilmenite, leucoxene and rutile. DuPont then signed a long-term lease with the State of Florida Armory Board. This lease allowed them to mine heavy minerals within the boundaries of Camp Banding, Florida. Heavy minerals are usually associated with ancient beach sands, flood planes and shorelines. The Trail Ridge minerals were formed as an ancient beach. It is very complicated to process the ore. There are two plants about 15 miles from each other on Camp Blanding. One was built in 1948 and another in 1956.

After about three miles I came to an intersection. There was another fence across the road that I was on....a sign proclaimed:

> **Road Closed**
> **Detour Impact Rd**
> **Travel Safely**
> **Stabilized by**
> **US Eng. Btn.**

I took the road, supposedly called Impact Road heading east. There was no street sign on a post. After a couple of miles on this bright, hot, sandy road, I came to a small creek and filled my canteens. I didn't know exactly where I was but I was heading in the right direction. In about 4 miles I came to a huge shiny aluminum tower on the left. I started to pass it but then reconsidered. I'd go up and look around, maybe I could see that forest tower that appeared on my map near the Mike Roess Gold Head Branch State Park. This would be my next destination and hopefully campsite for the evening. I set my pack down and started up. There were nice metal stairs and a handrail, freshly painted silver. On the top it had a roof and except for the posts holding it up and the metal locked shed, it was open with a railing all around. I was about 60 feet up and it was nice and windy up here This sure wasn't a fire tower! The view was great. There was a clearing, and I could see water towers to the north and lots of lakes. I couldn't see the fire tower southeast towards my destination. It was somewhat far away. I climbed down and was just about to put on my pack, when I saw a sign lying face down in the dirt at the base of the tower. My curiosity got the best of me and I flipped it over.

> **Navy Bombing Target Tower**

Oh...Oh! Now it makes sense, I had some how stumbled onto the Camp Blanding property. There had been no signs. However, there were a few other clues which I had not got...but this left no question, I was on the military base! What was I to do?

I couldn't go back, I guessed that I had been on the property since I left the railroad track. I knew that I just had a few miles to go. I had to go forward. A short distance farther down the road there was another sign:

> **Danger you are in an area formerly used as a bombing and firing range by US forces. If any unexploded ordinance is found it must be marked and reported to US Dept. of Engineers**

"Wow! Now I knew why they called it Impact Road!"
I didn't know just how I got here, but I had to move on. I started off, this time moving fast. In a mile I came to a road heading southeast to the right. I took it and very soon I could hear cars on highway 21 in the distance. Of special note, there was a sign on the side of Impact Road looking back the way I had come in. I read it and chuckled to myself.

> **Travel Safely**

A Walk Across Florida

A sample of the vegetation and terrain in Mike Roess Gold Head Branch State Park. A Pine sentinel in a field above and an oak draped with Spanish Moss near a pond lend themselves for picturesque variety.

Camp Blanding* is the Annual Training Site for the Florida Active and Reserve National Guard. It was established in 1939 with 30,000 acres. Before it could get started as a National Guard facility, the Federal Government took it over as a training site for troops for the Second World War in 1940. The Federal Government bought an additional 40,000 acres and leased 100,000 more. This made it the second largest training camp in the United States. At its peak strength it had as many as 100,000 troops on the base. The major divisions were the 31st and the 42nd infantries. In later years of the war, a small part of Camp Blanding held both German and Italian prisoners of war. After the war the 100,000 acres of leased land were returned to the owners and the 30,000 acres were returned to the Florida National Guard. In 1954 the Federal Government conveyed its 40,000 acres to the Florida Armory Board with the reservation that it could be take it over in the event of a national emergency.

Today the Navy and Air Force gunnery and bombing target area and the Du Pont mining lease are both operational. There is a state operated forest management program with the revenues from the timber and mineral rights going to Camp Blanding. The camp's primary use is for military training; however it also has other uses. These include a game management area (fish and wildlife) regulated by the Florida Department of Natural Resources*, recreational use by national guardsmen and their families, camping, county landfill and a Girl Scout Camp. In fact today the Florida Trail goes through the base near the very area where I hiked.

Soon I was on Highway 21. Luckily there was a sign pointing down the highway to Mike Roess Gold Head Branch State Park. Today was my day of many strange signs!

This highway 21 was busy! Lots of people looking at me as they sped by. It was the only way to go and thank goodness I could see the park in the distance. I went up to the park entrance building and paid my $2.50 fee. I walked back to the camping area and set up camp. I was sure tired. I was lulled to

Early morning, Mike Roess Gold Head Branch State Park. A dark oak stands guard over the many reflections in a small pond as its Spanish Moss droops down over a hauntingly fog-like backdrop.

sleep as I listened to the drip.....drip....drip of the raindrops falling from the trees onto my plastic tarp.

It was morning and I decided that I would check out the park. As I walked around I realized that I was almost alone. I had left my pack at the camp site and had only brought a canteen and some snacks. The trails were real sandy, typical Florida soil. Even as I sat writing these notes in my journal, I could hear and see Navy planes screaming overhead in groups of four as they headed for the targets at Camp Blanding. I was glad I wasn't over there now!

I ended up traversing a large portion of the park, at least 7 to 10 miles before I got to the old mill site I was seeking. The area which is called the ravine was very plush with dense undergrowth. In this location there once was a dam, a mill and the remains of a cotton gin that used the power from the dam. Gold Head Branch flows from a series of springs located along the ravine walls. This is what has formed the ravine. The flowing springs continue to erode the stream deeper and deeper. As I traversed the park I followed a lot of wide fire lanes. I crossed an old Burlington Railroad right of way and grade. The tracks had long since been removed.

I was surprised to find that the Florida Trail was marked through the park. I came upon their sign as I was following a faint vehicle trail. It consisted of a board attached to a tree with a footprint stenciled on it. Close by, near a small lake, there was a chickee shelter, a covered platform raised about a foot or two above the ground. It would be a great place to put one's sleeping bag for a night.

I found out that there is surprising little information about the original founder of Mike Roess Gold Head Branch State Park.* I have searched the internet and contacted both the park and the local town's library at Keystone Heights for information about Mike Roess.

What I am to mention is all that they know! Mike Roess' original name was Martin J. Roess. He donated the original 80 acres, the ravine area, to Florida for a park in the early 1930's.

Left:
The first Florida Trail marker I came upon during my cross Florida hike was in the Mike Roess Gold Head Branch State Park. I guess that this was the first style marker.

Below:
I found this covered chickee sitting next to a small pond and along the trail close to the Florida Trail marker. It would be a nice place to put one's sleeping bag since it is raised up off the ground.

I was intrigued by this lack of information and decided to call the Florida State Park's visitor information line. They suggested the Florida State Archives which in turn transferred me to the Florida State Library. It was there that I was helped by a very nice historian. She found the information for me in the *National Cyclopaedia of American Biography*. She did this in record time and was so very kind to scan the information and e-mail it to me.

Martin John Roess* was born in 1880 in Oil City, Pennsylvania. His father emigrated to the United States from Hanover, Germany. His father at first was a farmer and then later became an oilman. Martin Roess graduated from Cornell University in 1903. After graduation he went to Ocala, Florida and formed the Ocala Lumber and Supply Co. This business sold building supplies and cut lumber. One of its largest customers was the Atlantic Coast Line Railroad.

He became a very successful businessman. In 1908 he started the M. J. Roess Co. in Ocala which cut timber until his property's timber depletion. Then in 1917 he moved to Jacksonville and was general manager of a large lumber company until 1924. After that he started his own company and sold lumber and ties to the railroads. At this time he also started working with the Beverly D. Causey corporation from Virginia which managed 3,000,000 acres in north Florida. A large part of this land was sold to the U. S. Forest Service for the beginning of the Osceoa National Forest. The Virginia Corporation later became incorporated in Florida as the Columbia Forest & Farms Inc. In 1935 Causey retired and Roess became the owner.

More than once Roess served as chairman of the Forestry Division of the Florida State Chamber of Commerce and as president of the Florida Forest and Park Association. Because of this he became very interested in forest lands in the state of Florida. That is why he donated the initial land for the park. The Civilian Conservation Core (CCC) built a major portion of the park in 1935. They planted trees, cleared areas for campsites, built roads and many of the buildings still in use today, such as the rustic cabins and the bathhouse. One can recognize the buildings by the rugged look and the judicious use of stone.

9
Cross-Florida Barge Canal

I decided to stay over one more night and get an early start the next morning. Before I turned in, I went over to the ranger station. I needed to find a way to go south, but not on the busy highway I was on yesterday. There was a ranger there getting into his truck.

" Sir! Do you have a minute?"

"What can I do for you, sonny?"

"Possibly you can tell me the best way to go south and not get back on the busy highway 21. I'm backpacking."

He said, "It's easy, just go through the park and out the back gate."

That is exactly what I did in the morning. I walked back through the park on the now familiar trails that I had traversed yesterday. When I got past the gate I went left a couple of miles on a sand road to Hwy 315 and then went south. This appeared to be a little used, paved, two lane road. I stayed on this very quiet road. I had to laugh to myself when I walked by a house and two little girls and a boy were camping in their front lawn. One of the girls had a hammock draped over her shoulder. I thought, she is doing it right!

Late afternoon when I was passing by an ominous looking pond, a gator bellowed out…..it was a loud roar, kind of like an old bull in a field challenging one in the adjoining pasture. I had never heard alligators before. I looked around from the safety of the road. The pond looked like a leftover excavation, irregular sides, lots of brush and tall grass near the edge. I did not see the gator.

The largest reptile in North America is the Alligator.* Some say that it has survived on earth in the same form for 200 million years. It is a black-green color and has a rounded snout. It may be mistaken for a crocodile, but its teeth do not protrude from its lower jaw and its mouth is rounded. This is

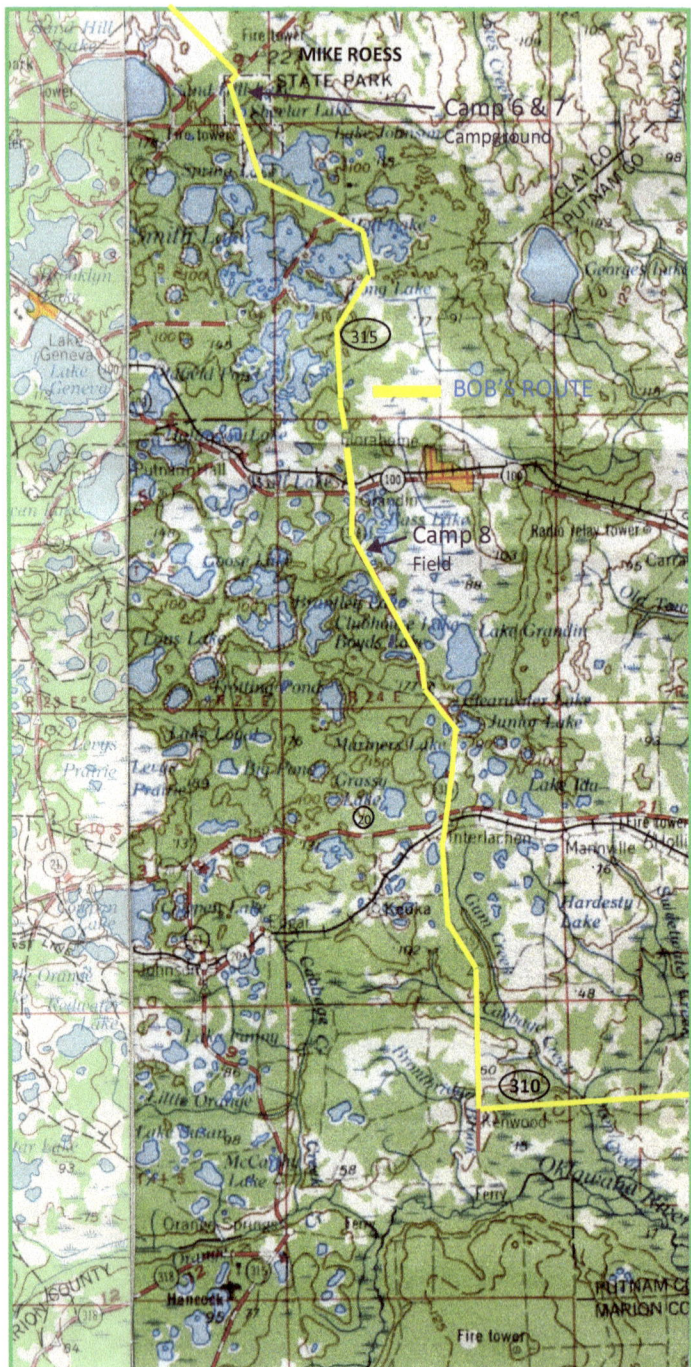

just the opposite of the crocodile. The alligator's jaws have a very strong bite. During a dry season the alligator helps the other aquatic animals by constructing "Alligator holes." These are depressions it makes in ponds with its tail and snout. The depressions provide both a source of water for insects and animals and a source of food for the alligator. They breed between April and June, and the roar or bellowing is used to attract a mate.

I continued on and came to a crossroads, Highway 103. It appeared to be another road like 315, and little used. I crossed over a mixed dirt, sand and gravel parking area to an old white faded-paint clapboard country store. I went up on the concrete porch and entered, one of the double screen doors slamming shut behind me. Dead center up front was a counter. The lady behind it standing next to an old push-button cash register told me that they were out of white gas, which I needed for my stove. I bought a sandwich and a coke, went back out and sat there on the front porch and ate my supper.

I continued on down 315, even though it was now dark. I did this because there was no suitable place to camp near the intersection. After I was some distance away, out of sight of the store and getting tired, I waded through the tall grass on my side of the road. I then slipped my pack under the barbed wire fence into a farmer's field, climbed the fence, laid my tarp on the ground and slept there next to the fence.

In the middle of the night I woke up hearing a strange noise. It was pitch black! Then I realized the noise was coming from the field. I could see strange dark shapes and the noise seemed even louder. It was a kind of a grinding-chewing sound. I was getting real scared. I scrambled for my flashlight which was under the shirt I was using for a pillow and shone it out into the field. Many pairs of eyes were shining back at me! At first I was shocked, then I realized…….they were just some curious cows.

I found out later that cows will graze at dark, especially if it is very hot in the day. They were chewing their cud as they

One doesn't want to go swimming in this pond. This is where I first heard an alligator bellowing. I never did see it.

I woke up in the middle of the night and heard a strange sound, kind of like chewing. I shone my flashlight out into the field and this is what I saw, talk about frightened......until I realized it was just a herd of curious cows.

were curiously watching me. It sure had given me a fright! I went back to sleep and in the morning the cows were nowhere to be seen. There was a heavy dew all over me, and I was wet.

I soon dried off, because this morning the Florida sun came out in force. The area I was traveling through was a mix of rolling hills and lots of small lakes. I saw some kids waiting for a school bus and a couple of miles farther, as the road wound around a lake, I passed the small country school. There weren't many vehicles on this road that day, and for that matter, there weren't many the day before. Since I had to take this road, I considered it a rewarding experience. I came to a picturesque area by the lake and rested as I sketched an old dock.

Hwy 315 took me through the small town of Interlachen. I crossed over State Road 20 and a railroad track, and kept right on going. I figured that in about three miles, I would be looking at the Ocala National Forest. I was soon to be surprised. The road ended and was barricaded. Ahead on the sides of the dirt road were the usual tall thin pine trees and lots of palmettos. In the far distance I could barely see an expanse of water.

The sign on the fence said that this area was part of the Cross Florida Barge Canal and:

> Posted No Admittance

The water was the back-up from the Rodman Dam and Reservoir. This certainly was not on my map. It just showed a road crossing the Oklawaha River. Now what do I do?

It was then that I remembered seeing a phone booth back about a half of a mile at an old gas station and a sand road crossing. I hiked back there and guess what…... I was in luck, there was a tattered, very worn and ragged phone book. I looked up the phone number for a local fire tower. The ranger recommended for me to go east to highway 19 and then south towards Ocala National Park and Salt Springs.

I took the sand road heading to the east from the gas station. A car raced by, not slowing down in the least, leaving me in a cloud of sand and dust. I assumed that they too were

A dock on a small lake along secondary road 315

Ghosts from the past. Worker's shacks on the north side of secondary road No. 310 heading towards State road 19 along the Rodman Dam Reservoir.

heading to highway 19. I figured that this road was Hwy 310 and would take me to 19. The next six miles or so the land on the right (south) was posted "Rodman Dam and Reservoir". It was a combination of pasture land, palmettos and pine forest. I couldn't see any of the reservoir water from this road.

As I walked along, I was surprised to see an unusually large number of run-down shacks in close proximity to one another. They were a desolate sight....ghosts from the past. These naked, never been painted, weather-beaten wood clapboard siding structures took on a life of their own, staring at me. I felt a strange premonition...a chill went through me. I could see small children playing in the dirt. Men with stooped backs sitting on the steps of porches with roofs of wind-bent rusty corrugated tin. And lastly, eyes watching me from the inside through the broken panes of dark windows. I felt the pain of living in impoverished conditions.

I headed south when I came to highway 19 and immediately came to, and crossed over, what was responsible for my detour, the Cross Florida Barge Canal.* If I excluded the occasional fire tower I have climbed, this would be the highest point I would attain on my hike across Florida.

The Cross Florida Barge Canal was first proposed as a ship canal. In fact as early as 1567 a canal was proposed by King Phillip II of Spain. They were having a lot of trouble with shipwrecks and piracy as their ships sailed around the southern tip of Florida and into the Caribbean. Again in 1818 Secretary of War John C. Calhoun proposed this for the same reasons. Nothing ever came of it until the 1900's.

In the 1930's, Florida politicians and businessmen worked to convinced the Federal Government that it would be a good idea. In 1935 President Franklin D. Roosevelt started work on the canal to provide work during the depression. Immediately 6,000 workers attacked the land, taking out ancient oaks and large longleaf pines, and driving out all forms of wildlife by clearing 4,000 acres. A year later work was stopped by the Congress and opponents of the canal. This was for two

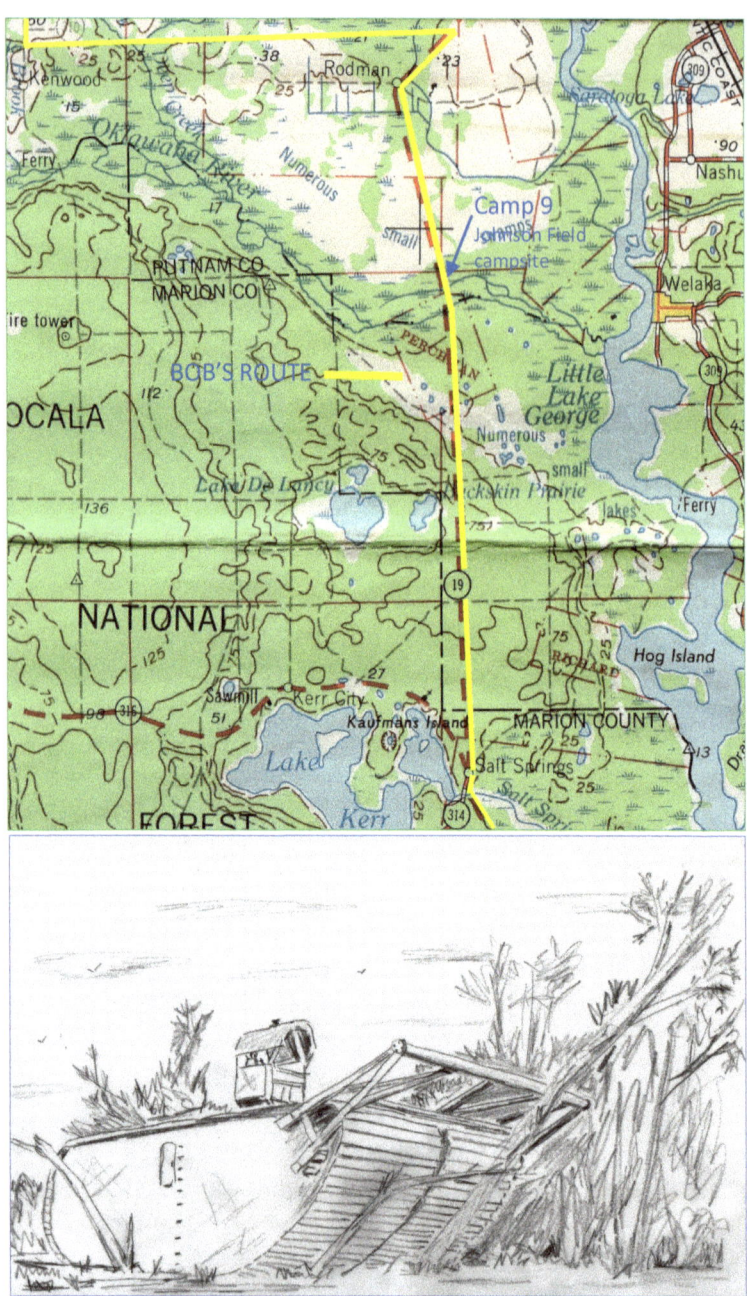

Crusher-crawler clearing land for the Rodman Dam & Reservoir.
Source for artist sketch: floridamemory.com. and Ring Power Cat photo.

reasons: Congress wanted to show the president who controlled the country's money, and it was thought the canal would deplete Florida's aquifers.

In 1963 President John F. Kennedy supported the canal for political reasons and in 1964 President Lyndon Johnson was present for the groundbreaking. Work continued by the Corps of Engineers on two locations: where the Withlacoohee River empties into the Gulf of Mexico east just south of Ocala to the Ocklawaha River, and the St. Johns River south of Palatka due west along the Ocklawaha River. Rodman Dam was constructed west of highway 19. The dam was named for a small community on a site that was flooded when the reservoir was filled. The dam was an integral part of the Cross Florida Barge Canal in providing water control to the canal.

To help in the construction of the dam and reservoir, the Corps of Engineers had a machine built that was called a crusher-crawler.* It was used to flatten thousands of valuable cypress trees along the Ocklawaha River. This destroyed 9,000+ acres of river and floodplain forest and backed up the river for 16 miles. This machine weighed 621,000 pounds, was amphibious and looked like a World War I tank, but much larger. It had two 10 foot wide tracks running the entire length of the machine and a tree pusher bar protruding out front. It was approximately 12-15 feet high by 40 feet long. On top was a control cabin which was an additional 12 feet high. The crusher-crawler was powered by two 270 horse power Caterpillar diesels.

The barge canal was opposed by environmental activist Marjorie Carr, grass roots environmentalists and a legal challenge by the Environmental Defense fund and the Florida Defenders of the Environment, so in 1971 President Nixon halted construction. The building of the canal was officially cancelled in 1991. Even so, the controversy has gone on, especially with the existing canal structures, the Rodman Dam and reservoir. In 1998 the Florida legislature renamed the Rodman Dam the George Kirkpatrick Dam and the water backup

Highway 19 Bridge over the Cross Florida Barge Canal looking south. Bob's pack leaning against the sign.

Cross Florida Barge Canal looking East from the Highway 19 overpass

Cross Florida Barge Canal looking West from the Highway 19 overpass. Today the cleared area is covered with large trees and vegetation up to the banks of the canal.

behind it the Rodman Reservoir. Kirkpatrick had fought to keep the dam and reservoir. The fight still goes on, because now the environmentalists are centered on preserving the Ocklawaha River by removing the dam and reservoir. All this information is just a short synopsis of the history of the canal and the struggle between population growth and preservation of a fragile environment.

Today the western part of the canal is a 110 mile preserve and park named the Marjorie Harris Carr Cross Florida Greenway. It has trails for hikers, bikers and horses, along with campgrounds and boat ramps The eastern part, the dam and Rodman Reservoir, has been set aside for recreation and conservation.

Here I was at the highway 19 bridge crossing the Cross State Barge Canal. The signs read:

> **CROSS FLORIDA BARGE CANAL**
>
> **NO STOPPING ON BRIDGE.**

Sometimes the literature I have researched said that this was the Cross State Barge Canal and other times the Cross Florida Barge Canal. I have used both names. As for the NO STOPPING ON BRIDGE, I wouldn't stop, but I would only be going about 3 miles per hour on the left side of the bridge facing traffic. I got my camera out, put on my pack, unfastened my hip belt and started my climb. I sure was fortunate, because no vehicles sped along during my crossing/climb. What a view! I got a couple of photos, one to the east and one to the west. I have since Googled this, and the wide areas that were cleared for the canal are now grown up with large trees and various vegetation up to the edge of the canal.

House boats on the Oklawaha River at the Johnson Field campsite and boat ramp. Just north of the Ocala National Forest.

10
Ocala National Forest

I got over the canal and off the bridge, then took a rest and had something to eat. I thought I must be near a Navy bombing target because silver stub nose Navy planes were streaking in overhead heading south. They would dive, pull up and circle around to do it over and over. They came in groups of two's and three's. They had red and green lights on their swept-back wings. What a great show!

I continued south on Highway 19. I soon decided that this road was too busy, with its fast moving logging trucks and other traffic. The only problem was that this was the only route I could take. I passed an intersection called Boys Ranch road. Because the road was becoming low and hemmed in by lots of wet growth, with cypress trees at least 50 feet high on both sides, I figured that I must be getting close to the Oklawaha River. I heard an alligator bellowing, and it echoed against the trees. I crossed a river bridge and saw a sign to Johnson Field boat ramp and campsite. I was sure glad to arrive even though it was dark I had hiked approximately 25 miles! Someone had a light bulb burning at their campsite. At first I thought it was a ranger, but it was just a camper. I picked a site and set up my camp. I made a small wood fire because I was out of white gas for my stove. Even though I had a good sound sleep, I did remember hearing and seeing raccoons scampering about in the middle of the night.

It was morning and the sunlight was filtering through the trees. A hoot owl sounded off in the distance. I got up and checked out the boat ramp and met some of my fellow campers in the process. One guy was on a trail bike. I bathed and lounged around in the sun . I surprised a snake in the water by the ramp. I was sure surprised that it could swim so fast, right on the top of the water.

There were a couple of house boats along the shore, one on the opposite bank and the other sunk on my side. This was a perfect opportunity to do some sketching. Later on I saw a guy working on his boat. I got to talking to him about the river and fishing. He said that he was going out later in the afternoon and invited me to go for a boat ride and fishing with him and his friends. I accepted and while waiting I spent some time polishing my boots, sewing some clothes and getting my gear in shape. A couple of the fisherman's friends, a girl and boy stopped by to talk.

Just a little past lunch, the fisherman came by and we went over to the boat ramp where he had his boat docked. His two friends were already on the boat. We launched the boat and headed up-river. From what little I know about boats, the boat was 12 foot long, looking like a flat-bottom boat with twin hulls. It went like a flash, a real thrill ride. My fisherman friend knew the river. There were many side channels. You could get lost if you didn't know the river, partly because of its sharp bends. It was beautiful scenery, a stark contrast to the canal I had just crossed yesterday. We stopped and dropped anchor in a back channel. There the cypress and water oaks formed a towering roof 40 feet above us.

The Oklawaha River,* is a Creek Indian name for "muddy." It is a little bit unusual because it flows north from Leesburg and then east where it dumps into the north-flowing St. Johns River. The river's original source is Lake Griffin (southwest corner of Ocala National Forest). Because of man-made canals and connecting streams it now receives water and pollutants from many other lakes in that area. Some parts of the river adjacent to Ocala are still wild and beautiful.

In the 19th and 20th centuries the river was used for steamboat transportation* from the St. Johns River mostly to the famous Silver Springs located center west of the now Ocala National Forest. In fact many famous figures traveled this way from Palatka to the springs: Ulysses S. Grant, Thomas Edison, and Harriet Beecher Stowe to name a few. These steam boats were very narrow. Many were only 18 feet wide at the waterline and 30 feet high above the water. They had to be small and have good turning capability to navigate the winding twisting river. The river is navigable for most of its length.

Many parts of the Oklawaha River's natural beauty are as they were when the Seminoles roamed and hunted years ago. One will see semi-tropical forest along the sides of the river. The forests are filled with maples, bald cypress, palmettos and pines of all types. In fact, it is so wild that one may see many animals such as bobcats, deer, otters, wild bore, black bear and turkeys. There are also plenty of fish, small mammals and birds.

However we did not catch any of those plentiful fish. We headed back before dark. Swarms of gnats were being pushed into our eyes as we sped back to camp. That night we had a pot of soup instead of fish. I talked way into the night with the fisherman. Seems he was a "Florida cracker" (A born-in-Florida country person). We talked about snakes, nature, hogs, deer, bear, cows and what have you. He finally left and I got into my hammock and didn't remember a thing until the next day. It sure had been busy.

It was early morning and I was out of rations. I had to get down the road, on to Salt Springs for resupply. As I left the boat ramp there was no sign of life at my friend's camp. The vegetation was changing as I got away from the Oklawaha watershed. Lots of scrub oaks, short needle pine "Jack Pine," some yellow pine. I didn't see any game except a black racer snake about 3 feet long that flashed across my path and then across the road. I was in Ocala National Forest. It seemed a very long time ago that I was in Osceola National Forest and didn't know if I would ever get here.

Ocala National Forest* gets its name from the name of a Seminole Indian chief, "Ocali," who lived in this area. It is located in central Florida between the Oklawaha and St. Johns rivers. It is approximately 600 square miles in size. Historically in 1539 DeSoto discovered an Indian village of about 600 homes at the present site of Ocala, which is about 10 miles

Johnson Field boat ramp and campsite is located just on the northern part of Ocala National Forest on Highway 19. Fisherman's campsite.

An early 1900's century steamboat on the Oklawaha River. They had to be extremely narrow to navigate the winding twisting river.

due center west of the Ocala National Forest.

The soil is mostly a coarse sand. Because it is very porous, it is absorbent and rainwater is soaked up almost immediately. The Ocala area has many wet prairies. They are low areas and have slash pine on the outer parts. Some of these lower areas are filled with water. They have no flow in or out, yet many of these ponds do not dry up and have water lilies growing in them.

This forest has the largest area of sand pine (scrub pine) in the world. Some people nickname this area the "Big Scrub." There are many valuable timber trees in this forest. Among these are longleaf, slash, loblolly and pond pines. There are also bald cypress and various hardwoods. Because of the large amount of longleaf and slash pine, the forest is able to produce "naval stores" operations.

As for the water, there are a lot of slow-moving rivers in the forest. The spring-fed rivers produce hammocks of evergreen and hardwood trees, and the prairies have many marshes. The Ocala forest has approximately 600 lakes and ponds.

The forest has many large animals and is a habitat for Florida's black bear, wolf, fox, wild boar, deer, alligator, bobcat, coyote and panther populations. For recreation the many lakes and beautiful clear springs make it a great area for hunting, fishing, camping, hiking and many other nature activities.

Salt Springs was a small town about 7 miles from my previous night's campsite at the Johnson boat ramp. It had lots of private property, not National Forest land. It was also on Lake Kerr. There was a fire tower there and you guessed it, I had to climb up and visit. This time I wasn't surprised to see a lady ranger. I climbed up and she opened the trap door and invited me in. She said that some time back she had injured her knee and the forest service was going to retire her. It seems that some of the towers had ladders to the platforms up to the top and no stairs. She said, "No way!" and had three operations and exercised her knee after the operations and here she was back on the job. She lived below this fire tower and this was

89 A Walk Across Florida

her job location. I thanked her for the visit and as I headed down, I couldn't help thinking that she was someone we could all admire.

It was resupply time, and the only food store in town, a 7-11, was the place to go. Whenever I went into a place to get supplies I always took my pack in with me. I couldn't take the chance of losing it. After all, now it was my home, just like a turtle's shell. As I was leaving the store and starting on my way walking along the road, an olive-drab 3/4 ton Army truck drove by and a Green Beret soldier driving it gave me a wave.

I continued down highway 19 towards Lake George. As the road was crossing a creek, I looked down and saw a small alligator casually swimming along. It was about a foot and a half long. Then here came another Army truck, and the two soldiers in it honked the horn and waved. I guess I must have impressed them--they might have thought that I was pretty tough! Ha!

After about 6 miles I arrived at Bill's Branch campsite. It was pretty rustic with an outhouse and an old-fashioned water pump. It was in a nice grove of oaks. I found out later that it was a hunters' camp. Today it can't be found on any map. I set up my camp--I sure was tired. After all, I now had an extra 10 pounds of food in my pack. That was about what I needed for a week's supply. Of course I had to buy whatever I could find in stock back at the 7-11. I hand washed some clothes and then as I was eating, I saw some Navy bombers overhead, slow and lumbering, heading south for their target.

The next morning I woke later than I had expected. I was just getting ready to leave when an old gentleman came up from the lake. He appeared to be an old farmer, wearing blue bib overalls with a vest made from a ripped brown shirt. He had white whiskers and was hard of hearing, but he wanted to talk, so I obliged him. In reference to the Navy planes I had seen, he said that he remembered during the Second World War that the bombing practice continued 24 hours a day. Army truck convoys would come through practicing with their

Navy fighter-bomber (more than likely a Vought A-7 Corsair, because that is what the navy was flying in 1969 and the silhouette has been ID'd by two military aircraft enthusiasts I work with) coming in over Lake George across Highway 19 for a run at the United States Navy's Pinecastle Bombing Range in the Ocala National Forest. The plane is either from the Jacksonville Naval Air Station or an aircraft carrier off the coast of Florida.

lights blacked out. He said that there was a Navy bombing range just southwest of us in the National Forest. As for his age, he remembered when the mail was delivered by horse and wagon. I said good-bye and he waved and hollered,

"If you are ever back this-away again, stop by for a visit."

As I started down Highway 19, the Navy fighters were overhead and at it again. I have since found out that the bombing range is the United States Navy's Pinecastle Bombing Range.* This is a restricted area of approximately 5700 acres. This is the only place on the East coast of the United States where the Navy can perform live bombing. The Navy drops approximately 20,000 bombs a year on this area. Most of them are duds, but a few, about 200 of them, are live. These fighters come in either from the Naval Air Station at Jacksonville or from aircraft carriers off the coast. They aim for the central 450 acres. They are authorized to drop up to 500 pound bombs. They have been using this area for the last 50 years with the U. S. Forest Service's permission.

Recently, since I work at a Naval laboratory, I asked a couple of my worker friends who are military aircraft enthusiasts if they could ID the silhouette of the Navy aircraft in the photo on page 91. Neither one hesitated a second. They both said,

"Definitely a carrier-based Vought A-7 Corsair." *

The A-7 is a single-seat tactical fighter-bomber. According to combataircraft.com, "The A-7 Corsair bears an uncanny resemblance to a drainage pipe with wings." It first flew in 1965. Even though it looks bulky, it had some real power and could deliver a large load of munitions. The "pipe" look comes from the large frontal intake. This was needed because the Pratt & Whitney turbofan engine requires a large amount of airflow, allowing it to attack targets at very high speeds.

I decided that I should get off this highway and see some of the backcountry. In a couple of miles I came upon a sand road entering the highway on the west side. I was sure that it was Forest Road (FR) 85, so I crossed over and took it, heading west. I hadn't gone very far, when I observed panther tracks

FR 85 heading west from highway 19. No wind, hot and not much shade.

One of the many prairies. They have marshes with prairie grass all around the sides. See the good size pines in the distance. There is lots of natural variety.

in the sand. It was walking, and then ran, and then according to the tracks it turned off apparently very fast. I also saw some bobcat tracks (which are smaller than a panther's by half yet larger than those of a common house cat) and lots of deer tracks. The area got more interesting when I got close to Hopkins Prairie. Now there were marshes with prairie grass all around the sides. Also there were a lot more larger pines. A lot of natural variety, and thank goodness, shade!

When I came to what I supposed was FR 86, I headed south. This should have taken me to Juniper Springs Recreation area, my destination for the night. As I headed south there were all kinds of hunters' roads heading this way and that. As the road was crossing a small stream, I surprised a beautiful buck which bounded off with his white tail waving. At the next pond there were a lot of large white and black birds wading in the water. A lot of the long-legged wading birds trample the bottom of the ponds, raising dirt and silt, and then scoop up the small fish that come gasping to the surface The sand road was getting hard to hike in, almost like walking down a beach in the dry sand.

It was a long, but another very eventful day and I arrived at Juniper Springs late in the evening. The ranger shack was closed. I could see by the entrance sign that it was 50 cents to swim and $2 to camp. I hung my hammock on some fair sized palmetto trees in the area. In the morning I could see that there was a mix of large pine and palmetto trees in the spring area. The spring had a small dam and a waterwheel where the water left the spring. I was rar'n to go so I got an early start and found the Florida trail at the entrance to the Juniper Springs Recreation Area heading to the east.

The Florida Trail Association* was formed in October of 1966, and the first orange blaze was marked in the Ocala National Forest at the Clearwater Lake Recreational Area. The original Ocala part was known as the "Ocala Trail" for many years. Today the Florida Trail is one of eleven National Scenic Trails in the United States and spans 1,400 miles from the

Camp site in the Juniper Springs area.

A Walk Across Florida

Florida panhandle at Pensacola Beach south to the Big Cypress National Preserve.

This all started in 1966 with Jim Kern who decided that Florida needed hiking trails. He made a 160 mile hike in 12 days from the Tamiami Trail to Highlands Hammock State Park near Sebring. The publicity from this and his persistence with the Forest Service helped him to form the nucleus of the Florida Trail Association. Their original goal of 500 miles has now turned into a plan for 1,800 miles of hiking trails with various loops and spurs. I didn't hike very much of the Florida Trail because I had never received the information I had requested from the Association before I started my cross state hike. I just didn't know where it was!

I know today it is hard to imagine not to be able to get the information, but in 1969 there was no Internet. Occasionally I came into contact with the trail on this trip. They were just starting the trail as I was hiking it. In the years since, the Florida Trail Association has done a remarkable job. Today it has 18 statewide chapters. Each chapter has its maintenance activities and meetings. It is a demanding job to keep up the trails because of the sub-tropical growth. The members are constantly doing whatever is necessary to keep the trails open.

As I hiked along I realized that I was looping around south-south east to bypass the two bombing ranges west of me. The trail went back and forth along hunting roads and new trail just like a snake. It passed through prairie which was covered with the most ponds I had seen yet. When I got to Farles Prairie Recreation Area, I stopped to rest and cool off. As I was sitting at that camping area, a lady and her little girl came over with a cup of ice water for me. A small but most refreshing act of kindness! We sat and had a nice talk.

I continued on the Florida Trail following the orange blazes. As I was traveling through fields of new pines near two sink holes I came upon a grandfather of an old pine, at least three feet across at the base. Now that's a good size! Suddenly I came upon what recently had been a logging operation.

The orange blazes of the Florida Trail in the Juniper Springs Recreation Area.

The Florida trail uses many old hunter roads. I did like being on the Florida Trail. It was much more scenic than highways.

There was slash everywhere, and guess what, I lost the trail. It was no-where to be found, no orange blazes, no trail! I was sure that the markings were on the trees that had been cut down. I saw where the logging trucks had been traveling to the east and since I was heading that way I decided to follow the truck tracks, cross highway 19, and proceed on to Alexander Spring.

It had been 16 miles, as I came up to the entrance to Alexander Spring. There was an admission shack and the very nice ranger said,

"No charge, and enjoy your visit."

We had a nice discussion. He was very congenial, and really knew his stuff about the area. We even talked some about catamounts, which is another name for panthers. He said that he was sure that they were around. I told him about the tracks I had seen.

I then had a nice cool swim. This was the most beautiful place to swim that I had been to so far on my adventure. I met a couple of college boys working part-time and they told me to set up my camp by the ranger house. I thanked them and did just that. It was a nice location and I had a good evening. It was uneventful except for some shots being fired way off in the distance in the middle of the night. I was to discover the cause for this later.

The next morning I took a blue-blazed trail which would have taken me to the Florida Trail. However I only followed it for a short distance until I came to another National Forest road, Clay Rd. I stayed on this until I came to the town of Paisley on secondary road No. 42. Along the way I came upon a bunch of spent military blank shells laying in the road. They must have been from the shots I heard last night I guessed the Green Berets had been practicing. That morning I had the trail all to myself, even on the small roads. Along the sand road I saw both deer and bobcat tracks.

I also noticed that I was seeing a lot of Sabal palmetto* trees. The Sabal can grow generally up to 65 feet high. They

On the left of my pack can be seen the two Florida Trail orange blazes designating trail direction change, similar to AT trail marking.

A very large old pine in the center of the trail with the Florida Trail orange blaze.

look ungainly, with a bent trunk and high up on the top a crown of fan-like leaves. Sabels were growing everywhere mixed in with pines and gnarled oaks. As a history reference, these are the same type of palmetto trunks that William Moultrie made a fort of in Charleston, South Carolina in 1776. The British men-of-war ships could not knock it down with their big guns because the trunks absorbed the shot. According to a Hessian soldier* who was on board one of the British ships during the bombardment, "The palmetto logs could not be razed by any gun on earth. For the point-blank shot of a twenty-four pounder strikes not even two inches into the wood and does no damage other than leaving the impression of the ball."

Another palmetto that is very prevalent in Florida is the Saw Palmetto.* It is the most common palm tree in the United States. It can grow up to 7 feet high but usually it is seen as a shrub type plant. Its name comes from the very sharp saw teeth along its fan type leaf supports. One does not want to bushwhack through an area of these plants. Besides the possibility of harboring snakes, the saw teeth will cut one's skin and rip one's clothes. You will definitely know when a Sable Palmetto gets-a-hold of you! The heart of the saw palmetto is edible. It was eaten by American Indians and Spanish settlers. The saw palmetto's berries are used for food by many animals. They are also made into extracts and powders and are used and sold as herbal medicines. Before using these people need to seek advice from their health care provider.

A short distance south on Hwy 42, I came to the Clearwater Lake tower. I went up and was invited in. I had a chance to look around the countryside and to see the stark contrast between the Ocala National Forest to the north and the developed private land to the south. The ranger told me to keep in mind as I hiked along, that the original Spanish land grants run at all angles along the coast of Florida and interfere with the mile sections. As we were talking, another tower ranger came up. It was the change of a shift. The new guy changed

The tallest Sabel Palmetto appears to be around 40 feet high.

A Sabal Palmetto with a trunk about 10 feet high.

the conversation to putting out fires with tanker planes. I thanked them both for the visit and hiked the way they had recommended, on a sand road to the Florida Trail and then a short distance to Clearwater Lake Recreation Area. There I decided to take a swim and just as I was setting my pack down I met a fellow hiker from Leesburg, Florida. He was the first Florida Trail hiker I had met. He was just getting ready to hike into Ocala National Forest on the Florida Trail. He told me that this was the start of the southern terminus of the Florida Trail in Ocala National Forest.

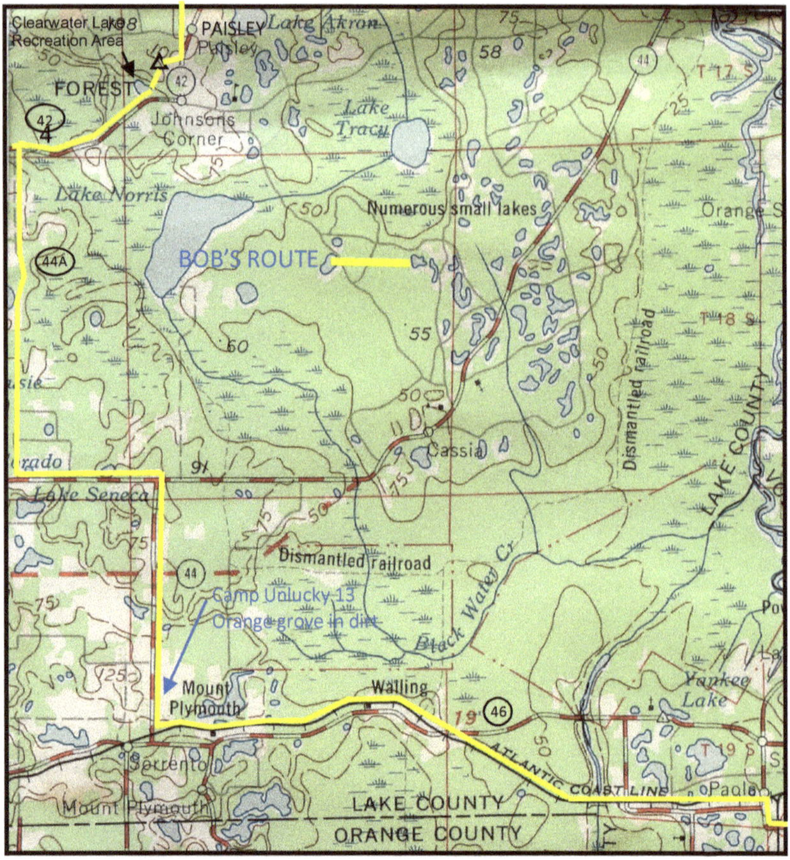

Old farmstead. The windmill was pumping water.

11
Bypassing Orlando

After I finishing my swim, I inquired where I could get some provisions. I then hiked an extra 2 miles each way along road 42 to get supplies. I couldn't see any town south where I was heading on my map. When I got back to where I started, I headed south west to a secondary paved road 44A. I then traveled east a short distance and then south again on another secondary paved road. Along these three roads I saw a boy with a homemade dune buggy, some air boats in a marsh area and a nice grove of oaks that I should have camped in. Six miles farther I had to settle for a campsite in an orange grove on the ground, in the dark. I was exhausted I had hiked 25 miles! I have a bad recommendation for anyone who wants to camp on the ground in an orange grove. If you like real dirty sand, old oranges on the ground, lots of cuttings from orange trees under your sleeping bag and the smell of oranges long since ripe, well, be my guest.

I started off very early the next morning so I wouldn't get caught camping in someone's orange grove. I was feeling a bit discouraged. Actually it was the first time I had felt that way. It was I think a combination of many things; the night's sleep on the ground, leaving the Ocala National Forest (I had liked the prairies and back country), and last of all, I was starting my loop around Orlando. I had to try to get around this big city without getting on any busy highways or in any business areas. After all where was I going to camp? This was going to be interesting.

I see that today the Florida Trail skirts Orlando on the east side, just what I was about to attempt. As I started to get moving, I was feeling much better. There was a sweet smell in the air of orange blossoms. I guessed that the groves were in bloom. I came to the railroad tracks just a bit before State Road 46. As I was now a veteran railroad spur hiker I took the Atlantic Coast Line east. I came to an old farmstead.

Under the Atlantic Coast Line trestle, Wekiua River

Railroad siding for pulp wood cars is all that remained of the town of Paola.

105   *A Walk Across Florida*

The place looked desolate, rundown and no one in sight. I was in need of water...again. I had been drinking a lot of it in the hot Florida sun. It was then that I heard...sweek-ah...sweek-ah...sweek-ah. I turned to look out past an old dilapidated barn, and there was my answer. An old fashioned windmill, standing at a corner of a fenced-in area, and it was pumping water with every turn of its blades. I cut across the overgrown dirt drive and back to the corner of the fence. The windmill was pumping water into an old claw-foot bathtub. I took this opportunity to fill both of my canteens and my belly with a very long, cool refreshing drink.

As I was walking back out to the tracks I looked over at the house. It was a derelict structure with just a hint of paint. It was in a somewhat better condition than my previous ghosts of the past. Then I saw something that really got my interest. Over to the side of it were two old Model "A" Ford sedans standing in tall grass. They were pretty much solid rust except for the chrome. The old Fords had nickel plating under the chrome which lasted a long time, not like today's vehicles. One of the old Fords was up on a trailer. I bet some antique collectors or hot rodders would have liked to be me at that moment.

I arrived at the Wekiua River, and there was a wooden trestle bridge crossing it. I decided that I would sit down there, eat and wash up. The river was slow moving with a lot of water oak, cypress, cabbage palms and pines growing along it. As I sat there listening to the occasional ripple, I felt like a proverbial hobo under the trestle waiting for the next train.

It was refreshing and I got some sketching in. Shouldering my pack, with hip belt dangling, I climbed back up the side of the steep river bank. Now up on the railroad grade I realized that I was very fortunate. The bridge had a kind of wood flooring along one side of it. I guessed it was for the repair men to walk easily on the bridge and it was a cinch for me to then quickly go across. I continued down the railroad line, but when I came to the town of Paole, it was gone. There was

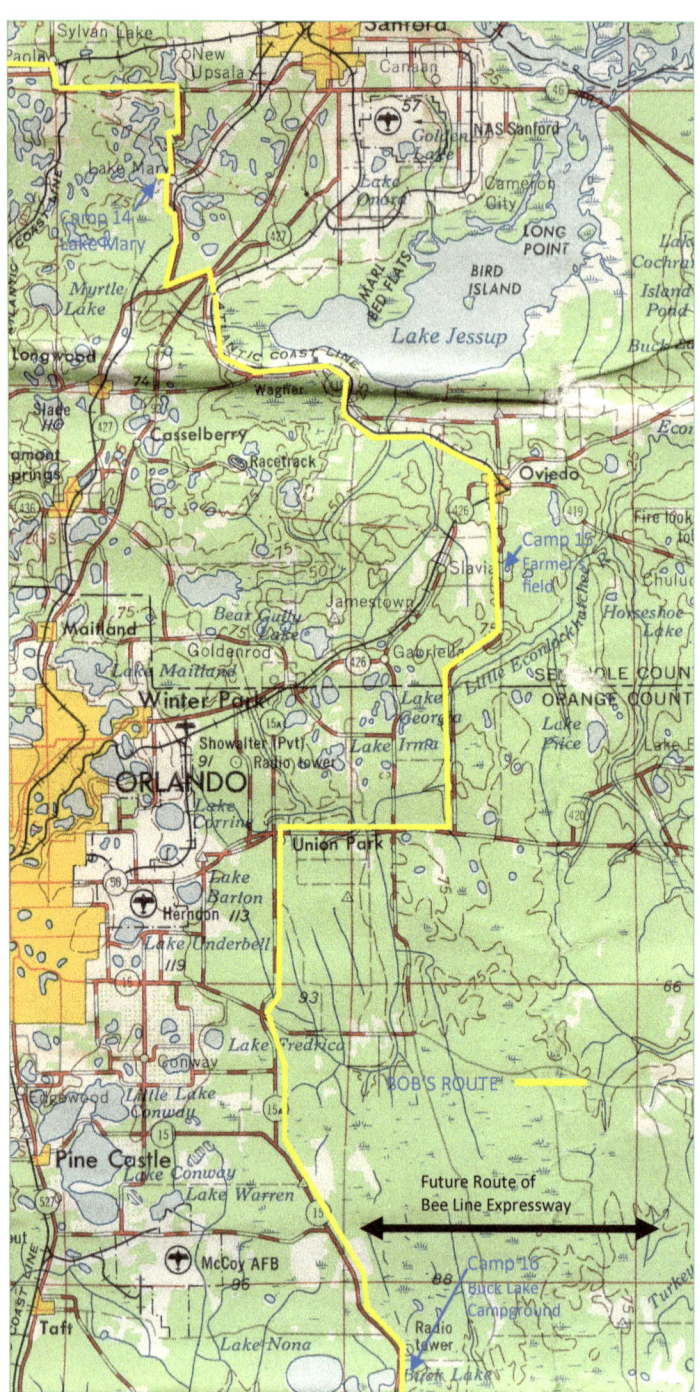

107 A Walk Across Florida

only a siding track with partially loaded pulp wood railroad cars sitting on it. They looked so lonely sitting there, with the 8 foot logs stacked crossways on the cars, ends sticking out. It was just a cleared dirt area, stomped flat from occasional trucks pulling up to the cars to unload. Not a sign of any buildings.

I left the Atlantic Coast Line tracks and took a south-bound road out of what was left of Paole. Immediately the road made a sharp 90 degree turn left, to the east, and crossed over another Atlantic Coast Line track heading north to intersect with the track I had been just following.

My map informed me that by turning east here and then taking the next road south, the town of Lake Mary would be ahead. Hopefully I would find some place there to resupply. Just before my turn south I came to a water storage and purification station. It must have been for the town of Stanford, about a mile straight down the road. I surprised a boy attendant and asked if I could fill my canteens. He definitely had plenty of water. I turned onto the next road. Lake Mary was a great little community. It had two stores, two filling stations, a post office and a laundromat. As I was buying some food at an open market, I met a boy called Butch and a couple of his friends. They asked me what I was doing and said if I wanted to camp at Lake Mary they would show me a great place on the lake.

They said that there were at least four or five lakes around Lake Mary and that it was a very nice area. While we are talking about lakes, I noticed that any one looking at maps of Florida could see that it is blessed with a surplus of lakes.* In fact, Florida has thousands of lakes. Approximately 7,800 of these are Natural Lakes of at least one acre. These lakes were formed by the limestone under the ground dissolving. This happened because the water above the limestone had an acid content. These Natural Lakes depend upon the ground water. There are usually no streams coming into or out of them. Some may be filled from underground springs. These lakes

Lake Mary in early morning

FRUIT GROWERS EXPRESS car sitting on a siding on the southwest corner of Lake Jessup. The fields of cabbage were ready to be picked and shipped.

are mostly less than 45 feet deep. Even though these lakes are mostly permanent, very dry times will affect their water level. Some lakes are as old as 8,000 years. There are even a couple that are over 30,000 years old.

I set up camp near the lake. It was all nice white sand. I could see by my map that there *were* a lot of lakes in this area. Butch and one of his buddies came by in the evening and we sat around a small campfire and talked late into the evening. They were both in their early twenties and seemed like good country boys. They lived at home and did odd jobs to put together some funds either to go to college or trade school or just to find a permanent job. They had a lot of questions about my travels.

I had a good sleep that night, and the morning burst forth with a beautiful red sky and a mist rolling across the lake. Butch came by about 7:45 in the morning. It seemed he was the guy with the car. We said our good-byes, as he had to get to work. I then took the opportunity to sketch the lake. While I was doing that, two boys went out with a small motorboat leaving a faint wake and a hint of oil smoke. As I was leaving, I asked a man and a boy if they could spare any water and they appeared more than happy to oblige. I had good memories of Lake Mary. I reminisced as I continued on.

I was approaching Orlando and my route now would be a zigzag, either west and south or east and south. I would have to be looking at my map a lot and trying to ascertain the road I would be taking. I would take railroad grades, sand or secondary roads. The name of the game was to stay away from civilization, business and busyness as much as possible.

I could see by my map that an Atlantic Coast Line railroad spur track ran around Lake Jessup, so I went to the east. When I got to a five road intersection, I could see the railroad track on the other side of the road. There was a small country store at the intersection. I stopped and while having a popsicle, I had a nice talk with the lady in charge.

As I walked along the railroad track it crossed over a

meandering stream. The water was crystal clear. Blue flowers were along the track and stream. The road here was very strange. It was a long curve paralleling the track and it was paved with red brick. But it was only about 10 feet wide! A real small road that I believed was very old.

I came around the bend and was heading in an easterly direction. I could smell something strange. Then I saw the fields: it was cabbage. It must have been ready for market. On a siding next to an old yellow shed was a refrigerated railroad car. The brick road had changed to a small paved secondary road and the railroad track came very close to it. That was when two good-looking girls in a new Ford Mustang passed by me...twice. They didn't stop, so I guessed I had missed my chance. Next I saw that there were a collection of identical, very small, plain houses along the tracks. My hunch was that they were for the migrant workers who would pick the cabbage. Where the railroad track crossed the secondary road there was a closed store, its better days long since passed —a perfect place for a rest.

I was on the south side of the road. Since it was time for lunch I stopped at a cool spot next to a small stream in an orange grove. I noticed a green Ford Ranchero pickup drive by a couple of times as I was sitting there. Oh no! I thought, it is probably the grove owner. He came by again, and this time the fella stopped to talk.

" Hi, what you up to?" he asked, "I'm a foreman for Seminole County and have a tractor crew cutting grass along the road you are walking on."

"Yes, now I remember seeing the tractors go by earlier," I responded.

"We were joking about hurrying ahead of you and cutting the grass so it would be easier for you to walk," he laughed.

He nodded toward the creek and said, "kind of makes you want to take your boots off and wade in."

He left, and after listening to his suggestion, I waded in.

A short distance farther, before the railroad track left the road and headed for the town of Oviedo, two ladies stopped me and wanted to talk about hiking. One had camped and hiked in New Hampshire, in the White Mountains, like the man I had met at Ocean Pond in Osceola National Forest. They were real nice and told me about a public park ahead where one could swim. I thanked them and told them that I would keep it in mind.

It is amazing to me, to think that many of the areas I hiked through 45 years ago were just back country. Today if you look at a Google map it is all built-up. I'm glad that I hiked when I did! Those old quaint country stores are now replaced by 7-11 stores. Many of the spur railroad tracks are gone, torn up or now owned by one large conglomerate. The fields and orange groves are now subdivisions and shopping centers.

I am very grateful and relieved that today you can hike on the Florida Trail and have some semblance of wilderness or at least a route to get through these congested places. In a way, I guess, it is to be expected. This area is on the outskirts of the large city of Orlando, and people want to work in the city and live in the country. Before they realize it, they have made the country the suburbs and then it becomes just another part of the city.

While we are on the subject of Orlando,* why is it here? It is not near a beach, a bay, a large river—so why just here in the middle of Florida? After all, it was fairly large even before Disney World located nearby in 1994-1995.

The first European settlers came to the Orlando area about 1837. Before that the Seminole tribe of Native Americans lived in the area. It is thought that the Seminoles lived in the Central Florida region for over 6,000 years, even as much as 12,000. Another Orlando history site says that the Seminoles migrated from Georgia and the Carolinas in the 18th century. I think that is a very large time difference. However, either way, we should be able to agree that the Seminoles were there first. The Seminoles and the settlers had violent clashes and in 1838 the U.S. Army established Fort Gatlin. The settlers then began to build outside of the fort. This was the beginning of Orlando. This Seminole War lasted until 1842 when the Seminoles, who were never defeated, accepted a treaty and were given land farther south towards the Everglades.

Throughout 1860 cotton plantations and cattle ranches were the main businesses. In fact the cattle business was just like the "Old West," with cattle rustling, cow towns and rowdy cowboys heading to the local saloons every Saturday night for entertainment. After the Civil War, the returning defeated soldiers found the cotton fields had gone to seed and there was no slave labor to work them. In 1870-1880 many of the cotton fields were replanted with citrus groves.

Now with the cattle and citrus industries doing very well, there came the need for better transportation to get the goods to markets. In 1881 the first railroads came to the city of Orlando. The railroads brought winter tourists down from the North. In 1920 Florida had a building boom, and during the Second World War many military training bases were established in Florida, including the Orlando Army Air Base and the Pinecastle Army Air Field (now Orlando International Airport). To top all this, in 1971 Walt Disney World started construction. So a military fort and then cattle and citrus gave this area its start, and today it is booming.

I left the railroad tracks in Oviedo and turned south. I stopped to talk to a nice group of people at a filling station as I filled up my canteens. I needed some film and for the next mile or two stopped at the few stations I came to--no film. I'd just have to sketch. I guess you might wonder, why did I have just a few rolls of film when I started out? Remember everything is weight. I figured I could find some whenever I needed, but I had so far kept off the main roads and away from shopping centers, thank goodness. I think of the digital 10.1 mega pixel point-and-shoot camera I have now (which is not much weight compared to the large 35 mm). Think of the weight savings, just about 1/3 of the weight of the 35 I had and I could have taken 1,000 plus pictures with just a miniature memory stick....... oh the technology of today.

I got to the park the ladies had told me about. A grouchy attendant told me that it was going to close in one hour. I thought I would hang around and camp there after the guy left. He never did. He kept driving his pick-up around and giving me the stare. Needless-to-say he wouldn't get the "Come to visit us in Florida" award. It had started to rain and thunder and lightning. I decided to just go a few blocks down the road and then put up my hammock in the middle of a field on a couple of trees and in sight of some houses. The rain stopped momentarily for this work, and I ate something cold and climbed into my hammock. It rained off and on the entire evening, including thunder and lightning. I was relieved when the lightning finally stopped.

I was up at 5:30 AM and went the few blocks back to the park and waited for it to open at 7:00 AM. Thank goodness the early shift was manned by a different person. Why go back? Well, I could bath in the bath house and then take a nice swim. After eating my hot breakfast, I packed up and continued on my route. When I got to today's Hwy. 50 I filled my camp stove up with Amoco white gas for only 4 cents. I sure did thank the gas station attendants for their patience. Of course I always bought something else.

I went west on 50 for about one mile and at 15A which today is 551 or N. Goldenrod Rd. I headed south. Again I remind you that this was all country, not congested like it is today. There was a huge oak shade tree, and it beckoned me to stop, drop my pack, sit down and lean against it for a rest. While I was sitting there near the road, the owner of the house came out to talk. He was an elderly man with very white hair, kind of like mine today. He didn't have much time to talk because his wife called him from the front porch. I guess she had some chores for him to do. I thanked him for the shade of his tree.

My next stop was an orange grove, where from behind some trees I hurriedly changed into my shorts as it was getting hot. I have to take a moment to go forward to the future. I can see as I sit by my computer today and look at a modern map that I was very close to Pershing Ave. That is by coincidence where the relatives I was hiking to visit in Key West were going to live when they retired in later years.

Some distance down the road I had a run-in with "Brutus," a huge, threatening, barking German Shepherd. How did I know his name? That was what she called him from her porch just before he lunged at me. I didn't know, but I might be beginning to like farmhouse dogs less and less. At least the horses in the next field were very friendly.

When I got to State Highway 15 I took it, because it was going to take me towards and under the Bee Line Expressway. At the underpass at the "Bee Line" the grass was too high, no fun to hike in. Lots of traffic and all the people stared. I guess they had never seen a backpacker before. I did get the sign of the times, the peace sign from lots of youngsters. I guessed that they didn't know that I was just discharged from the U.S. Army January 1968. They just didn't know an authentic cross-country hiker from a hippie. Even so, I acknowledged and waved at them.

I stopped at a gas station on the other side of the "Bee Line," *still no film*. About three miles farther I came to what in my trip diary says Butler Lake, but I bet it was Buck Lake campground. It looked like a good area and had a nice store and office combination, and charged only 50 cents to camp for the night. Now believe it or not, after talking to the man who owned it, he said he had to run over to the house for an hour. Would I stay here and tell any customers that he would be back soon and just pick a camp site and they could check in later. I was a campground manger! Wait till I write home to my mom, she will never believe it.

While running the store I had a very long talk with an Ohio man who had come down to live in Orlando. He was going to camp that night and then look around for a place to live and work. Something about having had enough snow. I guess that is why so many people have found their way to Florida.

That night and morning when the store was closed, I was able to cook with my stove on the front porch. I decided it was time to wash my clothes and I was fortunate that they had a very small laundromat in the back of the bath house. In the night it rained very hard, but in the morning the sunrise was wonderful! I had gone 22 miles the day before. I decided to rest some. There was a small, quaint church across the road and I sketched it. Then I couldn't resist drawing the old foot bridge along the lake over a small stream.

The day is beautiful, living is great and God is good, I thought to myself. I had packed up and was stopping back at the store one more time to tell the proprietor I was leaving. There were two families traveling together there and we got to talking. It seems that they were bikers and were also very interested in hiking. They wanted to know the weight of my pack. There was an old freight scale on the porch so I took it off and laid it on. They moved the weights until it balanced and read 56 pounds. By the time we finished talking and I got going it was a very late start, 11:30 AM.

I set a fast pace going on this old highway. I was rested and there wasn't any traffic. A lot of the countryside was cleared leaving only grassland for cattle grazing. There were also many types of palmetto and pines, cypress swamp stands, with a scattering of orange groves and lakes. I was in the real country again, and for a hiker it was a lot better than the "around Orlando" part of my trip.

Church across the road from the campground at Buck Lake.

Old foot bridge at the Buck Lake Campground.

12
Kissimmee Cooperative Bald Eagle Sanctuary

I made Narcoosee by 2:30 PM. I was traveling 2 1/2 miles per hour. When I got to 441 in Aston, I headed west towards St. Cloud. It was there that I met a couple of young boys on bicycles. They were astonished to see a real backpacker with a great big red pack. They wanted to talk and we did as we moved along. I saw them off by giving them some of the strawberry licorice I used for a treat as I hiked.

I guessed I made a hit in town. Everyone looked, and I in turn, waved. I must have startled a blonde girl in a truck at a stop light, because after her initial surprise, she laughed. A girl in a drug store waved and that is where I finally got the last three rolls of film I needed.

In the middle of town I picked up Secondary Road 523, which in town was known as Canoe Creek, and headed south. According to my map, it was a straight shot south on a real backcountry two-lane road, which after about 20 miles turned into a unpaved road and then on to Lake Okeechobee.

Once I got out of town a couple of miles, I started seeing a lot of scratch-off black tire marks on this deserted two-lane road. I figured it was a place for the local hot rodders to try out their cars, and then match off to see who was the fastest. I myself was a hot rodder once. In the late 60's and early 70's, I had a 1936 Ford 5 window coupe, channeled 4 inches, with motorcycle front fenders and a hundred horse flathead engine with a 3/4 cam. I never drag raced on the street, only on the strip. I am however guilty of scratching off and leaving black tire marks a few times.

It was late afternoon and I was tired. I stopped along the side of the road and just lay down in the sand and grass and put my head on my pack. While I was lying there I heard a car go by. It was the first one all afternoon.

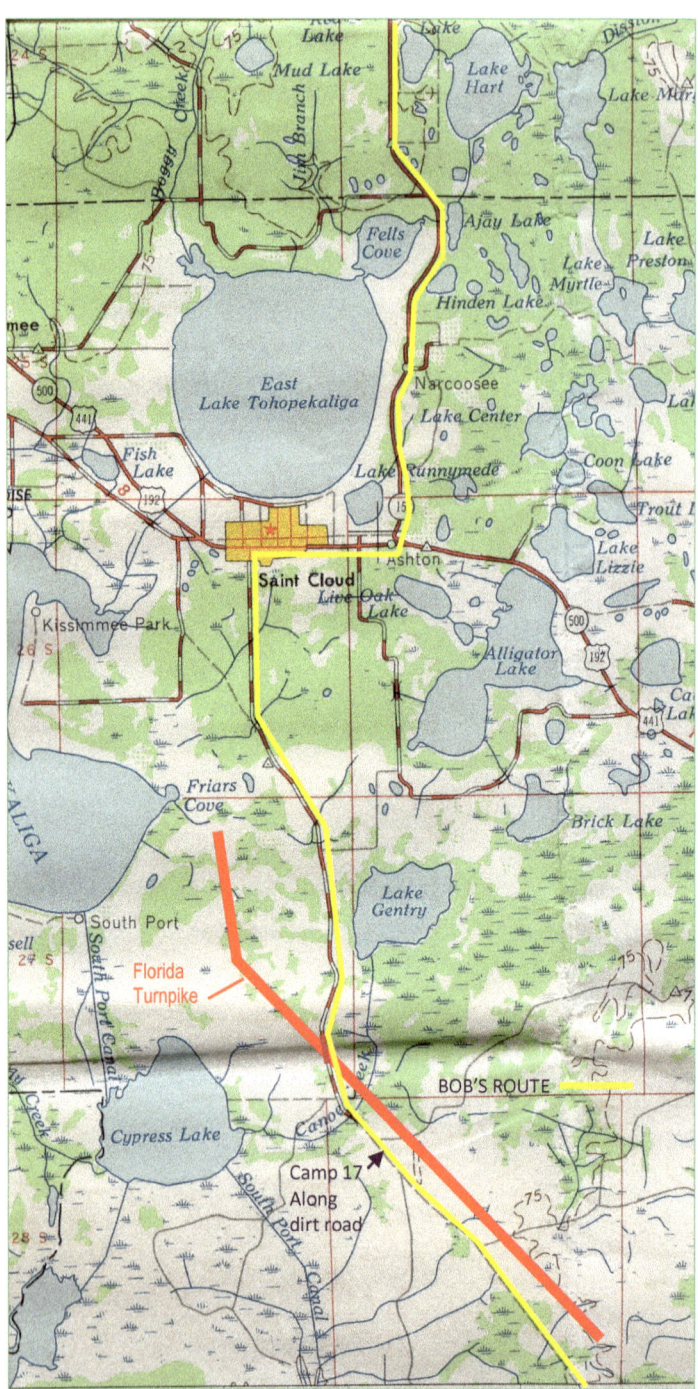

119   A Walk Across Florida

This sure was a quiet road I thought as I got back up and was off again. Guess what, just a few miles farther I noticed a car pulling off on the other side a short distance ahead of me. A man got out and put on his hat and I could see that he was a county sheriff's deputy. As I got closer to him he motioned for me to come over.

Oh Oh! I hope I don't get pulled over for speeding, I thought as I looked both ways and crossed over. I was hiking on the left side facing traffic.

"Hi, son. Where you going? What you do'n?"

" I'm backpacking from Georgia to Key West. I started the first of this month. I don't usually get out on the highway. Most of the time it's dirt roads, trails and railroad grades."

"Got any ID?" he questioned.

"Yes sir, but I have to put this pack down. It's in the side pocket, can't hike with a wallet in your back pocket and carry a pack," I explained.

I sat down and slipped off my pack, kneeled down, zipped open my small lower side pocket and came out with my wallet. I stood up.

"There it is sir." As I gave my driver's license, he took a long look and gave it back to me.

"Ok Bob, it looks fine to me. The reason I came by is because someone reported seeing a person lying along the highway, thought they might be hurt."

"I bet that was me sir. You see, sometimes when I'm tired and need a rest I just stop and sit down, sometimes I lay my head on my pack."

"Where you headed for tonight, Bob?"

"There is a campground about three miles ahead according to my map."

He introduced himself, we shook hands, and he said, "I could take you there if you want?"

"No thank you, sir, because I have to hike it all."

We got to talking. This guy was A-ok, a real fine law enforcement officer. Seems he had also been in Korea, in the

"A-frame" cabin that campers may rent in the Canoe Creek Campground.

Florida Brama-type cattle. Note hump behind neck and the horns pointing upwards.

U. S. Army, just like I had been. We had a lot to talk about.

"Well, I've got to go now. But here Bob, is my card, if anyone stops you have them give me a call."

"Thanks a lot." I looked at his card, it said Sheriff's Deputy, Osceola County, Florida.

"Take care now," he said as he headed back to his car.

I kneeled down and put my wallet back in my pack. I sat down, slipped my arms into the straps, leaned forward and stood up. The Deputy's car turned around. He waved as he passed by, and then fast disappeared in a roar of rich black gas smoke as he sped down the road. I wondered if he ever came out to Canoe Creek road to try out the cruiser?

It was getting dark when I got to the campground. I surprised the people hanging around the office. It was not every day they have a walk-in they said. The charge was only 50 cents for me to camp. Nice restrooms. This was the life. The water smelt kind of like eggs, but the hot shower sure felt good. That next morning I saw that this campground had some "A-frame" type cabins that people could rent.

I had got a little bit past Lake Gentry when I came upon my next adventure. I talked earlier about cattle being a major business that helped to start Orlando. This day I saw my first cattle drive. A bunch of commotion was happening in a field next to where I was hiking. I could hear a lot of noise and see dirt being stirred up. Then lots of moooos. Here came some cowboys driving a herd of Brahman cattle. One of them hollered over to me and asked me to please wait while they opened up a gate. The cows came out onto the road and headed south, the same way I was going. There were four cowboys driving about 150 cows. The back guy had a bull whip and was cracking it to keep them going. Even though I stayed over to the side of the road, the first two horses were spooked by me being there and the riders had a hard time holding them steady.

The introduction of cattle* to Florida is a very interesting story. It seems that the first cattle and also horses were

Two cowboys herding cattle right down Canoe Creek road. A real cattle drive! One of the cowboys in the rear had a bull whip, a real "cracker".

Two lane Canoe Creek Highway, cattle in the distance blocking the road as they head south to their new pasture. Three cowboys on horseback.

brought to north Florida by Spanish explorers in the early 1500's. They were from the costal areas of Andalusia, Spain. The cattle were left behind to roam after the Spaniards were forced to flee to their ships by the Calusa Indians. These cattle were not Brahma. This original Spanish stock were small and adapted to the Florida heat, parasites and the relatively low-quality forage of the grasslands, swamps and forests.

The Spanish explorers continued to bring more cattle to the new land. In fact, the Franciscan and Jesuit missionaries became the first Florida ranchers with the founding of St. Augustine in 1565. They used the Indians they were converting for the labor to work these herds throughout their various missions. By this time not only the Spanish had herds of cattle but Indians did also. A lot of wild cattle from the original expedition had multiplied and roamed the rangelands and prairies, and they were free for the taking.

In the 1600's the Spanish expanded their cattle production in Florida. This allowed them to export outside the country through the connections they had with Cuba. This trading with Cuba lasted for more than 300 years. Because of this a major commercial industry was started. It therefore was the first commercial industry to develop in the New World. It was the beginning of Florida's agriculture industry.

By the 1700's, Florida contained more than 30 ranches and thousands of head of cattle. The British began expanding into the Florida area in the very early part of the 1700's. This was detrimental to the Spanish cattle ranches. After that the Seminole Indians became the major livestock producers. The British ruled Florida from 1763-1783, then Spain. The U.S. took over from Spain in 1821. At this time according to a Florida Memory article, Florida was described as a "vast, untamed wilderness, plentifully stocked with wild cattle." From 1840 until the Civil War, Texas was first and Florida second in the U S cattle industry. About this time Florida cattle were sold to Cuba and the U.S. Naval Base in Key West. While the Civil War was raging, beef from Florida was smuggled to the

Confederates and also sold to the Union. After the Civil War Florida became the nation's leading cattle exporter to Cuba, Key West, and Nassau.

The cattle that descended from these first Spanish animals were later called Florida "Cracker" cattle.* It is believed that the name came from the Florida cowboys that herded the cows with their bull whips cracking in the air. In fact Florida had both the first cattle and cowboys in this new country!

As an interesting side note, the great western illustrator and artist of horses, cowboys and Indians, Frederick Remington, also wrote short stories. In the book, *Crooked Trails** which is a facsimile of his 1898 edition he wrote a story entitled "Cracker Cowboys of Florida." In it he describes the cowboys after the cattle trade had all but disappeared from Cuba and there was just a little money to be made from Key West and some local settlements. These cowboys were of a "generally bedraggled appearance." So he doesn't give the cracker cowboys very much credit at that time because his experience and love were naturally of the west. Even so, it is written with a local dialect and gives one insight into the life of the cowboys and the landscape of the times.

He was born in 1861 in Canton, New York. By 1890, Frederick Remington* was the most respected illustrator in America. In June of 1898 with a commission from Harpers Weekly he traveled with the invasion troops during the Spanish American war from Florida to Cuba. While he was in Florida he was able to write one of his few non-western stories including some great illustrations depicting the Florida cowboy.

One thing unusual about the Florida Cracker cattle is that their horns point up rather than out like the Texas Longhorns. This may be an adaptation for moving about the low-lying tree branches and through the scrubby Florida land.

In the early 1900's different types of Brahman cattle* were imported from India. They were cross bred with the Florida cracker cattle and produced an excellent breed of larger beef animal which were even more productive. In 1965, to save the original Florida Cracker cattle from cross-breeding and extinction, the Florida Agriculture Commission solicited donations from owners of the original herds. A State-of-Florida herd of Cracker cattle and a breeders association were started.

I let the cattle herd get a long ways ahead of me before I started walking again. The rest of the day I walked past lots of wide open spaces, some cypress swamps and clumps of pines not too large in diameter but up to 50 foot high. Later in the afternoon I was running low on water and came to a stream flowing out of a cypress swamp. As I was cautiously filling up my canteens I noticed a lot of game tracks. This area is great habitat for all kinds of wildlife.

I was about 10 miles south of St. Cloud when this two lane road I was traveling on crossed over the Florida Turnpike.* This toll road is 312 miles long. It goes from I-75 about 60 miles north of Tampa, at Wildwood, across the state a little southwest of Orlando to Fort Pierce. It then parallels the Atlantic beaches 5 to 10 miles inland to northwest Miami. One of the busiest highways in the country, the Florida Turnpike also ranks third in toll road use.

It was supposed to continue up the coast from Fort Pierce to Jacksonville, but Orlando citizens helped to change its direction to its present location. This was completed in 1964. This also helped to locate Disney World. Walt Disney was flying over Florida to find a location for his theme park when he saw the turnpike crossing Interstate 4. He decided that this deserted intersection was a great place to build his park—cheap land and excellent transportation access.

North of Fort Pierce the Turnpike enters a extremely rural area with cattle ranches and orange groves along the road. Between Fort Pierce and Kissimmee, a distance of approximately 90 miles, there is only one interchange at Yeehaw Junction. The section between Fort Pierce and Yeehaw Junction, 40.5 miles, is the second longest gap between two exits of any US expressway. The record of 48.9 miles for the longest gap without an exit, is between Yeehaw Junction and Kissimmee,

The Kissimmee Eagle Society had these two eagle nests posted. This was on N. Canoe Creek Rd. and not too far after I crossed over the Florida Turnpike.

the area I was now in.

This Florida Turnpike has something they call an "intelligent transportation system." It has two traffic management centers. They can monitor continuously by closed-circuit television traffic cameras, dynamic message signs, highway advisory radio and radar vehicle detection systems. In other words, "They got you covered!" It sure was eerie to stand on that overpass watching the four lanes of traffic speed by. It was high-tech. My world was a lot different as soon as I got far enough away to not see or hear it.

Large clumps of pine trees, open scrub pasture land--and what were those two large nests over by the grouping of dead trees? Then I saw the Kissimmee Eagle Society signs.

> Posted
> Eagle Nests
> No Trespassing

I didn't see any eagles but the nests were sure impressive. I took a photo from the road and continued on. I have not been able to locate a Kissimmee Eagle Society but there now is a Kissimmee Valley Audubon Society. It seems that eagles are so popular in the Kissimmee area that there are subdivisions, teams, streets, associations, streams etc. named after the eagle. Florida has one of the largest Bald Eagle* populations in the United States, 1,400 or more nesting pairs. The first is Alaska and then Minnesota and Florida compete for second and third place. The Kissimmee area in Osceola County is one of the most populated eagle areas in the state of Florida. Why do the eagles like this area? It has lots of lakes with fish for food, a good habitat of open land and secluded nesting areas.

By the late 1950's until early 1960's because of the use of the pesticide DDT, the eagle species in the lower 48 states was almost wiped out. It was interfering with the calcium of the bird's egg and making it brittle and was unable to withstand the weight of a nesting adult. After the pesticide was

End of N. Canoe Creek Rd. It was soon to get very rural.

My first stop after the pavement ended on N. Canoe Creek Rd. Here I ate supper, filled up my canteens and cleaned up. I camped about a half mile down the road, near the clump of pine trees in the distance.

banned in 1972 the total US population began a steady increase from a low of only 400 pairs to more than 5,000 breeding pairs today.

I have come upon a 1962 issue of *The Florida Naturalist*, a publication of the Florida Audubon Society. In this they had an *Immediate News Release* informing their readers that "Florida Ranchers were aiding the National Bird." The article stated that "More than a half million acres of ranch lands in the Kissimmee Prairie region of south central Florida have been established as a Bald Eagle Sanctuary." Fifty nine ranchers had entered into an agreement with the Florida Audubon Society. This area extended from the town of Kissimmee to the northwestern shore of Lake Okeechobee. The ranchers were going to maintain their properties in a manner to protect the Bald Eagles. In the same issue there was an *Open Letter* to all members of the "Kissimmee Cooperative Bald Eagle Sanctuary"* thanking the cattle men for providing this sanctuary. Here today, 50 plus years later, that agreement is still in effect!

In January of 2012 a new wildlife refuge had been developed. It was called the Everglades Headwaters National Wildlife Refuge and Conservation Area.* It is the combined efforts of the Audubon Society, the U.S. Fish and Wildlife Service, various Florida and other U.S. government agencies, the Nature Conservancy and ranchers. Elements of the program that Audubon encourages are:

1. Sale of perpetual conservation easements that provide funds to ranchers while assuring the land will always be available for ranching and not taken over by urban development.
2. Programs that compensate ranchland owners to restore wetlands, store water and reduce the amount of runoff from their tracts of land.

The locations for this newly proposed refuge fall within the original Kissimmee Cooperative Bald Eagle Sanctuary.

The Bald Eagle is the largest predatory bird in North

Camp site in the early morning in the Kissimmee Cooperative Bald Eagle Sanctuary area. Hammock strung up between two yet to be used fence posts. A tarp is suspended on parachute cord and by just pulling the tarp across I had a tent in the air. No worry about snakes while I slept.

One of the many wooden bridges along N. Canoe Creek Rd. The county or state hasn't spent very much of the taxpayers' money in keeping these bridges up. This was a very rustic Hwy 523. I really did enjoy it!

America. They can measure up to 43 inches in length with a wing span of up to 7.5 feet. Their weight can average between 7 and 14 pounds. Females are 25% larger than males on average. The smallest birds are in Florida. The males there weigh about 5 pounds and the wingspan is only about 6 feet. Eagles can fly very high and can see about 4 times better than a human. They can see their prey as far as a mile away. Their eyesight is excellent because they have very large pupils.

Bald Eagles are not bald as the name implies. They do have a white head and tail and the rest of the body is brown. Males and females will stay together all their lives. They return to the same area every year to mate and raise their young. They will use the same nest if it is available. Their food is primarily fish. They will eat small birds, small mammals, reptiles (mainly turtles) and dead animals if available. Florida's Bald Eagles nest in late September or early October and prefer high pine trees near water. The interesting fact to me, accented by the eagle nest signs, was that I was just entering into the Co-operative Bald Eagle Sanctuary.

I hadn't gone very much farther when a vehicle pulled up alongside me heading south. Another offer of a ride. Their eyes sure opened wide with disbelief and amazement when I said that I had come this far from Georgia already. I thanked them and they headed off down the road stirring up a miniature sand storm as they went.

It happened sooner that I had expected the pavement ended very abruptly, asphalt paving and then just a sand track, only about 10 foot wide. I knew that it was coming; my map had showed it. It was just like an Ocala National Forest sand road. It wasn't hard going and I was used to it. In fact I preferred it!

I came to a running stream. It was a light reddish brown colored water, real sweet. Just as the logger had told me, "Don't worry about the color, if it's moving, it's passed through a cypress swamp. It is ok to drink. I have drunk it all my life." So I filled up my canteens. The road here crossed over an old wooden bridge. Since it was getting dusk I

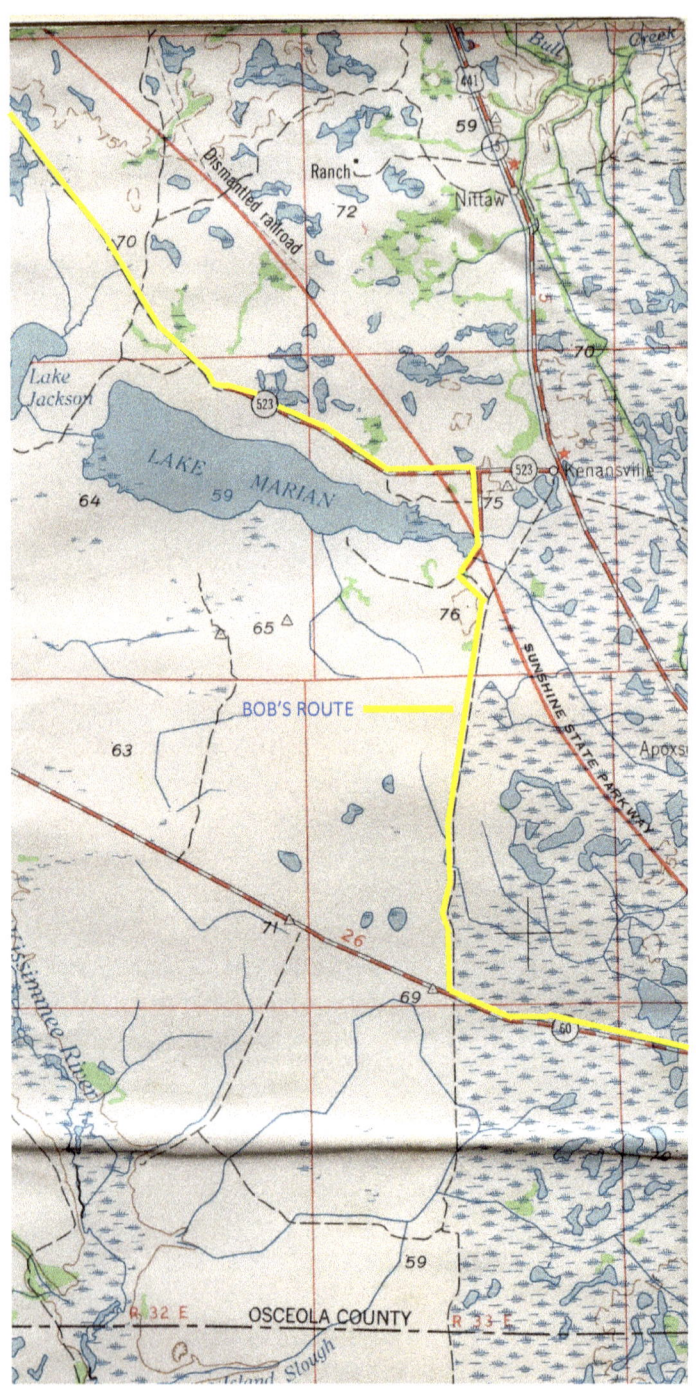

133 A Walk Across Florida

decided to eat my supper right there and then wash up. There wasn't any place near the stream to tie up my hammock so I packed up and hiked down the road another half a mile and found some fence posts which were not being used, so they had no barbed wire on them. A good place to hang my hammock. This would be my camp for the night, low brush, small palmettos and mostly field grass.

In the morning when I awoke I realized that last night the mosquitoes and I had a common goal--we both wanted to be in the same place at the same time. I should have bought and brought a mosquito net along. There wasn't much light that morning. It looked like rain. That big full moon the night before was now just a small faint glow in the far sky. The wind was gusting, and I was hoping that the big black clouds would blow over.

I started out and soon realized that this was perfect hiking weather for hot Florida. Overcast, sometimes sun, sometimes a very light rain and wind. I covered my pack with a ground cloth and put on my nylon water-resistant raincoat. This road was really almost like a trail, winding at times. Sometimes the road would traverse through a swamp, a pine forest or open prairie with occasional saw palmettos scattered throughout. This is why I was surprised to be passed by a fast moving, dust raising, large car. Inside were some guys with big cowboy hats. Something I would think of seeing in Texas, not here in Florida!

After the dust settled I was sure that I could see a large nest off in a distant pine tree. Then a little farther on I saw a huge bird flapping its wings and then gliding. I stopped and watched as the bird settled down in a pine tree in the distance. It started off again moving its wings and then gliding low across the field. I could see that its wings were brown. I was not close enough to make a positive identification but I was almost sure that it was an eagle. It made my day.

Sun then rain, then sun again. I'm-talking to hikers now…..ever stop, put your pack down, dig out your rain gear, put it on, only to have the sun come out? Then if you take all that stuff off and you put it up, it will start to rain again. That was my luck! I decided to just let it rain whenever it chose. I would just let the water come down, so I left my gear off.

I soon came to what I called the "Stream of Life." It was a brown-colored, but clear and clean running small stream. I could see that it was running from a Bald Cypress swamp area to a lake in the far distance. I decided to stop awhile and sit down on the edge of the small wooden bridge overlooking it. A one and a half foot long fish, a Gar, lazily waved his tail a few times and slithered and slipped along through the reeds toward the swamp. Small fishes and minnows darted along with the current. They kept constant and quick movements with the stream. A bumble bee buzzed busily by and then I saw a small water snake swimming and wriggling his way underwater.

A Red-Winged Blackbird, a glossy black male with its red shoulder patches, sat on a small bush's branch that overhung the stream. It let out its call, a liquid sounding gurgle *konk-la-ree* ending in a trill sound. Sometimes it just said *chack*. I just sat there and took it all in, the black bird, a water bug, the fish, the minnows, the cypress trees, the gar and the water eternally coming onward. Up I got, into my pack and turning my back on the little "Stream of Life," went on down the sand road, onto packed tan clay, and then onto the hard road.

I was near Lake Marion where the road turned east. I passed a few side roads. Canoe Creek was now a paved road that probably brought out the cars. There were now some people driving by. I came to a small country store, a good place for a break. I bought a sandwich and a coke. The store was so small that it was possible to talk to both the lady who served me and her husband while I sat in the booth eating my meal. He was a real country guy with a lot of tales and information. He talked about going wild pig hunting and then cooking it in a pit in the ground. Also he had done a lot of commercial cat fishing in the area. I reckoned so, this area had so many lakes!

He showed me a rig he had out back for commercial fishing. It was a wood box about 3 foot square with all kinds of hooks hanging down from it around the sides. It was for coiling his trout line inside and then placing each hook and drop line in a slot in the box. Then he had control of the hooks and he could clean them after each day of fishing. It seemed that a fisherman with a regular license could have 25 hooks, but commercial fishermen could have a lot more. He said that he was one of the fastest catfish cleaners in the county.

I bought some supplies and then sat down on the front porch of the store and cleaned my stove. I was sure surprised that he had a Coleman generator tube which my stove needed.

He said, "Camping and fishing supplies keep me busy here."

I thanked the owners of the little store and started off down the road. An old logging railroad came in along the right side of this road. The tall pine trees along the right-of-way had the "V" cuts and sap-collecting buckets attached beneath them, just like what I had seen along the railroad tracks in the Camp Blanding area.

Up ahead I saw that this road would cross the Florida Turnpike again. I crossed over and a little ways farther I came to a small and quaint old Florida church, still serving the Lord I could see. It was a small, one-story, wooden, white-painted German siding structure set up on concrete blocks, no basement. You don't find basements in Florida because the water table is close to the top of the ground. Usually if you dig a hole it will start filling up with water or be real moist. The belfry was only about 6 feet high, with an A-frame type roof on it. Around it were tall long-needle pines with Spanish moss draped on them, swaying in the breeze. On the other side of the church were some 15 foot high Cabbage palms. The grass, what there was of it, was neatly trimmed.

Spanish moss*--I had been seeing it hanging and swaying in the breeze ever since I left the Florida-Georgia line. Some times it was very picturesque like this day and other times it

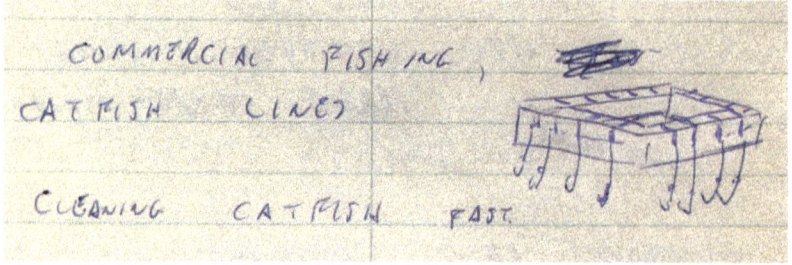

Notes and sketch right out of my trip diary. This is the box that holds his hooks separately so they can be cleaned after fishing. The trout line gets coiled inside and a drop line with hook is attached to each swivel on the trout line. The hooks are slipped into cuts in the box wood and face outside the box.

Small country church in the Kenansville area.

could be real spooky, like my first dark and foggy night on this trip as I walked through Lake City. Spanish moss is not a moss; strangely, it is related to the pineapple. It comes from South America, the Peruvian Andes. It prefers moist environments and when wet, it can absorb up to ten times its dry weight. It is not a parasite but uses trees only for support. It prefers trees with large horizontal branches and rough bark. Live oak and bald cypress are two which fit the requirements very well.

It reproduces from seeds that float on wind currents. It will grow on trees. But it will not grow on telephone poles, fences or buildings. The moss can grow as much as 20 feet long. It does its part in sheltering a number of animals such as bats and rat snakes. Other animals such as small mammals and birds use it for nests. It has been used by humans in many forms: building insulation, with mud and to chink settlers' cabins, mulch, fireplace kindling, packing material, mattress stuffing, car seat padding, fragile item packing and handicrafts. Some people use it as a tea.

In the 1970's Spanish moss began dying out, it was thought because of auto pollution. But that was not correct. It was from a mold. This mold killed off most of the moss but luckily a new type developed and now it thrives.

I didn't want to have to walk on highway 441. So before I came to Kennansville, which was on Highway 441, I checked my U.S. Geological Survey map. It showed that if I took a small paved road heading due south I could miss going into Kennansville and 441. That paved road was the one that crossed over the turnpike.

Just down the road I came upon a fair-sized Gopher Tortoise,* attempting in his casual sort of way to get across the road. I watched to make sure he made it. I found out that road kill is one of the major causes of death for adult tortoises. I could see why, they are sooo slooooow. They are amazing creatures. They can live up to 80 or more years. Their average length is 15 inches and their weight can be from 8 to 15 pounds. Gopher tortoises are very beneficial to other species. Their many burrows are made with their strong back legs and front feet which are very well suited for digging. The burrows can be anywhere from as little as 3 to as much as 50 feet long and 9 to 23 feet deep. Their front feet have scales to protect them when digging. These burrows are used by over 300 species such as rabbits, armadillos, burrowing owls, snakes, foxes, skinks, opossums and many invertebrates.

They also eat many kinds of plants. Among these are grasses, mushrooms, saw palmetto berries, prickly pear cactus

Gopher Tortoise crossing the road. Road kill is one of the major causes of death for adult tortoises.

Prickly pear cactus. The pads are a part of this plant that a Gopher Tortoise will eat.

pads, fruits and flowers, black and blue berries. In turn, they spread the seeds in their droppings. Their habitat is the longleaf pine and dry oak areas with dry and sandy soils. They also live in scrub, dry hammock, pine flat woods, dry prairie, coastal grasslands and dunes.

Today the Gopher tortoise is on the Endangered Species List in some parts of Mississippi and Louisiana. It and its burrow are protected under Florida state law. Gopher tortoises have been on human menus for thousands of years. In fact during the Great Depression they were called "Hoover Chickens" because they were eaten by poor people. Today it is illegal to bother them in any way. I took a photo of my new friend and then continued on my way. The road did turn perpendicular to and passed over the Florida Turnpike.

That made three times crossing the turnpike in just two days, and on very small roads. Immediately I had to make a left turn because the short dirt road would take me to the Peavine trail, which was also dirt.

It did say trail, why should I be surprised about the dirt. I had been in wide-open cattle country for the last couple of days. There had been lots of prairie with an occasional marsh. The land was cleared with some clumps of saw palmetto. Except for the occasional cow and wildlife, it was wide open and not a human in sight. It had been like hiking my own trail. If you look at a map you can see that even today this is still an area void of highways.

I soon came upon a very, very, huge Brahman Bull! He was lying down, but he *immediately* came to his feet when I stopped to get my camera out of my pack and take a couple of photos of him. He had this long brown-black mane which extended from his head back to and encompassing his hump. This made him look kind of like a buffalo. I thought that I could see short stubs of horns. I decided that it might be best to move on and not depend upon those few strands of barbed wire to keep us separated!

This was a becoming a long road. Just me, occasional cattle

Definitely the granddaddy of all Brahman Bulls. Thank goodness there is some barbed wire between us. He was wary of me as I passed by and took his photo.

in the distance, the sun and 10 miles. When I got to Highway 60, I had wanted to cross over and continue on. My map showed the road/trail/railroad grade straight as an arrow for at least 25 additional miles. It would have been much better than going on Highway 60 to 441. But it was not going to happened. I guess the Lord had other things in store for me. As it was, the extension of the Peavine Trail was blocked by a gate with a sign declaring...in fact, demanding:

> **NO ENTRY, POSTED**

Some rancher must have owned all of this land. Just when I was beginning to like the Peavine Trail. After all, it did have the convenience of no cars.

So on to Yeehaw Junction at Highways 60 and 441. It was getting dark and I had traveled 20 plus miles so far. I was out of water and there were just old drainage ditches along this road, nothing else. I was very fatigued when I finally staggered into the gas station at Yeehaw Junction. That is all there was then, and today there is not much more. Just the addition of a mom and pop motel.

There was a very nice boy and girl running the station and they let me camp on the side of it. I tied my hammock up in a tall thicket along the side of the building and I was so tired I didn't even eat, just fell asleep immediately. It was cool for a change and no mosquitoes. I woke up once in the middle of the night and I could hear big trucks running their engines across the street. They never even bothered me. In the morning I slept late. Then I got up, filled up my canteens and ate breakfast. I sure was hungry! I consulted my maps and figured that I must have traveled about 30 miles! Quite a lot, try that in the mountains.

The change of the shift at the station was an old fellow. He was very nice and very talkative. He told me that there used to

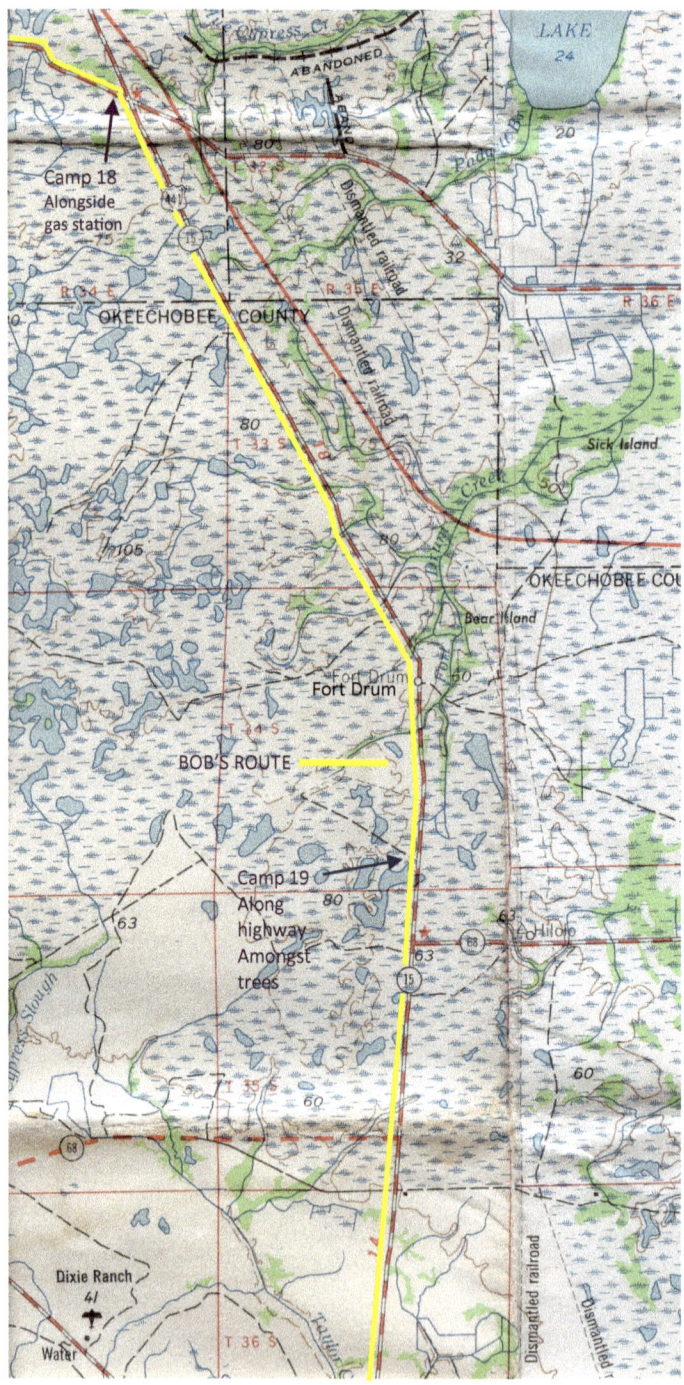

143   *A Walk Across Florida*

be a huge saw mill at Hodpaw, north on 441. He also said that many years ago there also were a lot of logging railroads, and plenty of large trees. That agreed with my map that showed a lot of dismantled railroads in the areas I had left and that I was hiking into.

There was a creek next to the station and I sat there and updated my journal for the day before. I noticed a young boy across the street sitting along 441 hitchhiking. He had a sack and a sleeping bag. He looked like a carpetbagger to me. I wondered what I looked like to him?

I could see that I was not the only one to have used this inviting, shaded spot by the creek. There was an old homemade fishing pole, a string attached and a red and white bobber lying there. Only problem, the pole was broken. It is amazing what you can see if you just slow down. The previous day at my *stream of life* I had seen all those wonderful creatures. This day a Florida buzzard was gliding effortlessly, circling and wheeling high overhead without moving a wing. I hoped that it was not a bad omen, although a buzzard is a wonder to watch. They make up for their looks by their fabulous maneuvers amongst the wind currents.

I packed up and had to face the inevitable, on to Highway 441 heading due south. I was sorry that so much of Florida was fenced. That is why today it is a blessing that the Florida Trail is developed. I would have liked one that day. There was lots of traffic for this two-lane road, both big trucks and cars. The young fella who was hitchhiking must have gotten a ride for he was nowhere in sight.

I was walking on the left, facing traffic, like one is supposed to for safety's sake. A group of young people in a car came towards me from the south and threw up the peace sign. I returned it, and lo-and-behold they stopped, turned around, came back, stopped, got out and crossed over. There were three of them, two boys and a girl. Naturally my attention was first turned toward the female. She was dressed in tight bluejeans and a tie-died shirt. She was the most talkative.

"Boy, you look great! I mean it! Real boss!"
I didn't know what to do at first. They looked like mild hippie types. No long hair. The bigger boy was barefooted, decent haircut, with a long-sleeved white shirt and blue jeans. The younger boy had a crazy hat and wanted to swap his love button for one of the blue jay feathers I had in my hat. We consummated the trade.

"Let's jam!" she says.

The older boy crossed over to the car and got her guitar, a twelve string, no less! Here we are, a beautiful, long-legged girl strumming a twelve string guitar, all sitting along Highway 441, out in the middle of nowhere, along the side of this busy two-lane highway (cars and trucks blasting by, both ways), in the grass, in the sun! *What a jam!* She was a gifted singer, really knew her folk songs of the day. We kept this up for about half an hour, exchanged addresses, talked some, and then they were gone. A high point of my day.

I never would have been able to do that in the backcountry on the trail, I thought to myself, What an experience! I just never knew what was coming next!

Just on the outskirts of Fort Drum there was a small picnic wayside. I was ready for a stop and rest. I talked for a while to a man and a boy sitting at a table. Another boy in his 20's sitting at a nearby table said that if I needed a ride he would take me as far as Miami. I thanked them, said my good byes and entered Fort Drum. Wasn't much there, even though it was the location of one of a string of forts built by the U.S. Army in 1842. The Florida East Coast Railroad had built a small depot in 1914.

Out of five gas stations only one was left open, the rest deserted and forlorn. One of the abandoned ones had an original hand-operated gas pump, with a 10 gallon glass bowl on the top. A real antique.

I stopped at the one station that was still open, it seemed for some friendly verbal abuse.

The station attendant said, "How's living with those

mosquitoes and rattlesnakes?"

A man in a cowboy hat said, "If you hike that a way tonight the Florida Highway Patrol will be visiting you."

I said, "That is the least of my worries."

I left Fort Drum and continued on. A couple of miles farther I came to Fort Drum Creek. It was clear and fast running, a perfect place to eat, bathe and resupply with water. It was getting dusk so I hiked a few more miles. As it got dark I came to a wide right-of-way with trees next to a fence. It gave me some concealment from the highway. A good place to set up camp if you have to set up along Highway 441.

The country the next day was flat and open. I had this for the next five miles. There was a milk cow dairy off in the distance. I have since found out that Okeechobee County is the county with the second largest number of dairy farms in Florida. One of the largest is the Larson dairy. It is composed of 37 different dairies that have been merged into one. They milk 6000 cows and if you include Mr. Larson's two sons' dairies near-by, that makes a family total of 10,000 cows. It takes 90 employees to milk three times a day the 6,000 cows on the Larson's dairy.

They have environmental controls on the farm consisting of a three-stage lagoon to process the manure. The water from that process is recycled to flush the barns or irrigate the fields. One additional requirement is that all rainwater from the farm must be captured. Consequently they have a ditch system to collect the water and it is then also pumped back to the farm. All these requirements have been put in place by the state and federal governments to protect Lake Okeechobee, the Everglades and the drinking water supply for the state of Florida.

During those five miles I had to turn down rides from three across-the-road truck drivers. It just shows how friendly and unafraid people were at that time.

13
Okeechobee, City and Lake

I must have been getting close to Okeechobee because I came to a small country store. The proprietor said that ahead on the lake, just past Okeechobee City and over the levee, there was real fine camping. There was an old couple on the front porch of the store giving away kittens. I got to talking to them and they told me that ahead near Taylor Creek was a black panther crossing.

I told them, "That is wild enough for me! I will keep my eyes open and my feet loose."

As I was hiking down the road I saw a funny sight. A boy with a cane pole was climbing a fence, and on that fence was a sign,

> *Posted*
> *No Fishing*

I came to a state fire tower I was surprised to see that they had a lot of new equipment. Four workers were just sitting around. I was really surprised by their lack of welcome. They were down-right not friendly. The reason I was taken aback, was that at all of the National Forest fire towers I had visited I had had a friendly chat with every person associated with them. By that time I sure had visited a lot of fire towers. It just must have been a bad day for those boys.

I didn't stay around there very long. I got back on 441. Shortly one of the truck drivers I had seen the day before came driving back towards me heading north this time. He had offered me a ride yesterday. He blasted his air horn and waved. I returned the friendly gesture.

I got to the city of Okeechobee. I took advantage of the Amoco gas station and filled up my white gas stove. The attendant had a lot of patience to pump me three cents worth of gas. But that is all my stove reservoir would hold.

It is hard to keep youngsters out of a good fishing pond!

Morning, Jaycee Park camp site, Hover Dike in the background. A small marshy area near the shore, with Florida wading birds.* The smallest bird appears to be a white Ibis and the larger one, an Egret or Heron. Middle one???

A young girl hanging around at the station said, "You remind me of a vet cong."

"Yea, sure," I replied. Even though I had never seen one, I felt certain that she hadn't seen one either!

In town, Highway 441 was designated Parrott Street. J. R. Parrott was the general manager of the Florida East Coast Railway.* In December of 1910, it was announced that the Florida East Coast Railway (FEC), would start work on a branch line called the Kissimmee River Valley Extension. This line would run from the main line at Titusville, up to Maytown. Then it would go south through Chulota, to Kenansville and then along the Kissimmee River Valley. This took it through Fort Drum and then to Lake Okeechobee. The completion of this spur line in 1915 was really the beginning of Okeechobee City's growth.

In December of 1911 officials from the FEC visited Lake Okeechobee to look over the area and announced that the next year they would survey and lay out the "new city of Okeechobee." In fact, they changed the name of the little town of Tantie to Okeechobee. The official of the FEC who had the primary responsibility for the project was James E. Ingram, who had a vision of a great city at the end of the FEC railroad at Okeechobee. The railroad's purpose from a monetary standpoint was to haul timber, turpentine and catfish, give a boost to the cattle industry, and naturally to sell lots, land, farms and ranches.

This branch line helped to develop all of the small towns along its route. The owner of the Florida East Coast railway actually was responsible for the development of the entire east coast of Florida. Henry Flagler was a partner in John D. Rockefeller's Standard Oil starting in 1878. He was advised by his wife's physician to visit Jacksonville that winter because of her health. She died in 1881 and two years later Flagler visited St. Augustine, Florida with his new wife. He liked the city, but he thought that the hotel facilities and transportation left much to be desired. He realized that there was much potential for Florida to attract visitors from out-of-state, especially in the winter months.

He returned to Florida in 1885 and built the Ponce de Leon Hotel in St. Augustine. He then purchased the Jacksonville, St. Augustine and Halifax River Railway because he realized that the solution to developing Florida was efficient transportation. This helped him in bringing in building materials for the many hotels he was about to construct. He then built a railroad depot and set about building schools, hospitals and churches. This renewed the historic city of St. Augustine. He then started a 30 hour Pullman service to and from New York City, making St. Augustine a winter destination for tourists.

In the next four years Flagler purchased three additional railroads. This got him as far as Daytona. He then bought and expanded the Ormond Hotel, north of Daytona. He continued to extend the railroad down the coast and by 1894 his railroad organization reached Palm Beach, where he built two more hotels and his private 55-room winter home.

Flagler had planned for this to be the end of his railroad development. However in both 1894 and 1895 Florida was hit by very low temperatures, in fact freezing! He was not happy with this because he wanted his railroad to terminate in a freeze-free area for his tourist business. At this time he was contacted by a landowner in the small town of Miami. This town only had, at the time, 50 inhabitants. Mrs. Tutle said that the freeze didn't hit her town. She said that if Mr. Flagler would extend his railroad to Miami, she and the other largest landowner, William Brickell, would give him half of their land north and south of the Miami River. They would also throw in an additional 50 acres for shops and yards.

They signed a contract. Flagler's railroad's name was changed to the Florida East Coast Railway Company. By April of 1896 the track reached Miami. Flagler then built a station, dredged a channel on the Miami River, built streets, and set up the first water and power systems. He financed the town's first newspaper and then built the Royal Palm Hotel.

This man Flagler was a real visionary.

Today, the story of the Florida East Coast Railway is the story of the east coast of Florida. They had some ups and downs. For example: the boom of the 1920, and then the bust in 1926, the Stock Market Crash of 1929 and then the Great Depression. This caused the Railroad to declare bankruptcy and become a ward of the court in 1931 lasting until 1961. A strike of the non-operating union employees in 1963 lasted until 1977. The strike got very violent and included bombings, shootings and vandalism, finally requiring federal intervention to calm things down.

During this time the railroad pioneered efficiency and cost savings. It was the first U.S. Railroad to operate two man crews, and to eliminate cabooses and unprofitable passenger service. This all helped the railroad to remain in the black. Therefor today the Florida East Coast Railway is one of the few remaining original United States railroads which has very dependable and efficient service.

I was getting ready to go into a small store to buy some socks (it seemed that I had pounded the pairs I had to shreds). Two boys stopped me and asked me about my pack and what I was doing. I said that I was going into the store to buy some socks. One of the kids said that he would get me some of his from home. I declined his offer of ultimate sacrifice. They were definitely a couple of good guys.

I had about three miles to go to get through town and to the lake. The sun was going down, but when I got to the end of Parrott Avenue, 441 intersected with State Route 78. There was a road just a short distance to the west of the intersection that went over the dike. Once I got over the dike it seemed to be lighter on that side. I had a refreshing dip, and as I was sitting there and resting two boys came by on a motorcycle and talked for a few minutes. They asked the usual, what was I doing?

A family came over and said that I could use their campfire because they were going and were done with It. I moved over to their site and sat there by the fire.

Then here came three boys in a white 58 chevy. They stopped, stayed in their vehicle and hollered to me as their two exhaust straight pipes roared....ah..thoomp, ah..thromp.

"What-sha-do'n? We saw you walking through town," they hollered, "we'll be right back." Off they went roaring and spinning out in the sand...and then sure enough, shortly they came back and brought me a coke and a snack. We sat around the campfire and talked.

Then they said, "Hey Bob we'll show you around the whole town."

It seemed like an interesting endeavor, so I cleaned up my camp, secured my pack and we all jumped in their Chevy.

We drove back over the levy and into Okeechobee. They showed me the old school house, a railroad grade and the railroad station. The railroad is now the Seaboard Air Line running from northwest to southeast. The Flagler Florida East Coast Railway is not active in Okeechobee any more. It does intersect and cross the Seaboard Air Line on the northeast side of the lake and then go south along the east side.

"Hey, let's take Bob over to the cattle auction," one of the guys said, and that is what they did. We parked and went inside. The auction pit had some selling activity going on and we watched for a while. There was a large scale next to it, I guess for weighing those large cows.

Today Okeechobee City* is a town which has a lot to do with the local cattle business. It supports dairy farmers, cattle ranchers, naturally tourists, and now the Florida Trail biker/hikers. Of course it wasn't always this way. Back 2 to 3,000 years ago native villages began to appear in the Okeechobee area. Mounds have been found and some excavated in various areas around and about Lake Okeechobee, and one has been found near Okeechobee City. The first white settlers arrived in the Okeechobee City area about the time of the canal dredging in the late 1800's. They settled along Taylor Creek about 3 1/2 miles from the Lake Okeechobee shore.

It was getting late so the boys took me back to the lake and my campsite. As they were leaving they spun out and turned a few donuts in the sand, their headlights drawing a rotating glow of sandy haze in the darkness.

The next morning I slept in and woke when the sun was high in the bright blue cloudless sky. I decided that I would spend the day and explore this beach and dike area. I came upon some beautiful birds wading in a marshy area near-by. These birds were standing on stick-like legs which kept their bodies above the water. I procured my sketching materials and sat as close as I dared to sketch them. I wasn't sure but I guessed that I was sketching some kind of a Heron. I have since found out that these were White Ibises and an Egret. Florida has some very amazing birds. All of these birds are being threatened because of loss of habitat. I finished sketching and continued off down the beach. There were small shells, millions of them crunching under my shoes as I walked along. They had been washed up by the big lake's many violent storms to form the beach.

I was heading away from Okeechobee City, in a southwest direction. It was becoming warm and I took off my shirt. I was carrying my pack. It had everything I needed in it and even though it was heavy I was very accustomed to it. In fact I was just like a turtle, I needed my home on my back. About a mile down the beach I could no longer see the lake. My view was blocked by a low land area and plenty of big trees. I decided to walk over to my right and climb up to the top of the dike for a better view. There was a faint vehicle trail on the top. I guessed it was for the Corps of Engineers inspection teams. On the land side was a canal from the building of the dike. I continued down the dike for a couple of miles. With the additional height of the dike I could look out over the spit of land and vegetation and see the lake again.

I got to a point where the dike headed north and here Highway 78 crossed it. I took the road and walked along the left side and soon came to the Kissimmee River. I walked out on the bridge. Here the dike traveled up both sides of the river for some distance. It was straight and devoid of trees or large vegetation along the shore, to keep the protective effect of the dike along the river. Almost all of the rivers and canals had dikes on both sides around the lake. That way any future storm or great wave would stay on the water and not damage any habitation on the land side.

However there would be a problem with this. The once meandering and beautiful Kissimmee River* is now a canal. In 1950 the U.S. Army Corps of Engineers began building these high flood control dikes along both sides of the river. They extended for miles and straightened out the river. Gone are the marshy floodplains, the birds, wildlife and the method that nature uses to filter out the pollutants that could flow into Lake Okeechobee. There is some hope, for there is now a project to restore the river though it will be some feat to duplicate the original twists and turns.

Why this Herbert Hoover Dike?* In 1926 a hurricane came from the Miami direction, causing considerable destruction there, then hit the Okeechobee area. The wind raised the water so much on the west side of the lake that it broke through a levee protecting the town of Moore Haven. Then just two years later, another powerful hurricane hit the lake, and flooding killed more than 2,500 people! President elect Herbert Hoover visited the area and because of his support for the project, in 1930 the U.S. Army Corps of Engineers began building the dike, finishing it in 1937. This dike is built with a lot of local materials: gravel, rock, limestone, sand and shell. It is 34 feet high and is around the entire lake. The U.S. Army Corps of Engineers has always kept the sides of the dike free of trees and brush. In fact, even today it is very manicured. For years they kept the public off the dike.

Since 1993 and through the work of the Florida Trail Association, today the public may hike or bike entirely around the lake on the dike, a total of 110 miles. There are many locations from which the trail can be accessed. There are primitive campsites and many commercial campsites, including hotels. In the future there may be a paved road along the top, and even an equestrian trail along the bottom. This area may become a very important recreation area.

I decided that I had better be getting back to the previous night's camp site. I returned the four or five miles along the top of the dike. I got back as it was getting dusk, set up my camp in the same place as the night before, and made my supper. As I was finishing, my friends from the night before made an appearance. We sat around and talked for quite a while. As they were leaving they told me why they liked to spin donuts.

"Yea, when the tourists pack in on the beach during fishing season, we like to come down in the evening and spin donuts to scare them Yankees off!"

This having been said, they took their leave in their Chevy with sand flying in a double-donut spin.

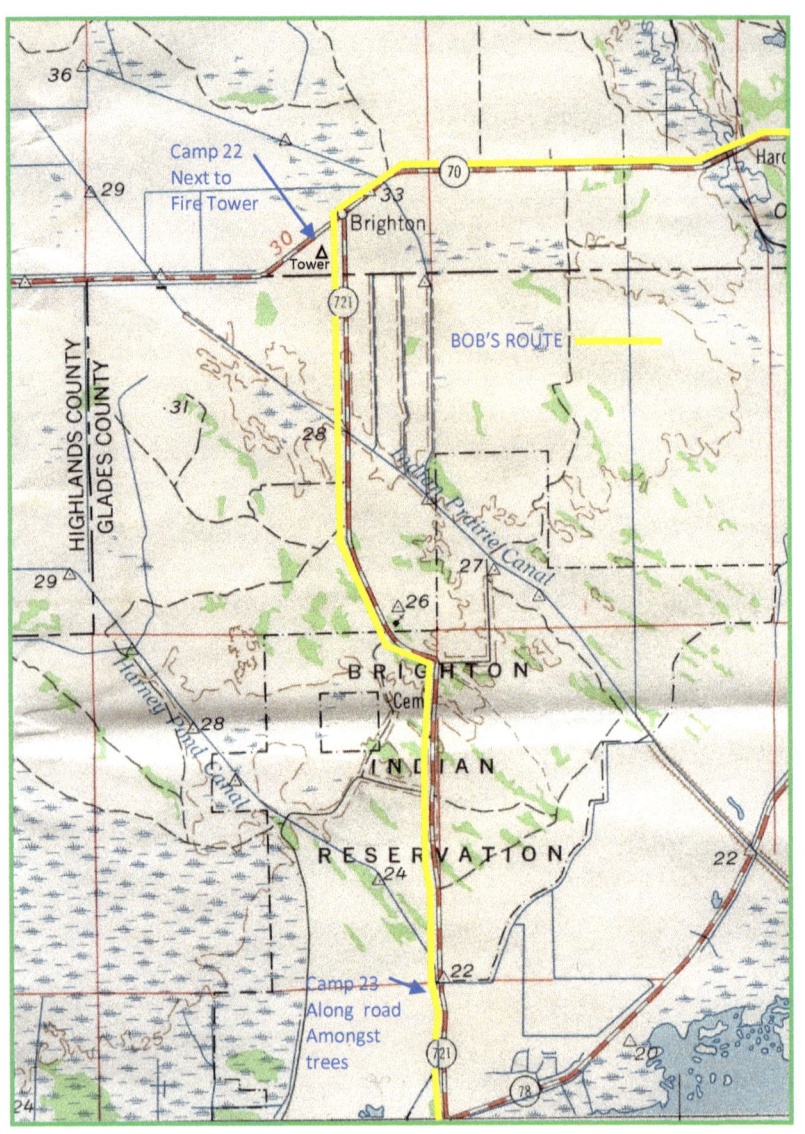

14
Brighton
Seminole Indian Reservation

By the time I woke up the next morning, ate my breakfast, packed up my pack, and picked up the area, it was late morning. I went up over the dike and north back through town. I was going to return to the lake and the Hoover Dike some time later, and it would be somewhere south of here. But first I was going to go west and then down through the Brighton Seminole Indian Reservation.

Back through town I stopped at a small grocery store. I put my pack in a cart and pushed it around. I sure got some looks! I was able to replenish my staples, a Cup of Soup, M & M's, raisins, oatmeal packs, nuts, a few cans of tinned meat, box of Graham crackers, Pop Tarts, powdered milk, Kool-Aid and 2 pounds of sugar to go with it. Then I took the opportunity to purchase and scarf down a few treats that you normally would not take on a hike, a soft drink and candy bar.

When I got back to the center of town I went west on Highway 70. Shortly I came to a country store and needing some more water in my canteens, I stopped and filled them at a water faucet on the side of the building. I went inside, and as I was shopping around a conversation with the man running the store commenced. He was well-traveled and a seemingly very educated person. I wondered later just why he was running an old country store in this out of the way place. He said something to me that I hadn't realized. I had not been looking at myself in my backpacking metal mirror very much lately, actually hardly any!

"Why you look just like an old man with that floppy hat and beard!"

"Well, I sure didn't look like this when I started!" I laughed.

I said goodbye and a couple of miles farther I came to

Popash Slough. It was a lazy, meandering, swampy stream heading towards the lake. I set my pack down on the side of the bridge and decided to go under it to get some well-deserved shade. That wasn't a very good idea I soon found out. There was a fat four-foot-long moccasin lying there. It appeared to be dead, but from a distance I could see some slight movement along its body. I wasn't taking a chance! I got back up on the road. Today you can hardly tell there is a bridge there as one rushes across a low modern concrete structure that looks just like the road.

I was about to put my pack back on when three well-dressed men in a big fancy car pulled up and stopped.

"Hey sonny, we're lost! We thought we could get to the Florida Turnpike this way."

I pulled out my maps. "If you go straight on into Okeechobee you can decide then if you want go north to the Yeehaw Junction ramp or go east to get to it to go south. It will be best for you to ask in town if you want to go south."

"Thanks a lot, take care." I guess that I was now a traveling Florida information station.

I put my pack on and continued on over the bridge and down the road. I soon came to an old abandoned homestead. There were large Australian pines on both sides. They were set in straight lines on either side of the remains of the house and foundation, barn, cattle pen and out-buildings. The wind was moaning through the tops of the trees. That together with the squeaking of the old wind-mill pump as the blades turned and with the sun going down made it an eerie experience.

Shortly the road veered southwest to make a perpendicular crossing of the Kissimmee River. The river was the same as I had seen at the dike the previous day--a straight, muddy, sterile canal with no trees on the sides. No beautiful wading birds or animal life in sight. A stark contrast to the scenic Ocklawaha River I had seen back in the Ocala area.

It was getting dark now and I could hear lots of cows mooing off in the distance on the north side. I just couldn't see any. A few dark building shapes appeared as I came into Brighton, and that's about all there was, a few buildings. The place was all dark, kind of deserted. I could see one exception. There was a faint glow coming from a window in a one-story building on the north side of the highway. I walked by a couple of beat-up pickup trucks. The door where the light was shining was an old wooden screen door. I looked in through the screen and saw what appeared to be a cook shack with a dining room. Since the screen was slightly ajar, I opened it, stuck my head in and hollered.

"How ya doin', I need some directions."

A guy with a real chef's hat looked up from a frying pan with some sizzling catfish in it and said,

"Come on in."

I walked in, pack and all. On the left was a sink built in a table and three large guys wearing cowboy hats, hunched around cleaning a mess of catfish.

"Here's one needs a shave," one of the cowboys said. I guess he thought at first I was a new hired hand.

"Don't mind him none," the cook said, "What-sha need?"

" I heard that there was a fire tower down the road towards the Seminole Indian Reservation."

"Yep, you're right, just a short distance."

"Well, thanks a lot," I said as I backed out.

I soon learned why I heard all those cows that night and why there were cowboys in that cook shack. If you look today on the north side of the intersection of Highway 70 and 721 you will see a bunch of metal shop buildings and a sign proclaiming:

> LYKES
> BRIGHTON
> RANCH DIV.

It sure was dark! I again started down the road. There were

more of those huge Australian pine trees on either side of me. As I neared the fire tower a dog was barking from the side of the house. The porch light came on, and a lady stuck her head out and commanded the dog to keep quiet.

"What do you need son?"

"I'm hiking across Florida and wondered if I could camp near the tower for the night?"

"Go right ahead. It's my job to watch the tower. I'll see you in the morning."

"Thanks, m'am."

She turned on a light near the bottom of the tower, and surprisingly the dog kept quiet. I started to tie my hammock to a cabbage palm near the tower. Then I found out that even though it looked smooth it was very fibrous and you could get slivers from its bark. I decided to tie it to the tower metal. I just ate a cold snack and climbed in my hammock.

In the morning I climbed the stairs to the tower and was surprised to see that the lady ranger was already at her post up top. She let me in, and I had a good chance to see the whole area. There were lots of tall cabbage palms in clumps with small palmetto thickets mixed with open spaces. I thanked her for her help the night before with my camp, wished her luck and went down. The dog was wagging its tail as I headed down the road towards the reservation.

I had some time to contemplate as I hiked along. Here I was about three-fourths of the way through my cross Florida adventure. Overall when I first started it sure seemed like an impossible endeavor, but if one takes a project or problem just one step at a time, it isn't so bad after all.

Little did I know that I was soon to have a forced hitchhike!

I was resting up against a huge Australian pine, when a cowboy drove up pulling a horse van with a jeep pickup. Now, this guy really looked the part, big hat, fancy shirt with those fancy pearl buttons and one of those small cigars dangling out of his mouth, A real sight! Kind of looked like Clint

Eastwood. He nodded.

"Howdy, I'm going to give you a ride about three miles down the road," he said.

"No thank you, I'm hiking," I said.

"But you don't understand. We're going to drive about 500 head of cattle down this road and with you walking along they'll go right through the fences."

Ok, that was enough of an explanation: "I'm with you!"

I put my pack in the truck. A short distance down the road we stopped and picked up a small, weather-beaten, tanned cowboy. He was just sitting on a fence rail. He also had his big hat and all the trimmings. In fact he looked like he had just stepped out of a movie, spurs and all! I was beginning to think that I was on a movie set. I found myself looking around for the cameras.

We drove about three miles, just over Indian Prairie Canal, and stopped. I got out, and they thanked me for my cooperation. They then drove through an open gate along the opposite side of the road, left their truck and trailer parked in the field, and rode off into the range on the two horses that they had tied there. I would like to have stayed and watched but that would have defeated their purpose. I then saw the sign on the side of their truck, *Lykes Ranch*. They must have been connected to the people I saw at the cook shack the night before.

As I hiked along, the vegetation in this area was mostly bunches of cabbage palm and some saw grass. There wasn't any cypress. I came to Joe Tigers Grocery store. It was a small country store. As I walked by a young girl appeared frightened when she saw me. Joe's was soon to be complemented by a trading post grocery a few miles down the road. I went inside and since business was slow, an Indian lady proprietor and I got to talking.

After I answered her question about what I was doing, she told me some interesting Indian stories and information. She talked about when she was a little girl living on a hammock* in the Everglades.

Under a chickee, showing the cypress log structure holding up a thatched roof of palmetto palms. This shelter style was started in the 1800's by the Seminole Indians. They needed a shelter that could be hurriedly build and abandoned if needed.

A Florida tropical hardwood hammock is a dense stand of tree vegetation that is a bit higher in elevation than the surrounding area. It has a rich humus type soil. The early settlers referred to a hammock as a "cool and shady place." The vegetation has many tropical species of evergreen or semi-deciduous trees intermixed with hardwoods such as live oak, red maple and hackberry. Today the remaining hammocks are found only in the most southern part of Florida and the Keys. Hammocks are usually surrounded by marsh, pinelands, saw grass and cypress swamps. They provide habitat for various species of birds and animals. Today the hammocks are fast disappearing, and the challenge is to preserve Florida's remaining tropical hardwood hammocks.

As a girl, the proprietor had many duties. One of them was to help grind corn meal. She said that her family would squeeze the juice out of the sugar cane to make syrup. They had a chickee (a palmetto thatched open side shelter over a cypress log frame.) She still had one next to her house to have picnics under.

Some of the early tribes making up the Seminoles were the Creeks and part of the Creek confederation, the Muskogee. She said that her children learned three languages. Some of their words today are the same as Spanish. Until 1821 Florida was under the control of the government of Spain. The Indians moving into Florida would have interacted with the Spanish, learned their language, and used some of their words.

She talked about a medicine man she knew who would pray to God when he made his herbs. She remembered when the first Christian Seminoles came from Oklahoma to visit him.

The Seminole Indians* have a very difficult but interesting history. They are made up of Creek Indians who moved to northern Florida from the Georgia and Alabama river valleys during the early 1700's and again in the early 1800's. They moved because of pressure from both other Indian tribes and the white men moving inland from the coast and wanting their land.

The story of these Indians was a ongoing saga of betrayal and deceit. It was a story of treaties made between the U S Army, the government, and the settlers with the Indians, with no intention of ever abiding by them. It was a story of the land set aside by these treaties not being protected from incursion by the land-hungry settlers. It was a story of meetings called under the pretense of a white flag of truce and then the Indians and their chiefs arrested and imprisoned. Their life journey was overwhelmingly sad.

The Indians were joined by runaway slaves* from southern plantations. Most of the slaves who escaped were from the colonies of Georgia, Alabama and Louisiana. They were originally from the West African coast. The Indians had their freedom (*they thought*), but these blacks were fighting for theirs and this together with their heritage made them fierce fighters. These runaways easily assimilated into the Indian tribes. After all, they had many similar customs: ownership of the land by the tribe, close family groups, drums and rattles as part of their customs, magic, headdresses used for special occasions, decorating of the face by painting, and animal stories and myths. They also brought to the Indian way of life their knowledge of agriculture. Their African system of tribal justice also served them well in the Indian formal meetings.

They were pretty much minding their own business when in 1817 a U.S. military commander attacked a Seminole Indian village to take their chief captive. Because the Indians fought back, President James Monroe sent Andrew Jackson and the army and they invaded Florida, which belonged to the Spanish. He pushed the Seminoles out of North Florida and took over the only two Spanish towns, St. Marks and Pensacola. This ultimately led to Spain formally relinquishing Florida to the United States in 1821. This was the beginning of the first of three wars the U.S. was to wage against the Seminoles.

In 1830 the U.S. government passed and President Andrew Jackson signed the Indian Removal Act. Then they attempted to do to the Seminoles the same disgraceful activity that they did to the Cherokees of North Carolina and Georgia: defeat, exterminate, or displace them to Oklahoma.

In 1832 some of the Seminoles were forced to sign a treaty called Payne's Landing, which required them to leave Florida and move to Oklahoma. The majority of the Seminoles did not agree with this treaty.

The Second Seminole War was from 1835-1842. There were 3,000 Seminoles fighting a guerrilla war against 20,000 to 30,000 U. S. troops. Even with the odds in their favor, the U.S. government had many embarrassing defeats. In October of 1837 their leader Osceola was captured by the U.S. Army using a ruse saying that they wanted to talk peace.

In November of 1837 Col. Zachary Taylor left Fort Brooke (Tampa), went east to the Kissimmee River, traveled south along the river three days, and built Fort Basinger. On Christmas day 1837, the Battle of Okeechobee, the largest one of the war, was fought, Col. Zachary Taylor's 1,000 soldiers against 500 Seminoles. Taylor said that he had won but it was really a draw, with most of the casualties being soldiers.

Nevertheless in 1838 Zachary Taylor, now promoted to general, became commander of all the forces in Florida. He began a fort-building project in the north and central areas, with a fort every 20 square miles. The total number of forts* established during all of the three Seminole Indian wars was anywhere between 250 and 400! (There are cities all over Florida with names, "Fort this" and "Fort that" and most people don't know that they were forts during the Seminole Indian wars.) This took its toll on the Seminoles and by the end of 1838 somewhere close to 3,000 had been captured and shipped to Oklahoma.

The third and final war was in 1855. The government used three methods to capture the last of the bulk of the Seminoles: the enormous number of forts manned with troops, boat patrols running up, down and around the Kissimmee River, Lake Okeechobee and the Big Cypress Swamp, and lastly a bounty system* put in place to bring them in, $500 for warriors,

$250 for women, and $100 for children. The money being offered in this bounty system was worth quite a lot in those times, so it was an incentive not only to the troops but also to civilian bounty hunters. By early 1858 the United States declared an end to the war with the Seminoles. That left between two and three hundred that they did not capture.

It is human nature, that if you encroach upon a people's property or try to remove them, they will fight back. It is also very strange that if the troops won a battle it was a war, but if the Indians won it was a massacre! Also it is common knowledge that atrocities were committed on *both* sides.

On December 28, 1835 Major Francis Dade was sent from Fort Brooke to reinforce Fort King. His 110 soldiers were attacked by the Seminoles and wiped out. The decimated party was later found, and a Major Ethan Allen Hitchcock was present at that time. He wrote in his journal:* *"The Government is in the wrong, and this is the chief cause of the persevering opposition of the Indians, who have nobly defended their country against our attempt to enforce a fraudulent treaty. The natives used every means to avoid a war, but were forced into it by the tyranny of our government."*

Major Ethan Allen Hitchcock, who was promoted during the Civil War to Major-General, was an advisor to President Abraham Lincoln. He was born in Vermont in May 1789. He was a grandson of the Revolutionary War hero, Ethan Allen. He was a graduate of West Point in 1817. He served in the Seminole, Mexican wars and later the Civil War.

In the early 1840's he was appointed by the government to investigate complaints from the Five Civilized Tribes over their removal to the West. He submitted a detailed report. Since it uncovered fraud and dishonest business practices by the government representatives, it was suppressed. This kind of unscrupulous activity was also a major cause for the Indians in the west to fight for their basic survival. Because of the government's overpowering military and the westward pressure of the settlers, the Indian tribes of the West and for that matter all the United States were ultimately depleted or wiped out. This can be verified in Dee Brown's book, *Bury My Heart At Wounded Knee.**

I think that Barbara Hershey playing Lillian Sloan, an expert in Native American culture in the movie, *Last of the Dogmen,** states it exactly on the *demise of the Indian tribes* resisting the advance of the settlers in the new world and their government: *"It was inevitable, but the method used was unconscionable."*

The Seminoles never surrendered as a nation. They call themselves the *"Unconquered* People." Most of the Seminole Indians living in Florida today are descendants of those 200-300 Indians who eluded capture.

The remaining Seminoles lived in the back country of the Everglades on the high areas called hammocks. There they could plant food and hunt. They only started to venture out to trade during the last part of the 18th to early 19th centuries. Today there are six Seminole Tribes on Florida reservations. These are Brighton, Big Cypress, Hollywood, Immokalee, Fort Pierce, and Tampa. The Brighton Seminole Indian Reservation* has a land area of approximately 57,000 square miles. Its population is somewhere in the area of 800 to 1,000 persons. There is vegetable, sugar cane, orange and grapefruit farming, along with cattle ranching.

I was truly enjoying talking to this Indian lady. We must have conversed a couple of hours. My detour to go through the Brighton Seminole reservation had been well worth it. She wished me well, and I was off.

As I hiked down this Reservation Road 721, I could see that it was being rebuilt by the State of Florida. I passed by a subdivision of small houses and could see tractors working the land for a vegetable farm. I came upon a survey crew marking grades for the road. Next a bunch of school busses came by. It was getting late in the afternoon. After this, the newly paved road ended, and it became dirt.

At a citrus grove a Native American boy yelled to me,

My friends in the 1946 green 3/4 ton Chevrolet pick-up truck waving to me again, in the Brighton Indian reservation area.

"Hey, have a grapefruit." He then threw it *to* me, thank goodness, not *at* me.

"Thanks a lot," I waved.

I camped along a levee, near the road but out of sight. The best that I could figure out was that it was the Harney Canal. That night the mosquitoes almost won! Now I knew why birds sing in the morning. I was sitting there eating my breakfast which was enhanced by my grapefruit. It was good and sweet. I had missed the ones my dad and I had been eating for the last month in the morning at home.

There were a couple of hawks flying by, turkey buzzards soaring above, and some ducks in the water in front of me. I heard a bird singing in the brush, che-da, che-da, but couldn't see it. A bob-a-link was also making its distinct sound. It must have been migrating, because I knew it summered and bred in the northeast and Canada.

Just then, I was startled when a diesel engine suddenly roared to life. My attention was directed to a huge dragline across the road. It had just gone into action. I hadn't seen it last night when I set up my camp in the dark. I presumed that they were working on the levee.

I decided that I had better get into action also. As I was walking down the road, an old 3/4 ton green pick-up truck that I had seen a couple of days before when coming out of Okeechobee came by. In it were a boy and a man. They both waved, and I returned the greeting.

I would be soon out of the Brighton Reservation. I could see the Hoover Dike in the distance up ahead.

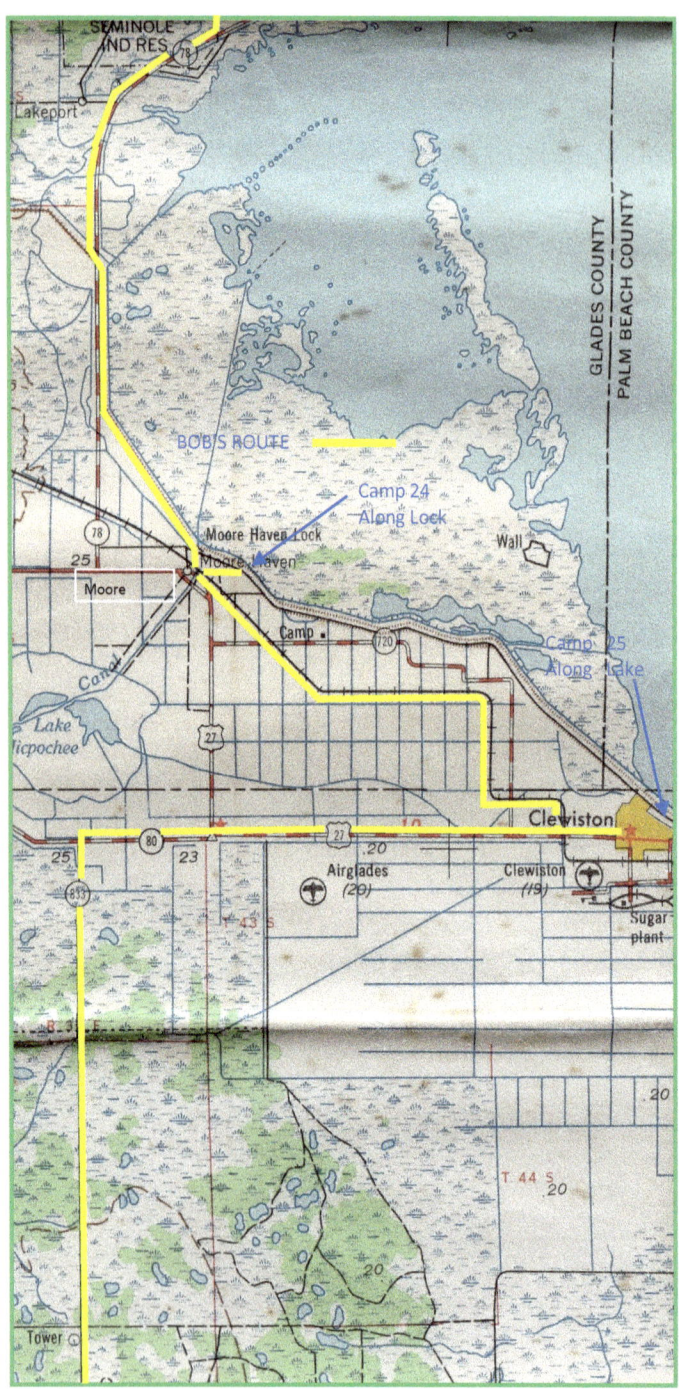

171   *A Walk Across Florida*

15
Hoover Dike and Clewiston Sugar

When I got to State Road 78 I had to go along the highway to get across the Harney Canal. I crossed the road and climbed up to the top of the dike. The dike then headed along the lake and the highway went straight and pulled away. I could see the lake from this vantage point every now and then when my view wasn't blocked by the dense stands of Melaleuca trees.*

These trees have a ragged, soft, paper–like, peeling tan bark and a very fleshy inside. Not sturdy like conventional hard or even soft wood trees, Melaleuca trees were first planted in the late 19th, early 20th centuries. They were brought from Australia to absorb and soak up the Everglades water. Today they grow so fast and thick that they are strangling the Everglades from the water it desperately needs. They can grow as high as 80 feet and turn into impenetrable thickets. This aggressive invader spreads rapidly and is a threat to the Everglades ecosystem. The U.S. Department of Agriculture is studying ways to eradicate the trees with natural insects and chemicals.

In about a mile the dike turned away from the lake and intersected with State Road 78. At this point I could see that the dike was heading west along with its constant partner, a large drainage canal. This drainage canal was made by removing the coral and dirt fill for the dike. The dike encompasses Fisheating Creek's seemingly endless marsh lands. This is one of the four areas where secondary dikes extend away from the lake. These areas are the Kissimmee River, Indian Prairie Canal, Harney Pond Canal and the Fisheating Creek floodplain. Because of this, I could see that I would have to hike along the side of the road. A note of caution, *there is only one way to hike along a road, <u>on the left side facing traffic</u>.*

I was told that Lakeport had been moved because of the dike. In the old days it was originally a port settlement of Belgian immigrants. Supplies were brought in from across

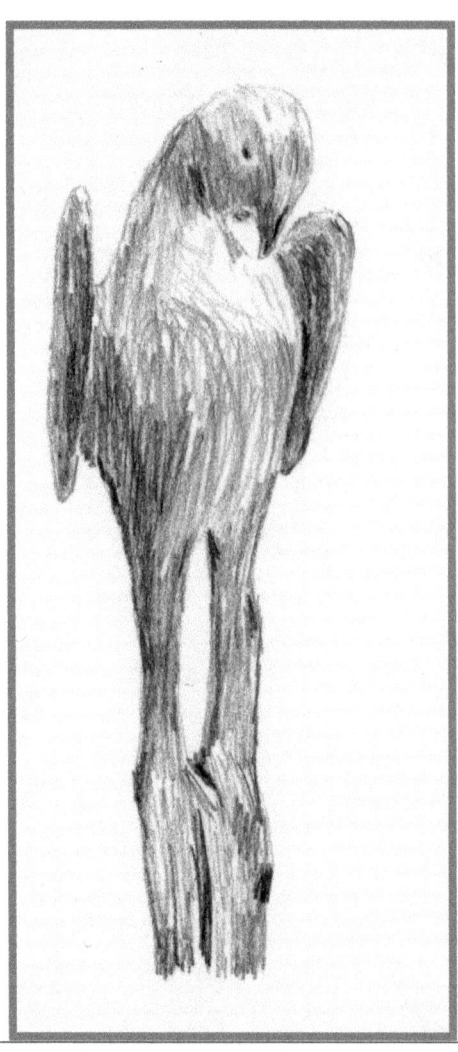

Life-size eagle carving from Fort Center archeological site, Fisheating Creek. It was uncovered along with other life-size wood carvings of foxes, bear, birds and other wildlife. The site consists of mounds, ponds, and circular ditches dating back to approximately 1,000 BC. The site and much of the land along Fisheating Creek came to be owned by the Lykes Brothers (the largest cattle ranching, shipping and meat packing company in Florida). Because they prohibited development along the creek it saved the site until in 1988 when the State of Florida purchased it and turned it into Fisheating Creek Wildlife Management Area.

Sketch model from: Florida Museum of Natural History, University of Florida, Gainesville

the lake. During the Second Seminole Indian War, the U S Military built a fort called Fort Center on Fisheating Creek. It was built two miles upstream, of cabbage palm logs on top of some old Indian mounds. These mounds raised the elevation of the area so it was a good site for the fort. During the Third Seminole Indian War the fort was rebuilt and used for the "boat companies" of military and bounty hunters searching for the Seminole Indians.

There have been some archeological digs in the fort and mound area, and many items have been found. This all started in 1926 when a carved wooden bird was found in a pond amongst the mounds. Archaeologists conducted surveys and test excavations in the 1930's, 1940's and again in the 1950's.

The area along the Fisheating Creek consists of floodplain swamp, natural levees, and wet prairies. It also has an abundance of oak, cabbage palm, and saw palmetto hammocks. The Fort Center archaeological mound* area consists of earthwork mounds, embankments, middens, circular ditches and an artificial pond about 1 mile long by 1/2 mile wide. There is an archaeological theory that these first settlers from the Belle Glade culture arrived from South America some time about 1,000 BC. The theory, based on pollen found in the ground and on the various artifacts, supports the fact that these peoples brought with them the cultivation of maize. If this is true it would be one of the earliest examples of agriculture in the United States. Besides corn these peoples subsisted on the abundant variety of the local fish and animals.

The people used the mound area until the 1700's, when the Spanish influence started to affect the peoples of Florida. In the 1700 and 1800's the various Indians making up the Seminoles roamed and lived in this area and throughout Florida. They also were forced to live here during the Third Seminole Indian War, when the Indians were being pushed farther south into remote locations.

In the early 20th century the Lykes Brothers acquired the land around Fisheating Creek and used it as a very basic

From the top of the Hoover Dike a stand of bamboo can be seen.

The top of the Herbert Hoover Dike as I viewed it. There is a faint inspection road along the top. The dike averages 34 feet high, and it is kept close cut and in very good repair. There is usually a water-filled canal paralleling it where some of the original fill came from to build the dike.

cattle range. In the 1980's Lykes Brothers closed the land because people were vandalizing and poaching. There was a lawsuit, and the court ruled that the creek was navigable and that the land belonged to the state. To avoid litigation, the State bought 18,300 acres and also a conservation easement of another 41,500 acres. This has become the Fisheating Creek Wildlife Management Area. Today there is a 5 mile hiking and nature trail* off of State Road 78 between Lakeport and Moore Haven that will take you to Fort Center and the mounds.

I hiked the three miles along the two-lane State Road. Here the lake view was blocked by marsh and trees and the land side was a marsh and swamp area. I came to a bridge that crossed the canal that ran alongside the dike and then was able to get off the road and back up on the dike.

It was a lot better hiking; I could see more now. There were cane fields off in the distance to the west. I passed some flood gates that I guessed were for a canal that drained those fields. The lake-side now had a mixture of punk, Australian, and other various assorted pine trees. I also came to a thick stand of very large bamboo. There was a wide and deep canal on the lake side. I had an enjoyable hike on top of the dike. During the seven miles to Moore Haven I could see alternating, on the land-side, cattle country and then cane fields. The highway continued due south when the dike and canal headed south-south-east towards Moore Haven. I found a nice camp area right next to town, but no water. I got to talking with two retired guys, one visiting from St. Petersburg, Florida. Both had travel trailers that they pulled with pickup trucks. They graciously let me have some water.

I got into my pack and decided to go to town for a look around Moore Haven. It is right on the Okeechobee Waterway, and the lock is now the second busiest on the waterway, with thousands of vessels going through yearly. Next to the lock is a flood gate bypass. The Caloosahatche River* wasn't always connected to Lake Okeechobee but the river was dredged to the lake by Hamilton Disston's developments in the late

Sunset along the Hoover Dike Looking across the Okeechobee Waterway.

1800's. This was partly for transportation and also to drain the Glades. Disston,* a rich businessman was interested in Florida's undeveloped natural resources. He formed the Atlantic and Gulf Coast Canal and Okeechobee Land Company. They then bought 4,000,000 acres of south Florida land from the state. Part of the deal was to dig a five-mile canal from the Callosahatchee through Lake Flirt and Lake Hicpochee to Lake Okeechobee. Lake Flirt and Hicpochee were the main collection and primary source for the Callosahatchee. Disston contracted for the canal to be dug. They dynamited the large rare waterfall at Lake Flirt, which drained the lake. They then dug a 48-foot-wide canal straight through Lake Hicpochee to Okeechobee. Later the Corps of Engineers widened the canal to its present width of 250 feet. This completed the canalizing of the Caloosahatchee river from east of Fort Meyers on the Gulf side of Florida through the original Disston canal to Lake Okeechobee.

Today you have a waterway with lots of recreational boating, and the canal has pretty much helped stop any flooding along the River. But as usual when man interferes with nature things get upset. The straight canal with spoil banks on both sides supports little aquatic or wildlife. The ill-timed freshwater releases have played havoc with reefs at the mouth in the Charlotte Harbor and Gulf. Also in times of low water the Corps has caused the Caloosahatchee problems by diverting water it needs to stay healthy to irrigate 500,000 acres of cane fields south of Lake Okeechobee. This has caused a smelly green algae to grow on the stagnated water, which in turn makes the water unfit to drink and the fish unfit to eat.

Moore Haven* was started in 1915 by James Moore as a land development. Two years later he had to sell out. One of the purchasing investors was Marian O'Brien who became the mayor of Moore Haven and the first elected female mayor in the United States. She helped promote the town as a farming center as it also had a sugar mill to support the cane fields. In 1921 they built a town, Clewiston, about 10 miles southeast of

them. It had better access to the lake, and they then ran a railroad called the Moore Haven and Clewiston to it. (It was later merged with the Atlantic Coast Line.)

Moore Haven had some very bad luck in the 1920's. First there was flooding in 1922. A bad hurricane in 1926 destroyed a levee between it and the lake and killed approximately 200 persons. The final blow came in 1928 when people there suffered in the devastating hurricane that affected the entire Lake Okeechobee area killing over 2,500 persons. This great hurricane was the impetus to building the Hoover Dike.

I took Canal Street to 1st Street and headed south towards Highway 27. I had to get across the Caloosahatchee River. Moore Haven is a typical small Florida town. Mostly two-lane asphalt paved streets. One–story concrete and some older wooden structures. I came to Highway 27, crossed over the bridge, and turned left along the canal. (The bridge was rebuilt in the mid 1990's and today I wouldn't recognize it, a large curving 4-lane span rising high above the canal. It also relocated Highway 27 through town.)

As soon as I crossed the bridge I turned left along the south side of the canal and headed towards the flood gate and dike in the distance. I came to a railroad grade and as I was crossing over, I could see a turntable style railroad bridge on the other side of the canal. (This railroad is now owned solely by U. S. Sugar.)

As I walked by I noticed that there was a lot of activity along this side of the canal. There were a couple of old dilapidated school-type busses with what appeared to be migrant workers milling about. Some of them were snacking and visiting with each other. I could tell that they were speaking English. But as I walked by, causing some attention, I caught an islander accent at times. I was just guessing, cane field workers? They might have been taking a break before heading south to the U.S. Sugar Cane fields. There was also some huge construction machinery loaded on two 18 wheelers, parked as I have seen many times along the highway in convenient places when the truckers have to take a legal driving break.

Once up and over the dike, I ate at a small beach area while I watched some people. It appeared to be a large family fishing in the canal. They seemed to be having a great time, two on lawn chairs with feet stretched out, their fishing poles in holders along side. Three children ran about with their small cane poles throwing their lines out and then impatiently trying another spot along the bank a few minutes later. An older teenager scolded them at times to be still or they would scare the fish away.

This was the section of the Okeechobee waterway that went south towards Clewiston. I decided to camp there in some Australian pines. It was a beautiful place but the mosquitoes were very bad that night.

In the morning I decided to pack up early, start hiking, and eat breakfast a little later. I started down the dike for a short distance and came to a gate across the road. There was a sign:

> POSTED
> FIRE HAZARD
> NO ADMITTANCE
> U.S. CORPS OF ENGINEERS

That took care of my nice hike to Clewiston on the Hoover Dike. Wait a minute, I had an idea. I crossed over the railroad on my way in here, I'd just take *it* to Clewiston.

I got out my maps and could see that it went to Clewiston. I turned around, and went back to where I had camped and decided that I would eat my breakfast and then get on the railroad right-of-way.

I set my pack down and reached in for the powdered milk without looking. Suddenly I felt something crawling on my hand. I gave my hand a fast pull out and a violent shake. It was just a natural reaction, and it was a lucky thing. A black scorpion was propelled off my hand and onto the ground. Before he could start running I stomped him. Again, another reflex. I looked very carefully in my pack and took everything out. The scorpion hadn't brought along any friends. He must have crawled in during the night.

I have done some research and found out that there are three scorpion species in Florida.* The reason I didn't know or actually care before my trip is because I had spent at least four years in two different boy scout troops in Florida. We hiked and camped all over the Tampa area and the center of the state and never encountered any scorpions. Scorpions can range in length from as little as one inch to a long four inches. They have ten legs but the front pair are not for walking but to hold the food they catch. The most respected part is the stinger on their tail that is held up over their body in an arched, ready-to-strike position.

Scorpion sting with a nerve poison. The good news is that no Florida scorpions are capable of a deadly sting. However it is reported that scorpion stings are very painful, much more than a wasp or yellow jacket. A scorpion sting usually swells up and sometimes the person infected will be dizzy. The only good thing about scorpions is that they eat spiders, mosquitoes, cockroaches, termites and all other varieties of insects. They are also nocturnal.

The *Hentz Striped Scorpion* is dark brown to tan. It has a greenish yellow stripe along the center of the body 2 to 3 inches long. The *Florida Bark Scorpion* is dark brown and a flat body up to 4 inches long, and the *Guiana Striped Scorpion* is yellow, 1 1/2 to 3 inches long and only found in south Florida. No positive ID of the one I just stomped--all I could tell was that it was a squishy dark color.

I repacked all of my gear, ate a Pop Tart, drank some water and got back on the road. The railroad track headed southeast. It didn't appear to be a main line. I saw a few markings occasionally that let me know that it belonged to the Atlantic Coast Line. I suddenly realized that I could have been walking on the original 1921 Moore Haven and Clewiston Railway (M.H. & C. Ry) right-of-way. This railroad was acquired by the Atlantic Coast Line Railroad Company (ACL) in July of

Former Florida East Coast Railway, now U.S. Sugar's "Pacific" 4-6-2 engine No. 113 starting to pull a string of sugarcane cars to the mill. See the loading beam arrangement in the background spanning the track.
State Archives of Florida, Florida Memory, 25987, Image RC02169

Loading beam arrangement I came upon while crossing the Moore Haven to Clewiston sugarcane fields. I was walking on U.S. Sugar's South Central Florida Express Railroad. Note the overgrown track. Units have since been replaced.

1923. It was then purchased by the CSX, sold to the Brandywine Railroad, and renamed the South Central Florida Railroad in 1990. In 1994 it was sold to U.S. Sugar and renamed the South Central Florida Express. Now prior to this time U.S. Sugar ran its own trains on these tracks from cane fields to the mills. In fact they acquired some of the Florida East Coast Railroad's 4-6-2 steam locomotives. In the late 1960's they donated two, numbers 113 and 153, to the Gold Coast Railroad Museum,* and they can be seen there today in south Miami, Florida.

Today U.S. Sugar's South Central Florida Express Railroad* owns 14 locomotives and over 1000 cane cars. They operate these on 120 plus miles of track and haul sugar cane to their two processing facilities. One is on the southeast side of Lake Okeechobee, the Bryant mill, and the other is on the southwest side in Clewiston.

Sugar cane* was introduced to the St. Augustine area by the Spanish in 1565. It took many years for it to become a commercial venture. Growing slowly, it moved south because of the cold weather. In the 1920's it finally became established around the southeastern shore of Lake Okeechobee, helped by the draining of those areas. The drained soil was rich black muck. In 1930 during the Great Depression, automotive pioneer and philanthropist Charles Stewart Mott bought out the Southern Sugar Company and started U.S. Sugar Corporation.* The growth of the industry in Florida was further enhanced by the Cuban sugar embargo in 1960. Today U.S. Sugar farms over 188,000 acres of land in Hendry, Glades and Palm Beach Counties. It is the largest producer of sugar cane in the U.S. with 1700 employees and annual capacity of 700,000 tons. It also has over 30,000 acres of citrus groves, making it the largest supplier of bulk, not from concentrate, orange juice in the United States.

In 2010 the company sold approximately 27,000 acres of land for the South Florida Water Management District's "River of Grass Restoration Project." In an effort to use

*Hey Bob—
Hope you had a rewarding hike — Sorry about scratch in forehead. Perhaps someday we'll meet again —
Carol + Fred Heineman*

This photo was taken by Carol and Fred Heineman from Miami. I was getting some white gas for my stove at an Amoco station in Clewiston when they saw me and asked me what I was doing. They were very amazed and interested that I was hiking across Florida. The photo was waiting for me when I got back home to Tampa. I sure had changed from the photo in the front of this book, and it had only been about 3 and one half weeks .

Wanting to use the photo in this book, I tried to locate Carol and Fred. I didn't have too much success on the internet. As a last resort I sent them a letter with a return addressed, stamped envelope inside to the address that was on their original letter. It was only about four days and here came my reply. I was so excited that they still lived at the same address in Miami and we were able to be back in contact. *Yes we have met again!*

renewable resources, they began using sugar cane bagasse. Bagasse is the sugar cane stalks. After the cane juice is squeezed out, it can burn in a boiler. The heat energy will then generate steam which in turn co-produces electricity for its plant. The company is also exploring the feasibility of producing ethanol from sugar cane waste material.

In less than a mile I crossed a secondary road, Number 720, and soon realized that I was cutting through sugar cane fields. The railroad track crossed rectangular field after field. Separating these fields were drainage/irrigation ditches There were dirt roads along the railroad track, and I came across some strange loading equipment on an overgrown spur track. There was a large beam bridging the track with supports, pulleys and cables. I guessed that it was a method to tip over and dump the sugar cane field wagons into the hopper cars, (see page 183). There were dried out cane stalks strewn about. No sugar cane was growing in the fields, as I had hoped to see. As I later found out, sugar cane planting and harvesting operations are conducted in the fall and winter.

It was a cloudy and windy day, and no was one around anywhere, just me. The railroad crossed over a larger ditch with a small bridge. I saw a fat dark cottonmouth moccasin sunning itself along the bridge. There were lots of rabbits in the thickets along the track. I stopped to rest at some cow loading pens. I was grateful for some very tall Australian pine trees in which I could finally get some shade. It was a perfect time to stop in the trees because along came a switching freight train. They didn't see me or even look my way. I was thankful for that. After all I was on U.S. Sugar Corporation's land and walking their railroad right-of-way.

The switching train having passed, I continued on. I found that it was a lot easier to walk on the dirt roads along the railway. I came to a track siding with a sign post proclaiming "Sugarton Station." Actually there wasn't any station there, but I'm sure it was a means of identifying a sugar cane loading location. The road took me across another canal, and I

could see railroad workers in the distance. I thought I might have a trespassing problem, but instead I was ok. The workers were really surprised when they saw me, but they didn't ask me any questions, and I didn't offer anything.

I took a left at the divided highway heading east. That was an interesting 10 miles, as I started down highway 27 towards Clewiston. I saw a sign to the Clewiston Post Office. I decided to stop by, get a few stamps, and send my mom and dad a postcard. It must have been slow that afternoon for there weren't any customers. I made quite a stir when I went in and set my pack down. The postal clerks, an older gentleman and a lady, wanted to talk. They wanted to know what I was doing, where I had been and where was I going.

They called to the sorter in the back, "Hey come out here. There is a guy wearing a pack just like you had to wear in the Marines."

It seems that he had been in the U.S. Marines and participated in the Incheon landing in the Korean War in the 50's. I've found out that everyone has a story to tell.

My next stop was at an Amoco gas station for 4 cents of white gas for my stove. This is where I met a young married couple, Carol and Fred Heineman from Miami. They were so excited and amazed that I was hiking across Florida. They just *had* to have my picture and said that they would send me a copy. I spent some time at the station there with them because they had all kinds of questions. As we were talking, a tourist bus slowed down and all the people just looked and looked! (By the way, when I returned to Tampa, that picture was there waiting for me. They had got it developed, printed and sent it May 19, the following month. They were true to their word. Now that I am looking at it I can see just why people would stare at me. I sure looked like I had been on the trail for more than 3 and 1/2 weeks.)

I continued down Sugarland Highway (US 27 through town), till I came to St. Francisco Street. I turned north to the Hoover Dike Rd. It took me up and over the Dike to some very nice camp sites along the canal. I put my hammock up on some concrete picnic table posts holding an overhead cover. I just rested. Some people came by and wanted to share my table. I obliged. It was nice to sit around and just talk and rest.

Late in the evening two boys came into the camping area. I helped them put up their hammocks at their campsite. In the middle of the night, half-asleep, I fell out onto the concrete. It sure happened fast! I lay there for a few moments, and then

Clewiston hurricane gate No. 2, looking towards Clewiston

A sketch of the mosquito net hat I bought at an army surplus store in Clewiston. It sure saved me later on in my hike. There were times in the Everglades that I would get into my sleeping bag and put this on and the mosquitoes would be all over it!

half-asleep I climbed back in. It is strange sleeping in a hammock. You learn to turn your whole body and stay in one place so you don't fall out. Sometimes when you wake up you will be in a strange position. It also seems that you wake up on the way down when you are falling. I was lucky: I did not hurt a thing.

Early the next morning I heard the two boys stirring. They shared their bacon and eggs with me, and then off they went fishing. I sat around resting and writing birthday wishes to my youngest sister, Denise. Her birthday was the 25th of the month. I would be late. I was having some stove trouble. It was real windy. Some campers sent their little boy over to borrow some sugar. I still had some left in my 2 pound bag and was able to help.

I wandered over to the hurricane gate and lock area. I worked my way out to the far side and was able to take a photo looking in towards Clewiston and the marina. It said that it was structure No. 2.

I decided to go into town and look for a shoe repair. I couldn't find one but I got some super glue from a hardware. I found a Cuban store and went in and bought a Cuban sandwich. Then I just sat and watched the activity around the marina. I noticed that there were some coconut palms. I was surprised but I guess I shouldn't have been, because I was far enough south.

I returned to my camp site, packed up and got ready to head out. The boys returned at that time. They hadn't had any luck fishing. I headed back through town. As I was dropping the letter to my sister into a post box I noticed an army surplus store. I decided that I had to go in and look around at the camping gear. It was there that I found a real life saver. There in a bin I saw a mosquito net hat. It appeared to be army surplus equipment. It was a tan and green color. I just had to have it. After all, the mosquitoes had been winning the war every night.

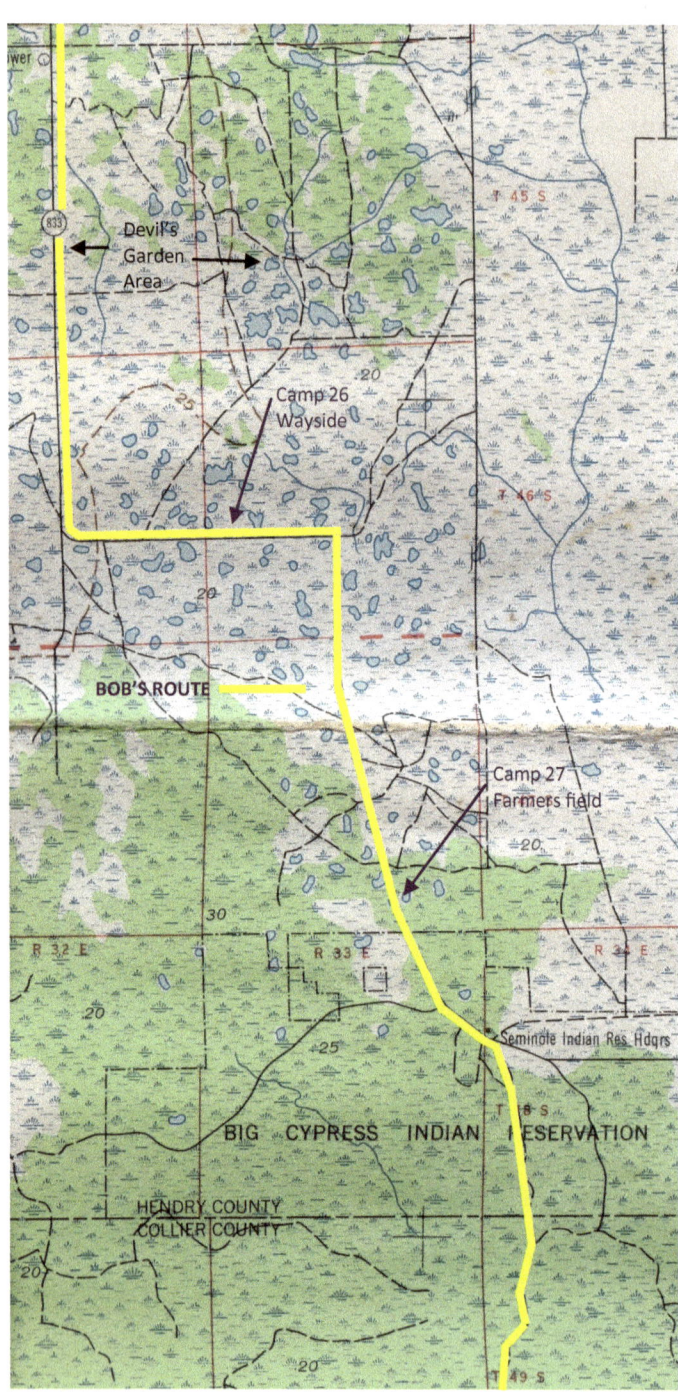

191 A Walk Across Florida

16
Devils Garden and Seminole Country

I went west out of Clewiston on U.S. Highway 27. Soon I was past the railroad tracks I came in on and then 27 turned north. It wasn't very far on State 80 before I came to my turn, Secondary Road 833 heading south. In this area I saw a lot of fields with new sugar cane plants starting to grow. This road had a canal running parallel to it. It seemed that every field had its drainage ditches around it, and then they ran into canals.

The sun was beginning to set when I came upon a parked car and four guys, two men and a couple of boys. They were standing along the canal with a 22-gauge single-action pump rifle, and were taking turns shooting at a big fat cotton mouth moccasin on the other side of the canal. I stopped to watch. This snake was big, not too long, but real fat! We got to talking as they took turns shooting. One of the men had been in Korea in the army. It seems that everywhere I went I met guys who were in the Korean war.

I continued. It was getting real dark now, and I would soon have to find a place to camp. There hadn't been any traffic on this road since I got on it. Just then a car's lights came by from behind, not one but two cars. They went down aways and then stopped, both of them. Then I realized that they were turning around! Oh, oh, this did not look good. Luckily my side of the road didn't have a canal. I crossed the slight depression in knee-high grass and then up and over into the field. I dropped my pack and got down low. My face pressed into the ground, beads of perspiration forming on my forehead mixing with the dirt. My heart was pounding. I hoped that they couldn't hear it! I had acted fast enough and had gotten out of sight before they got turned around and their lights shown my way.

They came back real slow. I hugged the ground! They went

It was too late at night to be hiking……..Here I was on a narrow, pitch black, deserted, two-lane road in the middle of nowhere……..in a swampy place called the Devils Garden. The two cars that had just passed me were stopping and starting to turn around Their taillights made the void turn into an eerie red…..*real spooky*. This did not look good. I hurriedly crossed the shallow ditch on my side of the road and went up and over into the deep grass in the field. I dropped my pack and hugged the ground.

down the road quite aways and then turned around and came back, this time as fast as they were going when they first went by me. I don't know just what they were up to, but I was sure they thought that they were seeing things when they couldn't find the guy that they thought they had seen walking along the highway.

I waited there for some time. The lights had disappeared in the distance. I needed to find a place to camp. I went about a mile and came to a curve to the left. A couple of miles farther and I stopped to sit on a bridge and rest. Then I saw the faint outline of picnic shelters just ahead on the left. Thank goodness! I needed to stop. There was a station wagon parked at one of the shelters. There was a carrier of some type on top. Not anything moving or anyone around. It appeared that this rest area was an access point to the canal. I set up my hammock and was soon fast asleep.

I really slept well because the next thing I knew it was early morning. I must have heard the two guys pulling their canoe up along the canal. I slipped out of my hammock and walked over to them.

"Been out fishing all night?" I asked.

"Yep and it paid off," the guy said as he pulled a large cooler out of the canoe. He opened it for me to look. Inside was a mess of big clunker large mouth Florida Black Bass. There were at least eight, and the one on top was about a foot and one half long!

All I could say was, "Wow! What in the world do you use to catch these!"

"Some times certain lures, but I really like to just use these cane poles and plastic worms."

The guy said that he had been a Michigan guide for most of his life, and now he was retired and lived in Fort Lauderdale. He said that fishing was his life. He showed me a picture of a bass he caught on a lake in Michigan that was three foot long! His buddy got out of the canoe with a smaller cooler and a couple of cane poles.

"John, give this guy a cold coke, and then we had better get somewhere to have breakfast. I'm starved."

John handed me a coke.

"Thanks," I said.

The guide leaned over and picked up the canoe portage style. John grabbed the large cooler with the fish and put them in the back of the vehicle. He then helped the guide put the canoe on the car carrier, tied it down and they were off. It did not take them very long. I guess they were really hungry!

The Florida Large Mouth Black Bass* is native to the Florida Everglades. Because it is a popular game fish, it has been introduced all over the United States and the world. To name the majority of places: Mexico, Central and South America, Europe, Guam, Japan, Lebanon, New Zealand, Philippines and South Africa. Black Bass like cover, such as weeds, submerged logs and stumps, and lily pads, where they can hide and surprise their prey. They feed on various small fish, and if available will eat frogs, snakes and salamanders. They are found in most of the waters of Florida.

I had a leisurely breakfast, to include the coke, packed up and headed down the road. It was wide open spaces. On my left, to the north, was an area called the Devils Garden Wildlife Management Area.* It is an tract of 82,000 acres of ranch land, non-forested wetlands, and prairie with ponds and marsh. There are also some occasional pine trees in the high locations. Florida's Fish and Wildlife Conservation Commission wants to incorporate it into a protected area. It will also be another way to give the endangered Florida panther some space.

I stopped to rest. As I sat there, real still looking at a pond, I suddenly saw a raccoon. Looking like the masked bandit, it slipped through the lily pads under some overhanging bushes along the bank. He saw me but kept on his way. Then a real low flying small plane startled both him and me, and he scurried off.

The sun was out in force. There were no trees along the road. I only had canal water to drink. I stopped at another pond area and watched as I rested. A moccasin slithered out. He was about three feet long. He saw me and then leisurely slithered back into the lily pads. These snakes are just as at home in water as they are on land. Next a red-winged blackbird took a cheerful bath, wings a-flutter. Just as soon as he was done he sang. There sure was a lot of wildlife around the ponds.

Around a curve there was a big canal. I ate and cleaned up under the bridge. Shortly an old car pulled up and a Native American man got out and began to fish on the other side of the canal. He threw in his line and sat down with his cane pole. We started to talk and ultimately he wanted to know,

"Just what is the purpose of this hike?"

A good question, I thought. It was kind of difficult to explain to him that it was just something I had to do.

"I hope that I don't get a crazy thought like that!" he said in jest.

I waved to him as I left. The sun was setting.

This had been a long day. There wasn't much traffic, even though I had turned down three rides and had made 18 miles. I put up my hammock on the fence corner posts in a farmer's posted field. When there were no trees these corner posts held my hammock up real well. It was kind of breezy and there were no mosquitoes until sometime late in the night. I put the mosquito net hat on and had to say, out loud,

"Knock yourselves out mosquitoes."

I was up early and got out of the field. I didn't want to be trespassing when the farmer came by. I had to eat my breakfast along the side of the road. As I started off, I realized that I would be entering the Big Cypress Reservation.

The Big Cypress Seminole Indian Reservation* is the largest of the six reservations of the Seminole Tribe of Florida. The land area is approximately 82,000 square miles. The census of 2010 showed a population of 591 persons. Today they have a very large cattle operation, a museum, an entertainment and rodeo complex, a swamp safari, an RV resort and campground, and a demonstration Indian village. When I went through, none of these attractions had been built. It was real quiet and quaint.

It wasn't very long after I crossed the reservation line before I came to a small trading post store. I went inside and the lady clerk was as nice as the lady I talked to at the Brighton

Chickees in the Big Cypress Indian Reservation

Seminole Indian Reservation. She was wearing the typical striking Seminole attire, a multicolored shirt and dress of red, yellow, pink and green. She really brightened up the scene. I talked to her and some Native American rancher-cowboy types who were interested in my hike. I got a lot of good information on the way ahead through the Big Cypress reservation and some tips on the Everglades ahead. The lady wanted me to send her a line when I got to Key West.

Continuing on my way, a light rain began. It wasn't very long before I came to another small store. A truck appeared to me to be the same green pick-up I had seen a couple of times in the last few days, parked out front. I definitely had to go inside there. Not only did I want to look for my waving friends, but it was also a nice way to meet people. I met the man and his boy. He said that he picked watermelons and then took them to the stores in Clewiston and also sold them along the side of the road.

There were also two teenage Native American boys who were inquisitive. One was tall and very silent and the other very talkative. His name was Frank. Two friends were opposites but seemed to complement each other. They thought that I was on a real adventure. However they said that it wasn't for them!

I continued on in the light rain. I passed a day school and then the U. S. Government Indian Bureau building. This must have been the headquarters area mentioned on my maps. There was a deserted chickee along the side of the road. I decided to rest, take some photos and sketch. I had the opportunity to study the construction. The roof was made from palmetto frons and it was amazing--it wasn't leaking!

It was still raining very lightly, in fact you could call it a mist. I decided that since I had a lot of day left I had better get started into the Everglades. I loaded my pack, made sure that it was covered well with a small plastic to keep everything dry, and left the chickee and the reservation.

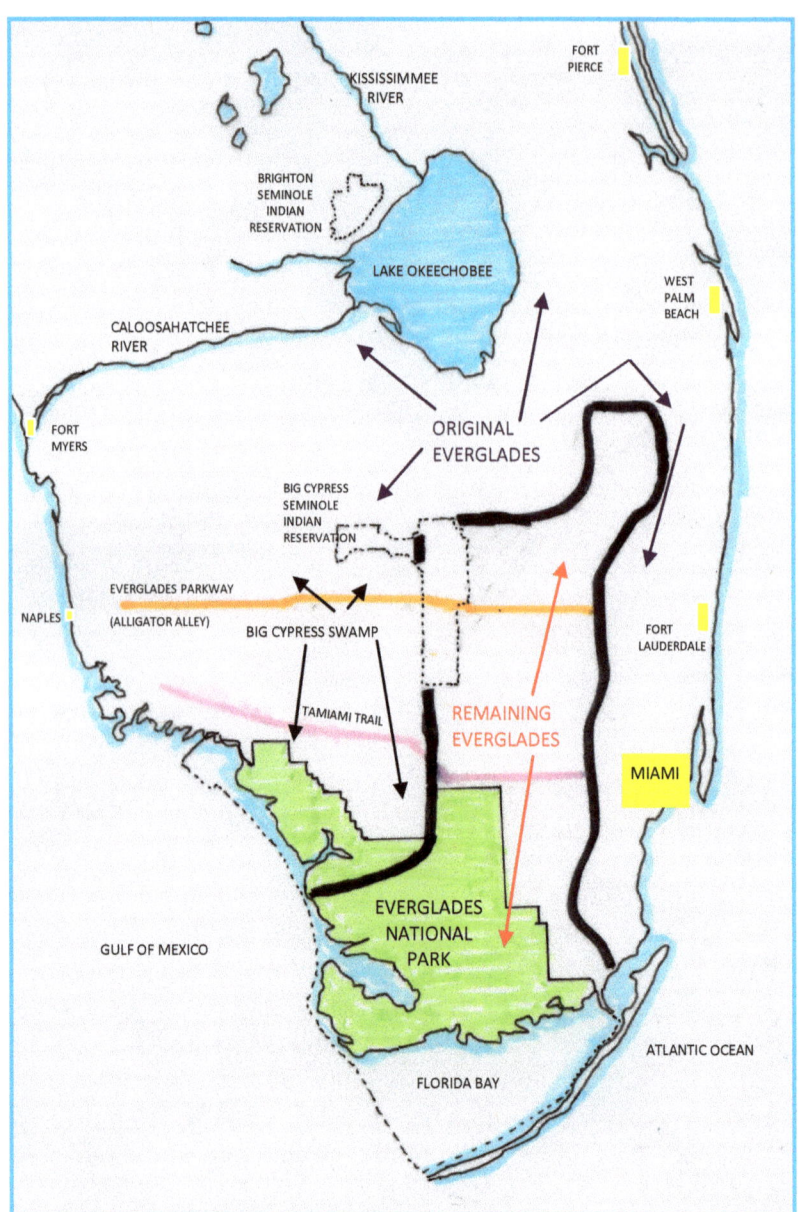

South Florida showing the remaining Everglades. The east and west coast were the original banks of the "River of Grass".

17
Big Cypress Swamp and the Everglades

For an excellent and fantastically concise history of central, southeast, southwest and southern Florida one *must* read *The Everglades: River of Grass* by Marjory Stoneman Douglas.*
This book will take you through the geology, the early explorers, the development, the almost total destruction of the water source for this area, the Everglades, and the battle to save it.

In 1847, two years after Florida became a state, Mr. Buckingham Smith from St. Augustine was appointed by Congress to make a report on the possibility of draining the Everglades. He submitted his *Report on the Everglades* the following year saying that it was feasible. Florida's surveyor general at the time, Colonel Robert Butler, also concurred. Neither one of these men or the others who came along later realized that it was a critical requirement that an adequate geological survey should be completed first!

So it became essential that the Everglades should be drained. After all, the people needed dry land to build and to farm. Later on came the large companies which needed land to raise cattle and grow sugar cane.

The first major draining started in 1882 when the State of Florida made an agreement with the Disston Company to bring in barges and dredge up through the Caloosahatche River into Lake Okeechobee. After that the U. S. Corps of Engineers came along. They straightened out the Kissimmee River from a meandering beautiful stream with fantastic wildlife populations to a sterile straight ditch. They then built a dike around Lake Okeechobee, stopping the natural flow of water into and out of the Everglades, and made hundreds of miles of drainage canals. Two roads were also built across the Everglades, the Tamiami Trail and the Everglades Parkway (Alligator Alley).

Since there never was an extensive geological survey on the results of drainage, and no realization that the Everglades

"River of Grass" was a ecological system, the balance of nature was upset. This brought about too much water, too little water, intrusion of salt water into the mainland, loss of fresh water wells, dying cypress trees, changing vegetation, drying out of the muck land, fires burning the dry muck, the runoff of phosphorus and chemicals from the cattle and vegetable farms, and loss of animal and bird populations. The Everglades were dying.

Mrs. Douglas's book takes you through the slow and arduous trail back to Everglades preservation. During her entire book she never mentions anything about herself. I believe she only had the well-being of Florida and the Everglades in mind. If you wish to read about her, I recommend: *Marjory Stoneman Douglas, Voice of the Everglades* by Jennifer Bryant.*

Marjory Stoneman Douglas was born in April of 1890, in Minneapolis, Minnesota. Her father's businesses failed, and they moved many times. When she was six her mother had a nervous breakdown. Later, when she was able, she took Marjory, and they left her father and went back to Minneapolis.

In 1908 she went to Wellesley College in Boston. The speaking and writing classes were to be a great aid to her in later years. She graduated in 1912. Shortly after her mother passed away, she got married to a Kenneth Douglas. He turned out to be a bad choice, became involved in illegal activities and soon was jailed. In 1915 at 25 she moved to Miami, Florida to live with her father and his new wife. He had finally gotten into a business in which he was succeeding. He had started the Miami Herald. Marjorie went to work for him writing about the people and happenings in Florida during the early 1900's.

It seems that all her life Marjorie was being prepared for the saving of the Everglades: her college training, working for her father in Miami by learning and writing about southern Florida, and getting out and into nature and being around events that were shaping the development of south Florida.

After all, at this time Miami had only 5,000 residents.

In 1924 she ventured out and began working for herself writing for magazines. In 1942, Hervey Allen, an author and editor, asked her to write about the Miami River. She said that she would rather write about the Everglades. So, *The Everglades, River of Grass* began. The book was popular, but the Everglades was still being destroyed in 1948 when it came out.

As early as 1928 a landscape architect, Mr. Ernest Cole, came up with the idea that the Everglades should be a national park. He campaigned tirelessly to keep the idea alive. Marjorie must have had the knowledge of this because she too had campaigned for almost 20 years for an Everglades National Park. She gave credit to her father for her earliest ideas about the Everglades. In 1947 this idea became a reality and the park was opened.

After this the Corps of Engineers continuously threatened the Everglades. They were straightening the Kissimmee River, building hundreds of canals, pumps and floodgates, constructing Dade County's huge jet port, and continuing the call for additional draining of the East Everglades. At 78 Marjorie founded a group called "Friends of the Everglades" to combat these Everglades intrusions and was still campaigning almost to the day she died.

Today the people and government representatives of Florida have come to their senses, and the environment of the Everglades is improving. However we need to be ever vigilant. For the last sentence in her book, Jennifer Bryant writes,

> "But even when Marjory Stoneman Douglas is gone, her legacy—an unwavering dedication to preserving the "river of grass"—will live on."

The problem is, *"Less we forget."* I found this book, "Marjory Stoneman Douglas," in a thrift shop in Winchester, Virginia, labeled from the library that no longer wanted it,

Earth *Keepers*

MARJORY STONEMAN DOUGLAS
Voice of the Everglades

Jennifer Bryant
Illustrated by Larry Raymond

Twenty-First Century Books
A Division of Henry Holt and Co., Inc.
Frederick, Maryland

> It was so sad that this wonderful book had been discarded by a library. One concession is that I might never have had the great opportunity to purchase it in a thrift shop, and to read and reference it in my book.

As I was walking along in the mist I came upon three armadillos. They were so busy looking for food with their noses in the dirt that I could have actually touched them. Now this is a strange looking animal! They look like prehistoric creatures. They are not native to Florida; the nine-banded Armadillo* has migrated from South America up into Central America. From there he has gone into Texas and then east across the south to Florida. They live in forests or partially-forested areas with soft soil in which to dig their burrows or hunt for food.

Their food source is many types of insects, including beetles, wasps and ants. They also eat earthworms, lizards, toads, frogs and small snakes. They have very poor eyesight but a great sense of smell. A strange characteristic is that they cross water by holding their breath for as much as six minutes and walking on the bottom. They also can inflate their bellies with air and dog-paddle across. If surprised they can leap high into the air, from 3 to 4 feet straight up! The good news is that they eat lots of insects. The bad news is, they have been known to carry leprosy and because of this they are used to study the disease.

I was leaving the Big Cypress Reservation and could see that I was heading into the Big Cypress Swamp. The road ended and straight ahead was a canal going south. Right next to it was my way across these glades. A huge dragline was parked alongside the canal. There was a rough marl (clay and calcium carbonate) road along the canal dredged by this great dragline. The road was made up of "Miami limestone"* with occasional bits of brain coral in it. It is a misconception of both the early scientists and even many people today, to think that lower Florida is an old coral reef. I, too, was one of those until I read Mrs. Douglas' book.

All I had to do was walk along this road. The Native American men I had talked to at the first store I had stopped in had told me about this canal. They knew just what they were talking about. There was also some shell mixed in with the limestone, and because it was raining the road was real sticky. I

A huge dragline that was along a canal on the south side of the Big Cypress Seminole Indian Reservation. This was the way I crossed the Big Cypress Swamp, all the way to The Everglades Parkway (Alligator Alley) and then on to the Tamami Trail. All I had to do was walk on the road made by draglines and construction vehicles. A sign read: Florida Drainage and Flood Control.

walked along just on the grass keeping a lookout for snakes. A sign at the start of the canal read:

> FLORIDA DRAINAGE AND FLOOD CONTROL

As I walked along I noticed that the canal zigzagged from southeast to southwest. Occasionally there would be gates in the canal with at least six feet difference in the water levels. There were also small concrete bridges to give access to the opposite side of the canal for the construction equipment and crews.

I was walking the eight miles to the Everglades Parkway (Alligator Alley) from the reservation. It was late afternoon when the rain finally stopped and the sun came out. I came upon some very large white birds along the edge of the canal and believe it or not, out here in the middle of nowhere, four white-faced cows! They just stood there staring at me and then went on grazing as I passed by. There were some small very dainty cypress trees on occasion and on them were growing some red flowering air plants, possibly some king of orchid. There was no Spanish moss on these trees. I also heard a gator bellowing off in the distance, or was it a bull?

I could see Alligator Alley ahead, and when I got to the two-lane the canal I was following intersected with the canal along-side of this road. The construction of the Everglades Parkway (Alligator Alley)* began officially on November of 1964. The studies and methods to finance were begun about four years before. A cross-state road was proposed way back in the 1920's but did not become a reality until then. In 1960 the opposition to the road started. This project pitted the Seminole Tribe of Florida against the American Automobile Association (AAA), and environmentalists against developers. The road was two-lane and had just opened when I set foot on it. It was widened to four lanes between 1986 and 1992. There are now bridges every mile or two to allow the uninterrupted

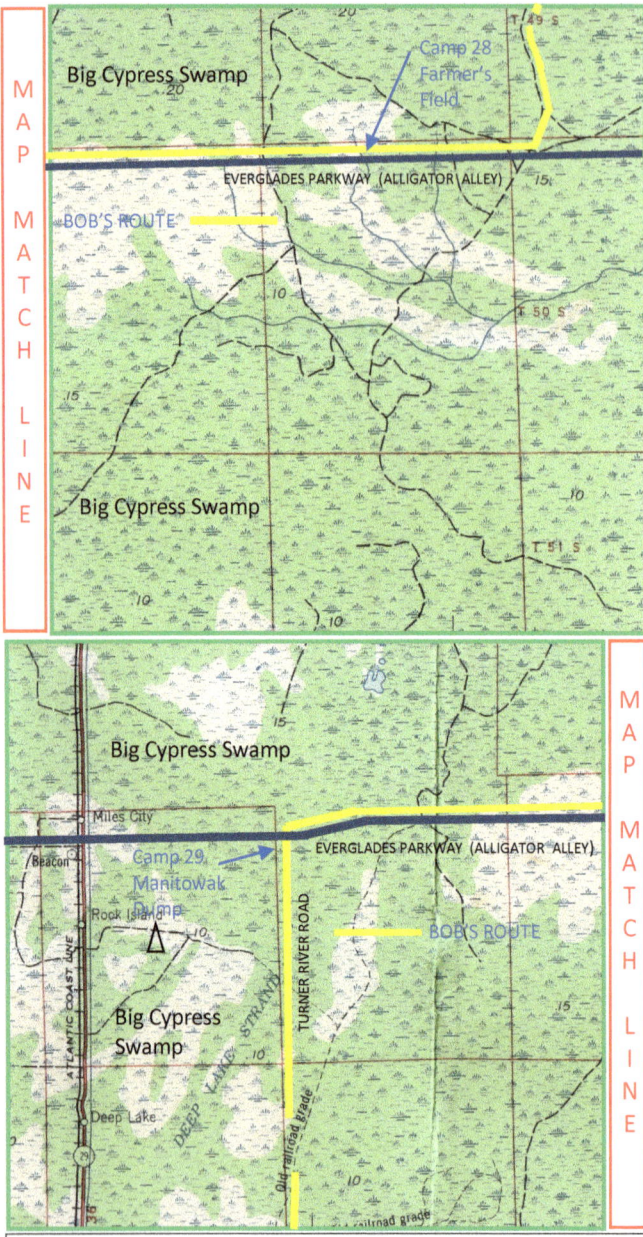

My U. S. Geological Survey map didn't have the Everglades Parkway located on it. I have marked its location in blue. It was just finished the year I was on this hike. That was good because there wasn't very much traffic and then it was only two lanes.

natural flow of water from Lake Okeechobee to the Everglades.

I came to another small bridge across the parkway's canal. There were four men, two on either side of the canal, fishing off this bridge. At first they seemed very surprised at my arrival. When I asked them for some information about the next canal crossing the Big Cypress Swamp they didn't know a thing. I bet they didn't even know where they were!

Actually the Big Cypress Swamp is the Big Cypress National Preserve.* It was one of the first national preserves established in October of 1974. It consists of 720,000 acres, borders the western side of the remaining Everglades, and is north of the Everglades National Park. When the Everglades National Park was established in 1947 Big Cypress was to be part of it. This did not happen because the land had not yet been purchased from private owners. Originally it was occupied by various Native Americans. In the late 19th and early 20th century the timber industry built railroads. They then proceeded to cut and haul out most of the virgin cypress trees. Today you will see on maps and find in the wilds these old railroad grades. Big Cypress National Preserve agreements allow both the Seminole and Miccosukee Indian tribes to have permanent rights to occupy and use the land. That is why in modern times, you will see swamp buggy rides and air boat tours by Native American people along Turner Road and the Tamiami Trail.

According to my maps, I couldn't go across the swamp due south. I would have to go west along the Parkway (Alligator Alley) for 20 miles. I should then come to Turner River Road and another canal just like the one I had been on, and then I would have to go about 20 miles south to the Tamiami Trail.

I set off heading west along Alligator Alley. It was getting late in the afternoon, and when I came to a bridge I stopped to eat. Just down the road I found some smooth trunk palmetto trees on which to tie my hammock in a posted field. I had hiked 15 miles.

35 foot Cypress tree. Big Cypress Preserve. (Pen and ink on paper.)

The next morning it was very hazy, not very light, and the mosquitoes were still out. I just left my mosquito net hat on. As I was crossing my first bridge, I saw a small two-foot alligator nonchalantly swimming along. This was my first alligator; at least Alligator Alley didn't let me down. Just over the bridge off in the grass I saw a young ground rattler. It was stretched out and was black, grey, maroon and red. It looked dead at first but was probably slow because it was early morning and cool. I watched it closely and it was definitely alive!

A few more bridges and I stopped at one for lunch. As I was sitting under the bridge for shade, another small alligator came swimming along in the reeds. He climbed up on a log to sun. All of sudden a hawk swooped down and splashed in the water trying to catch a fish. He missed and steadily climbed up out of the area with a strong beating of his wings. All the time he was emitting a shrill cry. Screech! Screech! probably to make up for the embarrassment of his failure.

As I hiked along, whenever I came to concrete bridges there were people fishing under them and in the canals alongside the road. Some people even looked like tourists; they said that they were fishing for bass. I don't think that they could do that today because now the Everglades Parkway is four-lane and part of U S I-75. At one place where people weren't fishing I got within 10 feet of a small gator. He jumped in but surfaced and stayed out in the center just looking at me. Don't ask me why I did that sort of a foolish thing, trying to sneak up on a gator, even if he was small!

The marl and shell along the side of the road were making it hot. I came upon a hammock stand. It was a few feet higher in elevation and had, instead of cypress and palms, scrub oak and pine on it. These small islands were occasionally set amongst the swamp with cypress trees. I stopped to sketch. I sure liked the dainty look of those cypress trees.

I came to a place where the forest service was starting to build a tower. Some people fishing there showed me a lot of bass. The water was murky and had a very bad smell.

Turner River road Canal.

The sun was going down as I came to the double bend in the turnpike. I stopped to eat something fast and then finished the distance to Turner River Road.

When I got there it was spooky with the large cypress stand, its Spanish moss swaying in the breeze and the swamp right next to it. The owl making hooting and screeching sounds in the distance didn't help any! Nothing else was moving or around when I camped in the Manitowak Dump and Junk Yard. I figured that I had done at least 22 miles that day.

In the morning I was heading south down Turner River Road. There was a hot breeze stirring. The shell along the side of the road was so bright that I walked in the grass to ease my eyes. Remember that I was looking down a lot because I didn't want to step on a snake. I was seeing small wooden bridges over the canal. At an old ferry-type bridge I stopped, looked around, bent down and dunked my head and arms in the canal. It was refreshingly cool. As I looked up a big moccasin was slipping into the reeds on the other side of the canal.

I saw some Mallard ducks swimming in a pond near a small run-down cattle pen. The cypress was beginning to thin out and now I saw prairie grass and pines just like the Ocala National Forrest, except for the cabbage palms. I came upon some county surveyors. I asked them how far it was to the Tamiami Trail. They said that it was three miles. It seemed like six miles by the time I hiked it! It was sure hot!

Gateway arch to Collier County traveling from Miami west along the Tamiami Trail, soon after the road was opened in 1928. Note the road is not paved and the canal is on the right, north side. The road was 30' from shoulder to shoulder and later paved 20' wide. This arch and its north to south mate on the Collier-Lee line was demolished in 1957 when the road was widened to 24'.
Photo: Big Cypress National Preserve, National Park

18
Tamiami Trail

I finally arrived at the Tamiami Trail.* This road officially is the 260 miles of U.S. Highway 41 from Tampa to U.S. Route 1 in Miami. There is some controversy about just who suggested the name, Tamiami Trail. Two different Tampa men claim this, but it is derived from "Tampa to Miami." After Naples the trail becomes an east-west road crossing the Everglades and forms part of the north border of the Everglades National Park. The north-south portion was begun in 1915. This portion was on higher ground and included many rough roads already in existence. The east-west portion was begun in 1923 across the Big Cypress Swamp. At that time the Everglades had only ox paths and Seminole Indian trails in existence.

People said that it was impossible to run cars across the Everglades swamp! On April 1923 Dade County land developer Captain James Franklin Jaudin started out with ten "Model-T" vehicles, 28 men and two Seminole Indian guides to prove that it was possible. They called themselves the "Trailblazers."* They were successful, but it took them 23 days. Much longer than they thought!

It took a lot of politics and positioning to arrive at the final location of the Tamiami Trail. In 1919, Lee County ran out of money. Captain Jaudon, the leader of the "Trailblazers," offered to build part of the road through Monroe County where he owned 207,000 plus acres. He wanted them to change the route through his land. He built the Loop Road. In 1922, the State of Florida ran out of funds. Barron Collier said that he would complete the Trail if the state would name a county (part of Lee County) after him and run the road through his county. He owned millions of acres of southwest Florida land. So in 1923 Collier County was formed.

Collier began immediately and in earnest. He started on what was to be the new county seat, the town of Everglades.*

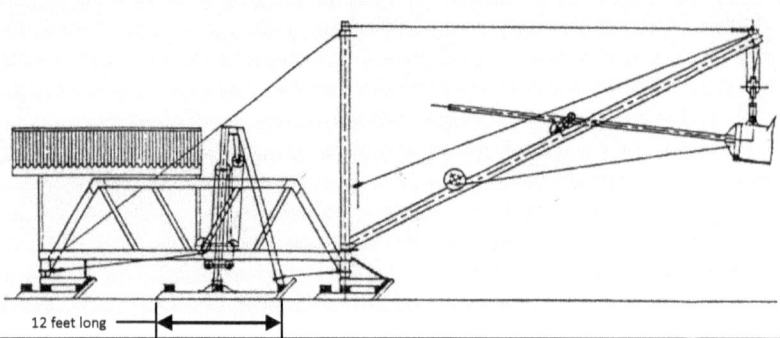

12 feet long

Bay City Walking Dredge
Built in Bay City, Michigan in 1924 and brought to work on the Tamiami Trail in 1927 for Barron Collier's construction company. The machine was light so it could work on the muck-swamp type land. With its approximate 36 foot width it could straddle the canal it was digging and then dump the fill for the road on the side. Two men could operate it using a system of cables, pulleys and sheaves. One of the most comprehensive sites to get additional information on this machine is the American Society of Mechanical Engineers (ASME) asme.org On a plaque at the Collier Seminole State Park is this drawing which also includes additional views and is provided by Agnoli, Barbe, Brundage Inc.

Swamp Buggy at the intersection of the Tamiami-Trail and Turner River road.

He brought thousands of workers in, raised the land and built the town up with docks, stores, schools, streets, and a base for his construction crews. He then dredged the river and built the road Highway 29 for four miles up to where his section of the Tamiami Trail would then head in both directions, west and to the difficult east.

Of particular interest is the type of dredge used in building the Trail through the Everglades. The Bay City Walking Dredge* sits on display in Collier Seminole State Park, which is 15 miles southeast of Naples on the Tamiami Trail. This machine was built in 1924 in Bay City, Michigan. It used pulleys and sheaves to move four wooden shoes and a central base forward in a walking motion that could cover five to ten feet at a time. The machine had a one-yard bucket, a 40–foot boom and was approximately 36 feet wide. Because of its width, it could straddle the canals it made.

In 1928 when the Tamiami Trail was completed it was considered a engineering marvel. However, it seems that no one had considered the potential damage that could be caused to the Everglades. The roadway and the canal became a dam to block the water flow from Lake Okeechobee to the Everglades. This was very bad for the ecology of the region. Since that time, in 1990 and today, some canals have been filled, extra culverts under the highway have been built, and a few miles of the highway have been raised onto a bridge to allow additional natural water to flow into the Everglades.

There was a small store at the intersection of Turner River Road and the Tamiami Trail. I went in and was amazed at the assortment of outdoors equipment hanging everywhere. It was a real menagerie. I dropped my pack near the entrance and before I could turn around a guy says,

"Howdy, what can I do fer ya?"

Came to find out, he was the owner. He once lived in Miami. He said that he made a good living by selling to the fishermen, hunters, and tourists and by storing swamp buggies. This fella had a floppy hat and talked real country. He

One black moccasin near a rock above and two moccasins sunning their selves on a rock along the canal below.

reminded me of one of the Hollywood Hillbillies. Especially with that hat! I bought a few snacks and a soda and asked him if I could look at the swamp vehicles outside.

"Them there's called swamp buggies," he said "and go right ahead, make yourself at home."

I looked around outside at one of the swamp buggies as I drank my soda. It was a crazy looking contraption, with an old 4-cylinder Model A Ford engine and chassis. There were real big tires with large chains on the rear wheels. Then there was a raised-up seating area behind the driver's seat. I guessed that was to have a good view and to hunt from.

I went east on the Tamiami Trail. I stopped at a roadside park and before I realized, it had turned into Grand Central Station. Some fishermen pulled up and started fishing on the nearby bridge. A car pulled up and some school kids got out and started running around. Two trucks pulled up and they started drilling holes in the dirt by the bridge. Bu...Bu...Bu...Tut! Bu...Bu...Bu...Tut! I had to get out of there!

In the next couple of miles I counted 30 moccasins in and on the side of the canal along the north side of the road. There weren't any gators, but these snakes were big, about the size of a man's arm, short and fat. Some were sunning themselves on rocks and sticks and some were swimming on top of the thick weeds.

There is a misconception that every dark-colored snake one sees in the water is a poisonous moccasin. Not the case. There are more harmless water snakes than moccasins. An adult Cottonmouth Moccasin* on average is between 20-48 inches long. Its body is very fat, and it has a short thick tail. Its head is distinctly broad and triangular shaped and much broader than the neck. Its pupil is vertical. Water snakes have a slender body, a long thin tail, a narrow head, and no neck, although a water snake can flatten its head out to look threatening, which will give it a triangular look.

Keep in mind that Cottonmouth bites* can be very

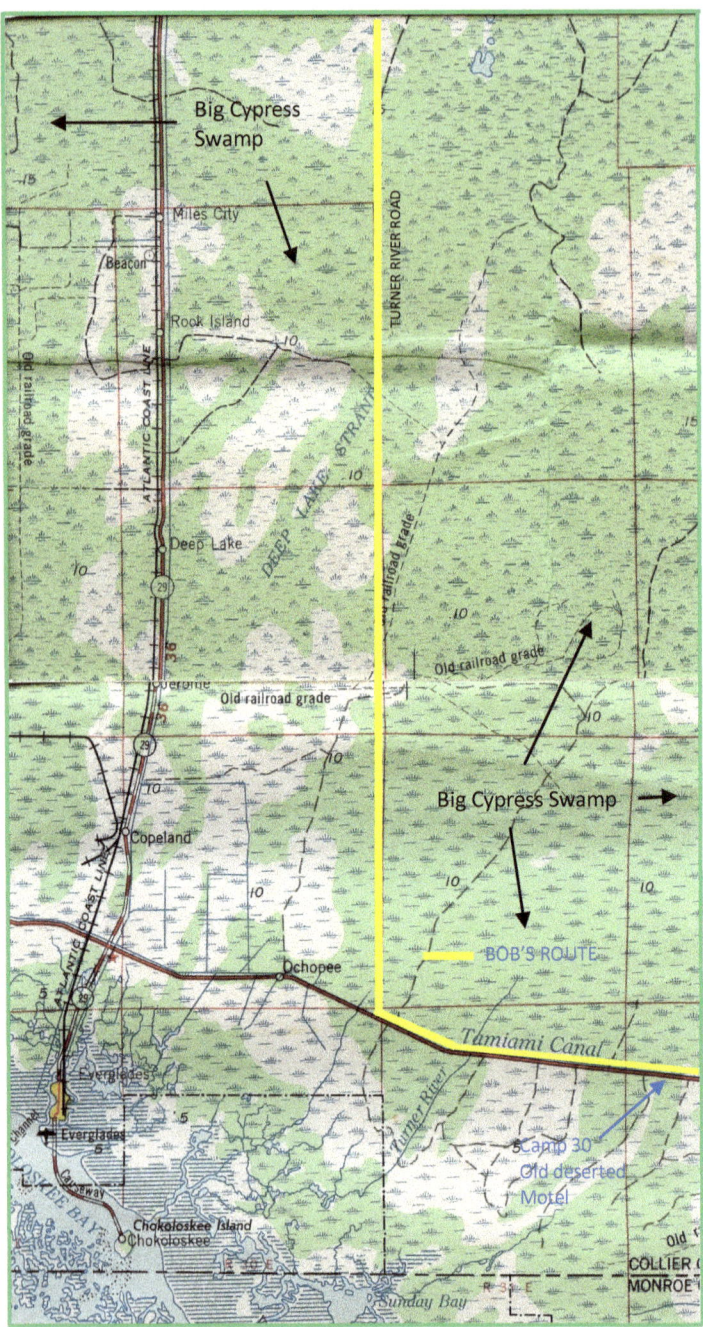

dangerous. They use a hemotoxic venom like copperheads and most rattlesnakes, which prevents the body's blood supply from coagulating and therefore a victim may experience a large blood loss. Bleeding may be from every opening of the body. There is extreme pain and possible permanent tissue and muscle damage or even loss of limb. The good news, if there is any, is that at least half of all venomous snake bites turn out to be "dry bites." This is a bite that doesn't have any venom in it. It is possible that they may save their venom for something they want to eat. Just remember that even non-poisonous snakes can bite, so it is best to leave snakes alone.

That day the mosquitoes and gnats were bad and so was the water. I was beginning to smell like an old canal!

I saw a couple of pairs of Coot* birds along the water's edge near a cypress stand. They are strange birds. In the water swimming they are mistaken for ducks but on land they appear more like, and walk more like, a chicken. Their rounded bodies are dark grey and rounded heads are black. Their bills are white, short and pointed with a dark band near the tip. They often mix with ducks and dive like them. They eat mostly algae and water plants. Because they have short wings, if they want to fly they must run a long way to get into the air.

It was about 9 miles along the Trail to Monroe Station.* Monroe Station opened in 1928. It was originally one of six stations built by Baron Collier every 10 to 12 miles along the most desolate part of the trail. They were to provide safety, comfort, supplies, gas, repairs and even a telephone. Collier planned these stations with husband-and-wife teams in mind. The wife pumped gas and took care of the commercial area, and the husband every hour would ride his Harley Davidson motorcycle the 5 to 6 miles each way from the station looking for motorists who needed help.

These buildings were all alike. They were modest structures, approximately 13' by 24,' with two stories and a hip roof. There was a one-story shed-roofed attachment in the rear. In the front there was a flat-roofed overhang across the

Monroe Station back in about 1933 (Note the Ford sedan on the left). The original main building only measured 13' x 24'. The stairs on the right went up to the living quarters. The bottom was commercial. There were sheds on the side and rear. Note the hand cranked glass-top gas pump on the left under the canopy. The front had two double doors that could be opened to give a kind of outside-inside feeling to the retail area. Barron Collier Planned the stations for husband and wife teams. You can see that this wife liked her flowers by the many flower boxes adorning the windows and front.
Sketch source: Original photo, U.S. National Park Service, nps.gov

entire front for a car to stop under. This was supported by three cross-braced posts. To get to the living quarters, there was a side stairway going up from the front and around to the rear. The commercial area on the first floor had two sets of doors with windows that could be opened to give it an indoor-outdoor atmosphere.

There is no deed stating when the property passed from Collier's ownership, but it is thought that it was some time in the late 1930's. The property changed hands a couple of times. By the 60's it had been added to in the rear which more than doubled the main building and also there were two side sheds. In approximately 1964 it was sold to Dixie Webb. Dixie sold the property to "Big Joe" and Susie Lord in 1972.

In 1974 the Big Cypress National Preserve was established

and sometime later the Lords were forced to remove their gas tanks because of possible pollution. This reduced the profitability of the Station. The Lords continued to live there until the early 1990's when the National Park Service took over the building. The bad news is that the building today is a boarded up dilapidated structure. The good news is that some money has been appropriated to do a study to restore the site. The Park Service is having meetings with architects and local people. Lastly the Everglades Society for Historic Preservation* has been formed and is working to preserve Monroe Station and also many buildings in Everglades City.

I could see Monroe Station in the distance across the road on the south side. As I was approaching the drive and preparing to cross I saw that there was what appeared to be a Seminole Miccosukee Indian settlement back behind the trees and brush on my side.. There were a lot of different chickees of all sizes. In the 1920's many of the Miccosukee Indians* started living along the Tamiami trail. Because of this, they were able to get jobs helping to build the road.

I crossed over and walked into the wide dirt and gravel drive. On the right a road was entering the Tamiami Trail from the south. It was then that I realized that it was the intersection of the original Tamiami Trail which went through Monroe County, the Loop Road. I could see over on the far side of the cleared property lots and lots of swamp buggies. There were all kinds and sizes. I could see some tow cars, trucks and even some campers. There must have been at least 60 or more vehicles parked there.

I walked inside and came face to face with Mr. Dixie Webb himself! A legend in his own time. I really didn't know just who I was talking to!

"Well look what we have here," he said, "What are you doin', and where did you come from?"

Hey, this guy looked like Buffalo Bill, with old cowboy-type hat, thick white hair down to his shoulders and a big white beard. He appeared to be 65 plus years, a real character.

Cypress tree in water with reeds and lily pads. Big Cypress Preserve. (Pencil on paper.)

"Just hiking from Georgia to Key West," I said.

" Well, glad to have you with us, young feller. Can I get you anything?"

"Thanks," I said, "I'll just look around."

"If you don't see it or we don't have it, we'll bring it in for you by alligator or dugout canoe," he exclaimed.

I looked around. This sure was a wild place. They had all kinds of odds and ends, from a stuffed tusk-bearing, ferocious looking wild swamp hog to a sign stating:

OUR COFFEY WILL FREEZE YOU AWAKE

I bought a Pepsi and a moon pie, and then hollered good bye to a flamboyant man in an unorthodox place! He was already talking to a tourist couple that had just come in.

I wandered out to the small shed-type garage on the side. There was a guy in there tinkering with a generator for a car. We got to talking and he made a statement that made me laugh,

" The tourists coming in here are scaring the gators off!"

He told me that his wife liked to hike back in the swamp on some of the dirt trails to get orchids. I asked him why he had so many airplane tires around.

"For the swamp buggies, they like to use em', real wide and put low air pressure in em' for bogging through the Glades."

I shouldered my pack, walked across the wide Monroe Station drive, looked both ways and got over onto the left side facing the two-lane traffic.

A few miles down the road I came to a small restaurant and went in, bought a sandwich and a coke, and talked for a while to the owner.

Next I came to a small Miccosukee Indian village along the road. I talked to a couple of Native American men and children there. They all had the wonderfully bright multicolored clothing. They were very congenial and we had a very nice conversation about many things, my hike and their home in

A chickee put up across the road from the Miccouskee Indian village next to the Tamiami Trail canal. It was a nice place to stop and rest out of the sun.

A 5 foot Diamond Back rattler' lying along the road in the grass. Lucky for me it was dead. It sure scared me at first!

the Glades.

It was becoming dusk when I stopped at a small gas station. The mechanic and sole person there had a small puppy in the bay where he was working. While I was petting the puppy I asked for some water and he said,

" Sure help yourself out of the spicket by the pumps."

There was an old torn up deserted motel building next door in the same drive. Since it was starting to rain and getting dark, I asked him if it would be ok if I stayed there for the night.

"Sure, it's ok with me, no one will bother you there."

So I took unit number one! There wasn't anything inside except bare concrete walls. I don't know just how I did I, but I found a way to string up my hammock. I did have a good sleep, but my friends the mosquitoes were out in force.

I got up early the next morning, and had to cross over to the left side to do my hiking. Everything except fishing places were on the south side of the Trail. I was moving along the road very briskly when all of a sudden, as I was putting my foot down, I spied a Diamond Back rattlesnake spread out in the grass. In a split second, without breaking my stride, that foot never came down; instead my other foot shot me up and through the air clear over that snake. It was probably an Olympic feat! What a scare! When my heart finally stopped pounding and I regained my composure, I very carefully crept back and looked over at that snake. It was still spread out. It wasn't moving. Possibly it had been hit by a car. I decided not to poke around and continued on my way.

Not very far down the road I came upon a man and a lady sitting on lawn chairs alongside the canal fishing. I told them to watch out for snakes because I had almost stepped on a 5-foot Diamond Back rattlesnake just a short distance back.

"Well ain't that a fact," he said, "I'm going to go back 'ere and see if I can't get a hold of it!"

As he said this he gave his wife his fishing pole, grabbed a cane pole, and started back the way I had come.

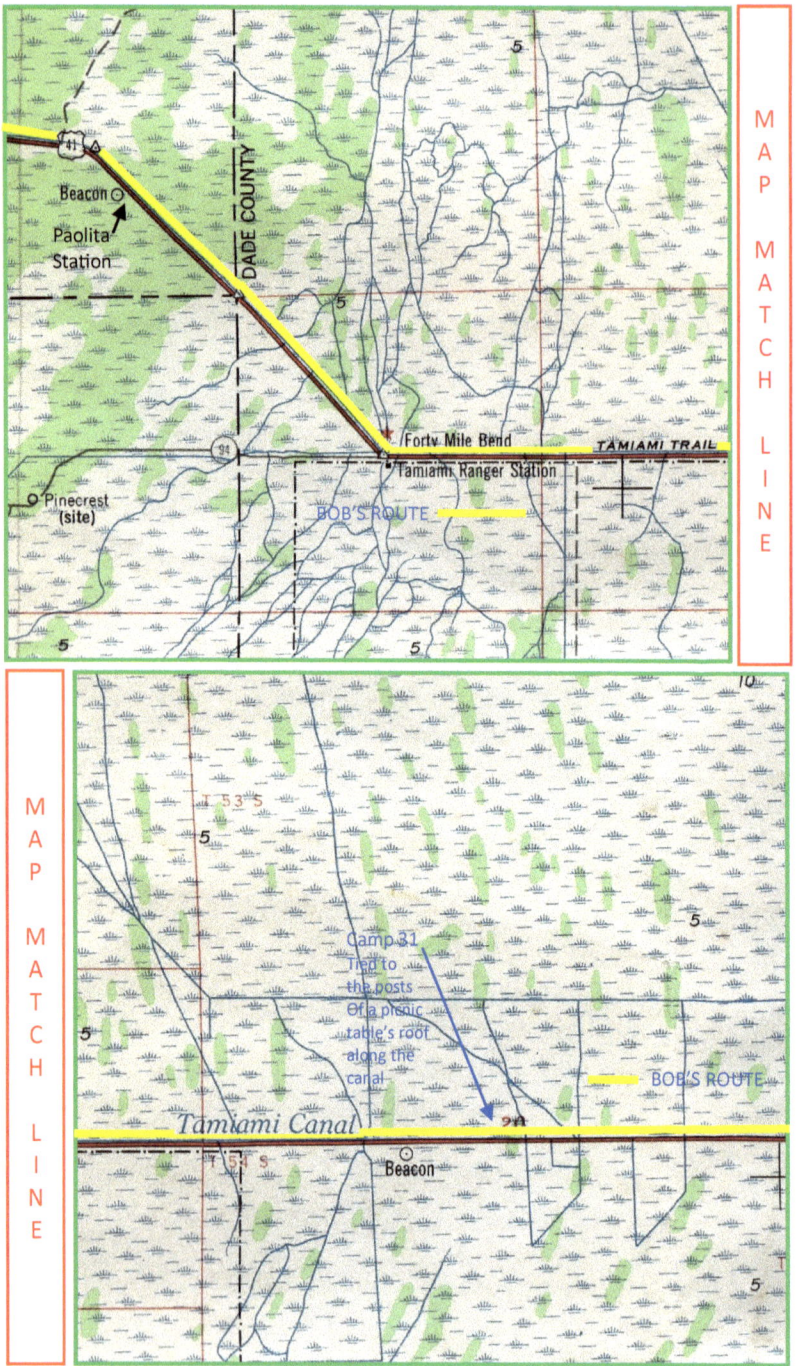

I decided that I was not going to touch that one with a 10 foot pole! So I continued on. When I got to Paolita Station, or where it was supposed to be, there was nothing there but an old building burned down.

Some ways north of there in the middle of the swamp was a place where in 1968 Miami-Dade Port Authority bought 39 square miles and started building a huge Jet Port.* They hurriedly threw up a training runway and had planned many more runways six miles long. The biggest airport in the world! To add insult to injury, they also wanted a wide transportation corridor from east coast to west with a new interstate, a high-speed mass transit system, and a waterway for boats. That is when Marjory Stoneman Douglas started the environmental group "Friends of the Everglades," and together with hunters and concerned citizens they stopped the Jet Port. This led to the creation of the Big Cypress National Preserve.

The one huge training runway that was built before it was stopped is still there, and the environmentalists have to keep vigilant. Occasionally someone gets the idea to start again on the jet port.

I moved along and soon was shaded by a long stand of Australian pines growing along the canal. This made the hiking real cool. It also kept me kind of close to the cars that occasionally came by, so I just stopped and stepped into the trees when one approached.

There were some small Seminole villages so I crossed over to the right to look as I walked by. At a place where the water was allowed to go under the Trail two little Seminole children were swimming in the canal next to a chickee house. This amazed me because all I could think of was the moccasins and alligators I had seen earlier swimming in the canal.

As I crossed back over to the other side I saw two small Screech owls* sitting on a limb near the trunk in an Australian pine. Screech owls are only from 7 to 10 inches tall but they have an 18 to 24 inch wingspan. They are nocturnal and fly fast with a steady wing beat. They don't glide but their

Screech Owl in an Australian Pine, Sketch by Bob Kranich
Original model for sketch, wikipedia.org, photo by Greg Hume

flight is erratic because they have to maneuver through the trees. They have two color phases, a gray and a reddish-brown. They will roost next to tree trunks as I had just observed. Their food includes insects, reptiles, bats, mice and other small birds. My *Field Guide to the Birds of North America* says that they can have two calls:* "a series of quavering whistles, descending in pitch; and a long single trill, all in one pitch." I did not hear them that day. Much later in my hiking career in the Smokey Mountains National Park I heard a Screech Owl while camping in the forest I can tell you right now, that it is an eerie sound when you are alone in the woods at night.

While looking up at them I almost stepped on a very large, very dead bobcat lying along the side of the road. Hit by a car, I'm sure. One of the casualties of man's progress. I have since read that vehicles on the highways are one of the greatest dangers to wild animals, especially large mammals.

I came to what is called the 40 Mile Bend, named that because it is naturally 40 miles due west from Miami. The other end of the 26-mile mostly gravel Loop Road came in at this point from Monroe Station. Here the Tamiami Trail was newer and much wider than the one I had been on. It also paralleled the original Trail on its way east to Miami. I would have liked to hike the old road but the canal flood gates cut it up. I could also see that there was an old main ranger station hidden from view behind some Australian pine trees. As I started hiking on the new road the canal was wide with no trees.

There were some chickees along the road for people waiting for airboat rides. Next to them was Bobby Tigers Snack House. I went inside and began talking to the couple who owned it. They told me that their little boy, who was there, had acted on a TV show with Mark and Gentle Ben the bear. They said that he had made $200 an hour! That would be good money today!

I went on, and there were more chickees and then Osceola's Air Boat Rides. I watched as some people loaded their airboat on a public ramp there. They had their trailer in the water. The driver of the airboat drove up onto the trailer, and then the airboat pushed the trailer up the ramp. It was amazing to watch. This thing was basically an aluminum flat bottom boat with two high seats, one in front for the driver, and the other behind which held about three passengers. There was a motor behind the seats with a large propeller mounted to it and a cage around the propeller to keep it away from people.

My camp along the Tamiami Trail. Note the hammock strung between the two concrete pillars over the picnic table and the canal in the background.

I came to a man working on his car engine in a roadside park. The next thing I knew I was siting down at a picnic table with his entire family, wife and three young children, just talking. They gave me some water because they said they had a lot with them. They were hauling the water to their house because their well had been condemned. It continually amazed me just how much people would help and be just down-right friendly.

I looked around and decided I would spend the night there at the roadside. I worked up a real crazy method to tie my hammock to the two end posts of a cast concrete picnic shelter. I was hanging way up in the air over the picnic table. That evening the mosquitoes were the worst that they had ever been. Another thanks to my mosquito net hat. It was getting hot in my sleeping bag when I slept at night, but I couldn't sleep outside of it because the mosquitoes would carry me off!

In the morning I decided to get an early start. I could see by the passing cars that there were a lot of weekend travelers and pleasure-seekers on the road. I came to a family and some of their friends who were fishing in the canal.

We got to talking for quite a long time. The one lady insisted that I was getting paid to take this trip and that she would see me pretty soon on TV! It went something like this:

A very large lady and the most vocal of the group, "I know that you aren't just doing this for the fun, Nooo Sir...re. I'm going to see you on TV."

"No mam, I'm just hiking for the fun of it."

Ha...Ha...Ho...Ho, I'll bet so... How much are they paying you?"

"***You are going to be on TV***, I know I'm right, I'll bet I'm right!" They all said, "Yea, Yea."

"Did they tell you what station you will be on? What time?"

"M'am, I've got to go, but honestly, I'm just a hiker on a trip."

"Well bye and good luck, we will be looking for you on TV."

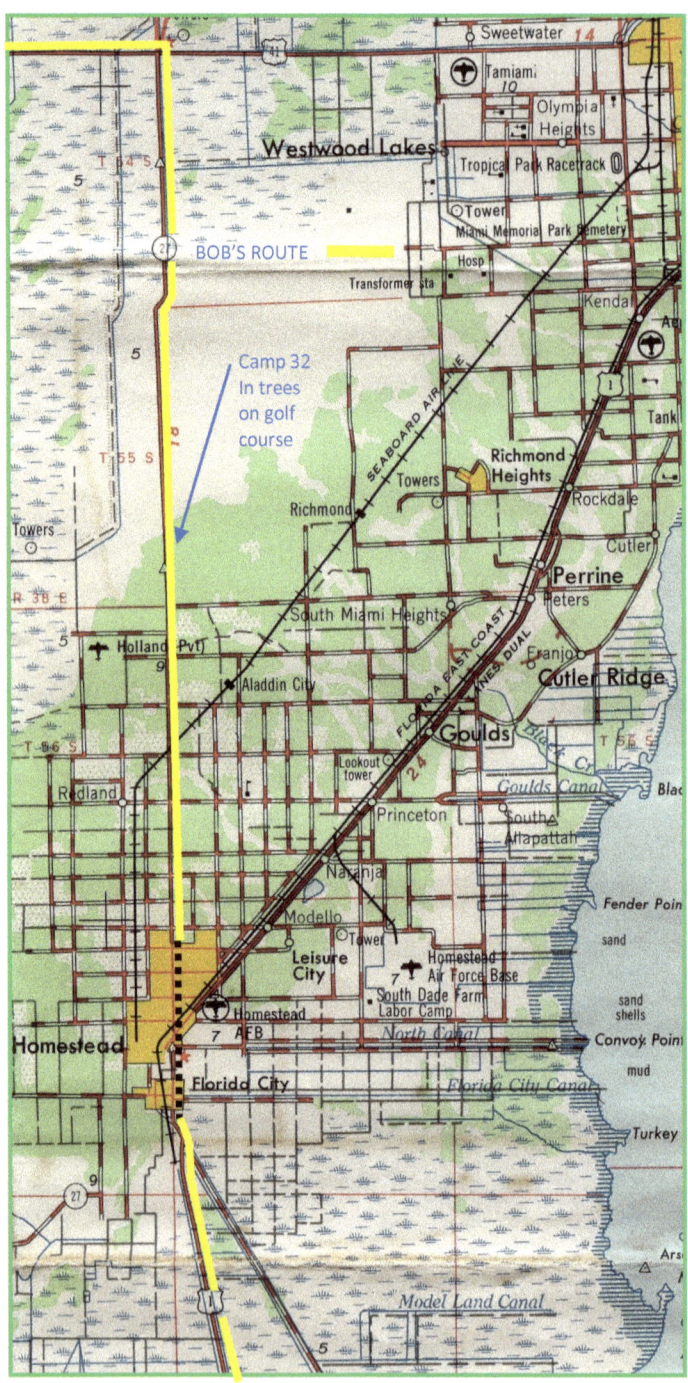

233 A Walk Across Florida

19
Homestead and Florida City

It wasn't too long before I came to my turn: it was highway 27 heading towards the south and Homestead. There was a sign along the road stating Nike Missile Air Defense Station. Coincidentally an Air Force convoy of trucks passed me by heading south. This caught my attention because it had been just two years since I was in Korea and in the U. S. Army assigned to a Nike-Hercules rear echelon repair depot. I was trained in chassis repair in 1966 at Redstone Arsenal in Huntsville, Alabama.

This Nike Missile Site was number HM-69.* It was located in the Everglades National Park in 1964 in response to the Cuban Missile Crisis. It was the last stationary air defense missile system to remain in operation in the United States until it closed in 1979. Today it is on the U.S. National Register of Historic Places, and the National Park Service gives tours in the winter.

This was a long straight road with tall Australian pines on the left (east side) on the other side of the canal. They had been there a very long time because the trees were quite tall. I could see off in the distance that a big blow was coming in. The sky was getting dark, and a front was moving across. The wind blowing me along felt good. The land was flat, strangely no fences...it was a pretty sight. There were small truck farms for growing vegetables. Here the canal was crystal clear and I could see the limestone on the sides and bottom. I stopped at a farmer's roadside stand and bought some tomatoes. I ate some of those tomatoes and some other snacks. Then I walked for a few more miles, saw what appeared to be a real nice area and put up my hammock in the dark. I figured that I had gone at least 22 miles.

In the morning, I was suddenly and rudely awakened to a word called out very loud……. "FORE!"

A truck farm north of Homestead. The storm was blowing up across the field. If you look close you can see the small coral/limestone rocks that are a main part of the field for growing the vegetable crops.

A small Royal Palm along the road on the golf course north of Homestead. It is about 30 feet to the top of the frons. The trunk is so smooth that it appears to be concrete. The part that the frons are growing out of is bright green. They are beautiful trees and just their presence gives one a feeling of being in the Tropics. Some trees attain a height of 100 ft.

I jumped out of my hammock. I looked around and guess what? I had camped on a golf course! No wonder it was such a nice place. I heard water sprinklers and mowers cutting grass. I hurriedly packed up my gear and shouldered my pack. No one had seen me. I guessed some people wanted to get on the golf course very early.

I ate breakfast along the side of the road by the golf course. I was sure that I must be just on the outskirts of Homestead. As I hiked along I could see people going to pick vegetables. A lot of the small farms had "pick your own" signs. The soil on these Homestead vegetable farms* looked like it was filled with rocks. The land around Homestead is very flat and the soil is marl, a limestone and shell mixed with sand. In fact, most plants can grow very well in the marl soil around Homestead. It is composed of minerals such as silica and calcium carbonate. Some of this soil which was at first hard limestone had to be made by using giant bulldozers with specially designed blades* that would cut off the rock one inch at a time. This made a mix of soil with rocks in it.

Nearly half of the winter vegetables eaten in the US. are grown in tropical south Florida in the Dade county area. The region near Homestead has a long growing season, abundant supplies of fresh water, and the absence of freezing temperatures. Vegetables are planted in their peak growing time from October to May when the warm and sunny days create a perfect growing environment.* Some fruits or vegetables that will grow in Homestead will not grow anywhere else in the United States, except possibly Hawaii.

I was beginning to feel that I was in the tropics. There were huge Royal Palm* trees lining the highway. These were about 30 feet high, but I knew that they could grow as high as 90 feet. They had a very smooth grey trunk which looked like they were made from concrete. Blend that with beautiful bright green frons on top and you have a very striking palm tree. The Royal Palm has a religious place in Christianity, palms for Palm Sunday.

The Florida Pioneer Museum* is located in the old Homestead East Coast Railroad Station Agent's house that was built in 1904. It was donated by the Florida East Coast railroad in 1962 and had to be moved from Flagler Ave. to land donated by Henry and Jacqueline Brooker. These are photos of the original house I took in early May of 1969. It was blown down by hurricane Andrew in 1992, and the museum reconstructed the building using the original drawings from the Florida East Coast Railway.

It was Sunday and beautiful weather as I walked through Homestead. Not too many people around. Still when people saw me they seemed surprised.

How did this area get its name? In 1898 it was open to homesteading.* To get to this area there was only a trail. It was called the "Homesteaders Trail." This all changed when in 1904 Henry Flagler decided to extend his railroad south from Miami to this location. The engineers who did the mapping for the railroad marked this area as Homestead. A story tells of Henry Flagler standing on the southernmost point of land in Florida, (and it could have very well have been in the Homestead Florida City area), with five of his most important executives. He said, as he extended his arm in a broad sweep south towards the water, "Gentlemen: the railroad will go to sea."*

Henry Flagler then extended his Florida East Coast Railroad south through the swamps, and mangroves, across the sounds, and then from Key Largo to Key West. This made Homestead the hub of the railroad expansion. The name Homestead originated from the supplies and construction materials being sent to the "Homestead area." Florida City and Homestead are so close that they are almost one. That was what I thought as I hiked through. It is the southernmost city in the U.S. that is not on an island, and it is the jumping off place for the Florida Keys.

When I got to the Florida Pioneer Museum, it was closed. There was an old, large, one-story, restored Florida City house on the property. Sitting next to it on a short section of railroad track was a railroad caboose from the old Flagler Florida East Coast Railroad. Even though the museum was closed I had the next best thing,....maybe the best! I started by dropping my pack on the large front porch and then taking a seat there and just resting. When I had my fill of resting, I took some photos of the Florida City pioneer house. Also since I could't resist railroads, I had to take photos of the old Florida East Coast caboose and sketch it. Some literature there said that the house

Historic Flagler System Florida East Coast Railroad Caboose. It is still behind the Florida Pioneer Museum, It looks good here, but today it is badly in need of some tender love and repairs.

was the old Homestead Florida East Coast Railroad Station Agent's home and was built in 1904. This structure had to be moved to its present location from Flagler Ave. in 1962 to donated land.

I noticed as I started off on Highway 27, that it was named Krome Ave. It ran through Homestead and Florida City. I was sure it was in honor of William Krome who became the chief construction engineer on the overseas railroad after Joseph Meredith died. Meredith was stressed and over-worked from the job. Krome had been a member of the original survey party that went through the Everglades looking for a route for the railroad.

I was through Florida City before I knew it. I filled up my stove for 4 cents at an Amoco gas station. It was there that I saw that I was on U. S. Highway No. 1. There was also an old railroad grade on my right, the west side of the road. There weren't any rails, but the old ties were still there. I had this feeling that where I was standing was historic. I was sure that it was the jumping-off place for the overseas railroad, *the railroad that went to sea.*

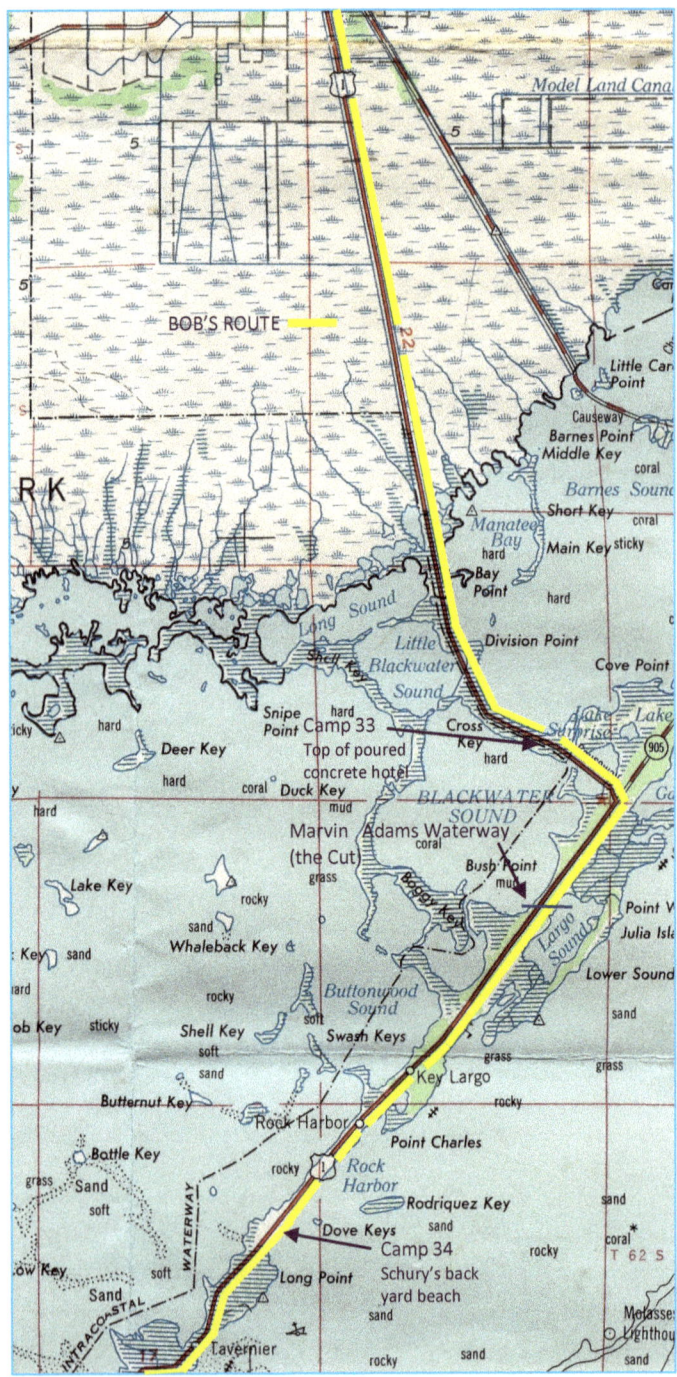

241   A Walk Across Florida

20
The Hike That Went to Sea

I checked my map and looked south down the highway towards the Keys. I could expect a raised causeway, about 10 miles of Everglades swamp, and 10 miles of mangroves. It looked like the mangroves would be high on each side, so I couldn't expect much breeze. The raised causeway is what Flagler's two dredges* built. The railroad was built on it where the highway is now. In April of 1905 two of Flagler's huge traveling dredges set out from what now is the Florida City area, south heading for Cross Key to Jewfish Creek. The dredges worked side by side with the marked right-of-way in the middle. They piled up the fill between them making a canal on each side and the raised causeway in the center.

As the dredges moved along, rock was brought in and spread on top of the causeway and then tracks laid. They built two stations, Woodall and Everglade, along the way. When they got to Jewfish Creek, which is the Intercostal Waterway now, they had to build a drawbridge for boat traffic. There was an area called Lake Surprise just before they got to Jewfish Creek, and there they had a tremendous time. In fact it took 15 months to build the causeway through it. They barged tracks, engine, and railroad work cars across to Key Largo and then began working on the 27 miles of railroad grade needed there. They also started working in other places along the route especially where the bridging was to go, by boating and barging in equipment. In Key West they started on the final terminal by dredging in fill from the ocean.

Why build a railroad to Key West?* One may ask.

There were a few reasons. We would be able to trade with Cuba. The Spanish American War with Spain was over, thus the Panama Canal could be completed. Key West, which was then the largest city in Florida with approximately 20,000 inhabitants, had a very nice economy and a natural deep-water harbor. That harbor and its location in the Caribbean would make it an obvious choice for trade from the Panama Canal and the Caribbean nations.

I started off with Australian pines lining the road on both sides. It was a narrow two-lane road so I was on the left side facing traffic. The Sunday traffic was fierce and heavy, but most of it was coming from behind me going to the beaches. Some kids went by in an open flatbed truck playing drums and mariachis. I got hot and stopped to cool off in the canal. I saw a big bass dart away and then some small minnows nibbled on my feet. Since I had left the Australian pines behind me there was no shade, so I just sat there and evaporated off.

All day, as I hiked along, I had to wave back at people. I guessed they didn't see many hikers. When there was a break in the mangroves, I could feel an occasional breeze as well as a salt smell in the air, not entirely ocean, still some Everglades memories. I tried to get a photo of the ospreys which had some nests on the poles along the highway, but they seemed to scare easily and stayed away. This was sure a long straight stretch. The side of the road was marl and rough coral rocks, really putting my boot soles to the test. I almost felt like I would flake out! Then up ahead I saw a rise in the road. I figured that it must be a Florida flood control canal. It was at least a mile or so away but I poured on the speed and moved out with a last thrust of energy

It was nice under the bridge, real cool with the breeze moving up the canal. I lay down like I was about to die. After a nice rest I ate my meager rations and drank some old canal water. I was back out on the highway, and in a couple of miles I came to a marina. I stopped for snacks and some fresh water. I had a long talk with some people who had seen me in the morning, on their way out to the beaches. I guessed that is why so many people waved at me the next five miles. They had seen me in the morning when they were driving out to have some fun and relaxation. Here it was late in the afternoon, and this guy *is still hiking in the sun!*

The traffic coming back from the Keys towards me was solid. Sometimes it stopped, bumper to bumper. Every one was waving and hollering at me, actually encouraging me. It was like I was a one-man parade and they were all bystanders waving, hollering and whooping. What a time! The enthusiasm just carried me along.

In the distance far ahead I could see that it was raining from some big storm clouds. The wind sprang up, and it got cool. At last I came to Jewfish Creek. I crossed over the drawbridge. There was a gas station, restaurant, marina, and a large unfinished poured concrete hotel under construction at this island in the mangrove swamp. The poured concrete mass gave me the impression of a huge monument to man's continued quest for domination over nature.

I went right over to a phone booth by the marina and called home. I was so excited about almost being in the Keys. My mom and dad were glad to hear from me.

I saw a man standing out front of the marina. He had on an all-white tropics outfit with a short sleeved sport shirt, dress pants, and one of those Panama wide brim hats. Looked like he had just stepped out of a movie. I asked him for suggestions for a place to camp since there were only private business areas and rocky fill amongst the mangroves. He suggested the top of the huge hotel being built. He was named Francis and had a French accent. He said that he was from Quebec and was running the marina.

He said, "Bob, this is not my usual running the marina outfit. But later on tonight I'm going to go to the mainland, pick up my girl and another couple, and we're going out on the town. Miami to be exact. Dancing all night!"

I took a look at the huge concrete structure, thanked him and climbed up the 6 flights of stairs to the top. What a view! I was really thrilled by what I could see, a long string of lights stretching out towards the southwest along the Keys. That was my destination….my goal.

I had just finished eating supper when Francis called up,

Looking at U. S. Highway No. 1 drawbridge over Jewfish Creek on the way to Key Largo from the Florida mainland, (in the distance). This photo was shot from a unfinished 6 story poured concrete hotel. Today there is an overpass that has replaced the drawbridge so that now cars do not have to stop when a bridge goes up for boat traffic.

Bob's sleeping bag laid out next to a bent over rebar. His camp was on the top of a unfinished poured concrete 6-story hotel. He tied a line of rope to the rebar and around his waist so in the middle of the night he would not wake up and half awake walk off the roof of the building.

"Hey Bob, you wanna some wine and a hot shower? Come on down."

What a gift, I didn't drink, but the hot shower was like heaven, a newfound luxury. It had been weeks since I had had a hot shower! Sure I sponged off every night and got in the water at times for a swim, but this was the best! What nice people I met.

The top of the unfinished hotel was nice, no mosquitoes and a cool breeze. I had to sleep on the concrete but it was worth it. I saw that the roof hadn't been finished. It would be real easy to get up in the middle of the night, and being half asleep walk right off the top. I tied my hank of 3/16 thick 500 pound test, nylon rope to a bent reinforcing rod protruding out of the concrete and then around my waist. I was now tethered to the hotel. The moon was out and illuminating the top of the hotel. I could hear the traffic way down below, but up here it was like another world...and with a cool breeze. I crawled into my sleeping bag and drifted off to sleep thinking of that song by the Drifters, *Up On The Roof*.

It was early morning, and it seemed that I saw the sunrise from the top of the world. I ate some breakfast, packed up and went downstairs. As I walked by, the restaurant manager said,

"Hey, wait just a sec, I'll get you a drink of ice water."

He came back with a large drink cup filled to top with ice and cold water.

He looked a little sleepy.

I thanked him and in two miles, I was on Key Largo and heading down the Keys.

Unfinished poured concrete 6 story hotel at Jewfish Creek and U.S. Highway 1.

21
Keys At Last!

Well I was finally in the Keys.* They were originally inhabited by the Caloosa and Tequesta Indians. The name Key is derived from a Spanish word, cayo.* Its definition is "small island." When the Spaniards first arrived they were naturally looking for gold. There was none of that here. There also was not any drinking water in the Keys. What they did do was to log the very old Mahogany trees. They took some of the Caloosas that they could capture as slaves to do their work for them in Cuba and some of the other islands in the Caribbean that they were settling.

The Keys have a true tropical climate and are similar to the Caribbean. They were built by plants and animals.* The Florida Keys are exposed parts of ancient coral reefs. This reef was along the edge of the Florida Straights and according to Wikipedia, "It is the third largest barrier reef system in the world."

I started to see signs along the road, that read:

```
NO HUNTING
NO SPEARFISHING
GAME PRESERVES
```

This was because the John Pennekamp Coral Reef State Park's* center is just about where U. S. 1 comes onto Key Largo. This park came about through the efforts of the Miami Herald's associate editor John Pennekamp. He headed up the Park Commission, and the park was named after him in 1959/60. At that time the boundaries were moved out to the ocean bottom's three-mile limit. Mr. Pennekamp was able to get two families to donate to the park. The Crane family donated land with shoreline and a strategically located island, and the Shaws donated access from U. S. 1 to the park.

An old road paralleled the new highway. It was very possible that this old road was on the original

The old highway on the Keys. It was very narrow. In many cases this was on the old Florida East Coast railway road bed. The mangroves would at times hide the new U. S. 1 and the commercial establishments and block the ocean breeze.

roadbed of the Florida East Coast Railway. I decided that I would hike it as much as I could. As I walked along, sometimes the thick and impenetrable mangroves would hide the busy main road and commercial establishments and block the refreshing ocean breeze. At other times the road ventured near the ocean and the beach, and then the hiking was ideal. I came upon a sailboat being loaded to go out. It had two sails and was a real nice-looking outfit. There was a lady, a man and their two high school age boys. The boat had an unusual name:

RAT HOLE BOYS

They were loading diving gear and other supplies. They said that they were going out to explore the reef.

I guessed that this was a public access area to the Gulf and the reef because another car was parked there. As I walked by, a lady who seemed to be just watching the action, started talking to me. It seemed that she was here from Clearwater and had spent a lot of time in the Key Largo area. She said that her son was just starting U. S. Air Force basic training.

I continued on. It was great weather with a cool breeze under clear Florida skies. I noticed that the water was turquoise blue-green. I came to a barricade and had to follow a footpath to the main highway. I found out why: there was a fairly short bridge, but it crossed a waterway. The waterway had shear vertical walls cut down into the coral of the island. The walls looked to be around 15 feet high. I was lucky--just as I got my camera out a motor boat blasted by. It made a good size comparison.

I found out that this waterway is called the "Cut." Officially it is the Marvin Adams Waterway.* It seems that in the early 50's Mr. Adams was able to purchase 50 acres of land on Key Largo at both the narrowest point on the Key and the middle. Mr. Adams had the idea that they needed a shortcut through the Key which would cut in half the distance and time to go from Black Water Sound (Florida side), to Largo Sound

Old overgrown Key Largo house along the old highway I was hiking on.

The "Cut" across Key Largo. Formerly named the Marvin Adams Waterway because it took Mr. Adams a year and half to excavate this. In some places the vertical walls are 15 feet high. When the tide comes in or out the water runs through this cut just like rapids.

(Atlantic side). He did the cost study and worked on the permits and then was introduced to Matthew "Barney" Waldin. Mr. Waldin was inventor and builder, and he had patented a machine that could cut deeply into coral rock. This machine had two huge caterpillar diesels. One would move the machine and the other would cut on the side just like a saw.

It took one and one half years to complete the digging and blasting. What "Barney" Waldin did was cut the sides down to where the water line was going to be and then blast out the center. Neither end went out into the Sounds until the entire cut was finished in 1961. He did not charge Marvin Adams for the work. Instead they made an agreement that he would do it for the valuable fill that was removed.

After I got close to Key Largo, the town, a Boy Scout on a bicycle rode along with me all the way through town. He had the usual questions. On the south side of town I came to a small store and stopped to shop for supplies. I felt that it was kind of a special occasion, me being on the Keys and everything. It was a small store and wasn't very busy. Because of this I was able to talk for a long time with the manager and some customers. Everyone was very interested in what I was doing.

Shortly after I left the town of Key Largo I found the old road again. The land was narrow along here and I found myself walking close to the ocean. In the Dove Key area I came upon a man working in his woodworking shop. He hailed me and said,

" Where you going?"

Dusting a bunch of wood shavings off his arms he introduced himself.

It seemed that Mr. Schry was retired and kept himself busy with various wood projects, and I found out later some other businesses.

"It's getting pretty late, you need a place to camp?"

"Sounds like a good idea," I answered.

"Come along back here. The water is right behind my

Dove Key sketches, a couple miles south of the town of Key Largo,

house. The breeze will keep the mosquitoes away tonight."

I'm happy to hear that." I told him where I had camped last night, up on the top of the motel, and he was amazed.

"I'm an old Keys man, some might call me a Conch," (born and raised in the Keys), he said, "I'm 69 years old, been here a long time. In fact I remember the railroad running along here. I'll leave you to your camp. You can get some water up behind the house. There's a spigot there."

I dropped my pack in back of the house down towards the shore, grabbed both of my canteens and headed for the water spigot. A real break! While I was getting some water Mr. Schry came out with a heaping paper plate of lasagna.

" The missus wants you to have this," he said.

"Gee thank you, I haven't eaten this good since I started my hike over a month ago!"

Thank the Lord for Mrs. Schry's good cooking! I thought, as I scarfed up the delicious food.

After that great supper, I had a swim in the boat basin area. There was no beach back there and the coral rock was too rough to sleep on. I looked around and found a partial sheet of drift plywood. It worked ok for a place to put my sleeping bag on. I set up camp and then settled down to sketch. There was a broken lobster trap amongst the coral rocks and a real nice palm tree nearby. While I was doing this, I watched as a long legged bird fished and sea gulls swooped down for fish–on-the-fly. As I lay down I was serenaded by a bird in the distant trees.

In the night I woke and noticed that the tide was up. The moon was bright and beautiful. The mosquitoes were very light but I still used my mosquito-net hat.

I was up early in the morning. As I was walking by the house, Mr. Schry waved and hollered out,

"Bye and good luck,"

"Thanks for everything," I said.

I had a later experience with Mr. Schry. When I got to Key West and settled in with my uncle and aunt, I wrote and sent a

The coral rock strewn shore of Key Largo. My backpack in the foreground.

Old Keys home along the highway in the Tavernier area. Note storm shutters.

thank-you card to Mr. and Mrs. Schry. I told them that I was so very thankful for their wonderful hospitality. They had gone the extra mile by letting me, a perfect stranger, stay in their backyard...and then serving me that wonderful plate of lasagna. To my great surprise they wrote back to me immediately in care of my uncle and aunt's address.

The Schry's letter…..

> Dear Bob,
>
> Your nice letter was received as we were getting ready for a short business trip here and other places in Fla, in relation to my TV Tower business.
>
> It's seldom, these days, that one, like yourself, will take the time to write and thank one for a favor. Pleased to know that you enjoyed your nite in "Dove Key", especially the lasagna.
>
> If your by this way, anytime in the future, your welcome to stay by the ocean and perhaps have another dish of lasagna.
>
> Good luck on the balance of your trip.
>
> Very truly yours,
>
> The Schry's

As I got back up on the road, I noticed the mile marker to be 95 miles to Key West. The markers begin at Key West and

A desolate, windswept and weather-beaten large structure along the old road near Tavernier.

In Tavernier I came upon what I thought was an old church. Later research proved to me that it was an old Masonic lodge building. The symbol above the door appears to be a mason sign. (see inset)

were started by the FEC Railway. It also let me know that I had covered 18 miles the day before.

In about 5 miles I came to Tavernier. This was an old city originally composed of a couple of communities and dating back to the coming of the railroad in 1905-1908. There were remains of small old Key houses with hurricane shutters and steep roofs. There was what appeared to be an old church along the original road I was on. (I have since found out that it was an old Masonic lodge building.) I just couldn't resist using some of my precious film to take a few photos of these early structures.

I crossed the bridge over Tavernier Creek Waterway. I was now on Plantation Key. In 1871 an article written in *Harper's Monthly Magazine** reported that since Plantation Key had very good soil it was able to have large trees and a plantation of coconut palms and pineapples. This is the reason for the name *Plantation*. Plantation Key once had a large Indian mound on it—meaning that it must have supported a group of natives for a long time but the ravages of time and development have obliterated it. This Key was also one of only two island locations other than Key West that had a boat building operation on it in the early 1900's.

As I walked along I saw that there were lots of small shops, motels and boat-bait-fishing marinas. Everyone was looking at me so I waved. It was lots of fun!

On the left side on the road I saw a sign, Coral Shores School. A man on the side of the school with a bunch of kids around him saw me and waved me over. He said that his name was David Monroe* and he was the DCT* vocational teacher. (The Diversified Career Technology program was for students in 9-12th grades. It gave them an opportunity to receive on-the-job training through the cooperative efforts of employers in the business/industry community.) He was interested in hiking and asked if I would talk to his kids on the subject. It sounded real interesting to me, and I sure didn't have anything else to do. So I held a class right there on the spot.

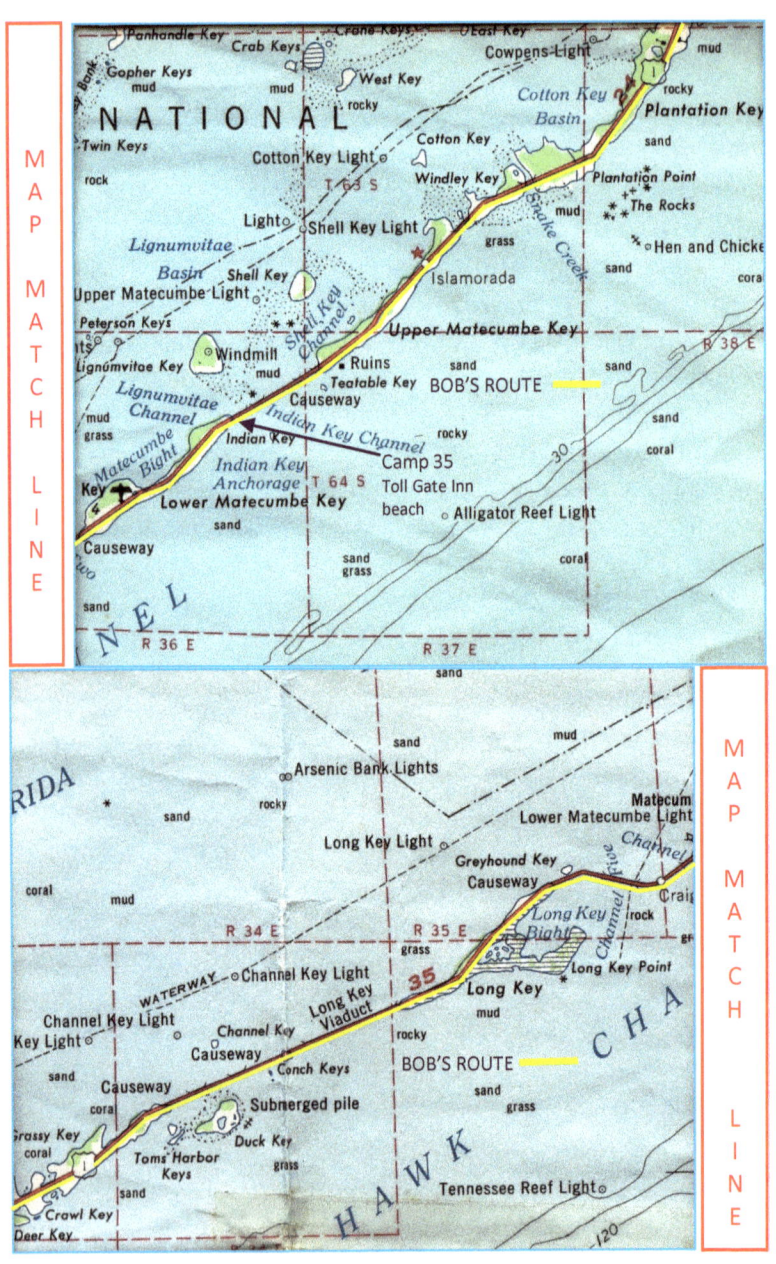

In crossing the many bridges, I had to step up on the concrete curb when a car came towards me, holding on desperately to the side of the bridge. The highway built upon the original FEC Railway bridges* was a very narrow two-lane. The Overseas Highway bridges were laid on top of the railroad bridges. Steel beams were laid across the top of the railroad bridges and then encased in reinforced concrete. Each side had a 9 inch high by 20 inch wide curb. The road was 20 feet from curb to curb.

The topics included gear, trip planning, map reading, food and supplies. I showed them my sketches, told them what I was doing and described some of my adventures. Then, as to be expected, every one of them wanted to try on the pack.

After I finished the class and everyone had the chance to try on the pack, I bid farewell. A few miles farther I came to the Snake Creek Bridge. This was a bridge similar to one I would be crossing over many times the rest of the way to Key West. It was very narrow and when a car approached me, I had to step up onto the concrete ledge on the side and frantically hold on to the rail. Since the rail was low when I stood up on it, I once almost lost my balance towards the water. I was sure that it would be real difficult to swim with the pack I

The Florida Keys Memorial.
Bronze plaque reads: "Dedicated To The Memory Of The Civilians And The War Veterans whose Lives Were Lost In The Hurricane Of September Second 1935."
The local quarried "keystone" coral slabs of rock rise 18 feet tall. It was dedicated Sunday November 14, 1937 at mile marker 81.5 just east of U. S. Route 1 in Islamorada, Florida Keys. The memorial was designed by the Florida Division of the Federal Art Project and was built by the Works Progress Administration.

had on. For that reason I always loosened my hip belt and dropped my pack onto my shoulders when crossing a bridge. This kept my center of gravity low.

I was now on Small Windley Key, and before I knew it I was crossing another bridge and was on Upper Matecumbe Key. In about a mile I arrived in Islamorada. There along the road at mile marker 81.5 was the Florida Keys Memorial (Hurricane Monument).* This was a memorial to the local civilians and WWI American veterans lost during the 1935 hurricane.* This hurricane was ferocious, the strongest hurricane ever on record to assault the United States. It came ashore on Labor Day, September 2, 1935 with 200+ mile per hour winds and a 12 to 20 foot surge. The storm devastated a large part of the upper and middle Keys with the worst destruction in the mile post 60 to 80 area.

The unemployed veterans had been sent there by the Government's Works Progress Administration, WPA. Their job was a work project during the Great Depression to build the overseas highway and bridges. There were 600 or more men working in these particular camps, but many were on holiday at that time. This storm killed more than 400 people, wiped out buildings, ruined the land, and destroyed the Florida East Coast Railway in the Keys.

The end of August 1935 people were warned that a hurricane was building in the Atlantic. However in those days there wasn't any hurricane warning system, like today's satellites, radar, or computers. In fact, old timers in the Keys watched for natural hurricane signs:* ants climbing up walls, land crabs heading for higher ground, or animals acting strange.

The morning of the day of the hurricane the weather was becoming very upsetting. The camp supervisor requested a train to take the residents and veterans off Islamorada. However many things went wrong. It was 1:30 PM when the message reached the Miami railroad yards. It took until 4:30 PM to assemble the train crew, locomotive, six passenger cars, two baggage cars and three boxcars. Then there were some serious delays along the way. The train arrived at the Islamorada area after 8:00 PM, just as the surge hit. The entire train except the engine and tender was thrown off the track together with the people they had picked up. A great book to read this complete narrative is: Les Standiford's book, *Last Train to Paradise*.

Just a short distance after I left the Memorial, I came upon a man standing out front of a barber shop.

He asked me with a jovial sound in his voice "What are you celebrating?"

I said, proudly, "Five weeks from Georgia to here!"

He sure looked surprised. Then the barber came out, white hair, mustache, apron and all, and wanted to take my picture.

He exclaimed, "Hey, I saw you last Sunday on the causeway." (That was when I was crossing over from the mainland to the Keys, my kind of a one-man parade.)

The barber took my picture and then proceeded to tell me about concrete hurricane houses nearby. He said that they were 12" poured reinforced concrete walls, floors and roofs. The only problem was that they were made with sea water which rusted the reinforcing iron. They were all cracking. But they were still sturdy and the floors were 5 feet higher than other houses. They were called "Red Cross houses" and were built by the Federal Emergency Relief Administration and the Red Cross right after the 1935 hurricane. The houses had four rooms, contained tons of steel in the concrete, and were anchored to the bedrock.

This guy was an encyclopedia of historic information! He went on, "The railroad fills were responsible for the damages because the tides and water couldn't get by the islands fast enough.... The storm just rolled right over. The railroad had 15 feet fills, just like a huge dam."

He knew a 90-year-old man whose father lived on the Keys 40 years before, and his father had told him that the water had never crossed the Keys.

I finished my invigorating conversation with the barber and

his friend. I continued my walk along the old highway. It was not long before I came to a small group of the Red Cross hurricane houses. I couldn't go inside because they were private residences. But they were just like the barber had described.

Between Upper and Lower Matecumbe Keys was a causeway. It was the original Florida East Coast Railway fill, and there were three short bridges to allow the tides to flow through at the channels. Not too far out on that causeway was another, smaller causeway that went south about a quarter of a mile to Tea Table Key. Tea Table was just one of many, many keys. However it had a road leading to it, a private island. I mused that it must be nice to have your own island!

These innumerable Keys were mostly formed by a coral outcrop stopping a mangrove seed. This cigar shaped seed drops off its parent and then floats vertical. Usually its roots are partially grown, are on the bottom, and will float until it is stopped and caught by something sticking out of the water. Over time sand and sediment will collect and this begins the process of Key building. The red mangrove* is the species
most prevalent in the Florida Keys. Its roots slow down tidal water and build its own environment. As they grow, their roots and branches provide a protective area for all kinds of water birds. The roots also provide a habitat for many kinds of marine fish and animals. Their leaves are able to process salt water into fresh by an osmotic process. Mangrove plants have many uses such as tea, medicine, wood for boats because it is water resistant, furniture, houses, charcoal, and dyes.

There was a park area on the causeway near the Tea Table Key fill. I stopped there to rest and read a historic marker. I would like to have seen those wells. (see the next page)

I crossed the three bridges over Tea Table, Indian Key and Lignumvitae channels. I then came to a new establishment at the north end of Lower Matecumbe Key. The sign said:

> New Establishment
> Toll Gate Inn.

A island on its way. A mangrove has got a foothold amongst some coral outcrop and has grown to about four feet. Its roots are dug in and it is going to drop a seed to either start growing next to the parent or float away to catch hold somewhere else and start the process all over.

> **HISTORIC MARKER (Tea Table Key)**
> - NE end of Lower Matecumbe Key, ancient water wells, only fresh water on upper keys. Used by Indians, sailors and traders, 17th century. Huge Indian midden (kitchen) near wells.
> - Indian Key, Spanish trading post. Started by Antonio Gomez, 1695.
> - Lignumvitae Key, Spanish outpost, Indian burial grounds.
> - 1549 Hernando de Escalante Fontaneda, son of Spanish-Comendero serving King Phillip II in Carthenda. En route to Spain for schooling, shipwrecked on the Keys. Held prisoner by Caloosa Indians for 17 years. His memoirs, were the first detailed description of Florida.

This was where the toll booth for the bridges to Key West on the Overseas Highway was first built. Before that the ferry used to dock here.

A man was standing out front, and as I walked up, he said,

"Hey it's getting late, if you want, you can camp here tonight. Just set up camp out back of the inn and use the showers back there and the dock and swimming area."

Came to find out he was the new owner. I thanked him, and we talked for a few minutes. He was a very interesting person and said that he was a swimming instructor as well as an innkeeper. I went around back, set up my camp, took a refreshing swim and then a shower. What a great favor for a tired hiker!

In the morning, as I was picking and packing up, here came the innkeeper and his helper with some coffee for me. Now I didn't drink coffee but I sipped it and listened to him as he warned me,

"Don't hike the bridges, it will be best to ride over them."

I told him that I would take that into consideration and be very careful. That seemed to satisfy him.

As I was crossing the drive, a large boat was being pulled

Indian Key off the south side of the causeway between Indian Key and Lignumvitae channels. Note that the beach appears to be improving from the beach I slept on the previous night near Tavernier, south end of Key Largo. A real picturesque coconut palm.

Florida East Coast Railway railroad track in the upper Keys. More than likely from the 1935 hurricane. Now a perch of convenience for a sea bird.

up to the inn…..it said Memphis, Tennessee on the transom. It looked as if they came from all over the U.S.A. to fish and dive here.

I hiked the three and one half miles through Lower Matecumbe Key. I was back on a causeway for about a mile and a half, then a short bridge over Channel No. 2.

After crossing Channel No. 2, I sat down to rest. I watched a couple of birds drying their wings as they too sat on pilings that were at the start of my first long bridge. It was a mile across Channel No. 5. from where I sat on Craig Key. I also could see that it was a very, very long distance.

An artist's rendering of a Florida East Coast passenger train crossing the Long Key Viaduct. This bridge was composed of 180 arches and was over two miles long.

22
Flagler's Monumental Bridges

As I looked out across the water and the bridge, I remembered the innkeeper's warning at the Toll Gate Inn, *"Don't walk those bridges!"* I didn't know what to do. All the short bridges had been ok, except for the occasional vehicle.

As I was sitting there contemplating hiking across this mile-long bridge, a car pulled up.

"You need a ride?" he offered.

"You know, that seems like a good Idea," I said. He had just solved my problem.

"Not too far," I said, "I just need to get to the next land."

I put my pack in the back seat and got in. It seems that this young fella had seen me a couple of times on his way to Miami. From a car point of view, I could see as we sped along just how beautiful the clear emerald blue-green water was. Between the looking, and talking I suddenly realized that we were covering too much distance. I would be in Key West before I realized it!

"You had better let me out at the next causeway or land!" I suddenly exclaimed.

It had been so very long since I was in a vehicle, that when you think about it, 50 to 60 miles an hour is a mile a minute! In just a few minutes, we had gone 9 miles.

He let me out at Conch Key, at the very end of the Long Key Viaduct. We had blasted through Long Key!

I thanked him for the ride and off he went, in a flash.

I just sat there looking back at the two-mile Long Key viaduct and said out loud, "Not going back."

I was looking back at the highway bridge built on top of the old railroad bridge and suddenly realized that this was the famous arch bridge. It was one of Flagler's favorites. Photographs and posters of a passenger train speeding across it were used on stationary, the sides of freight cars, and innumerable

Sketch showing the spandrel arch construction over Long Key viaduct and Channel No. 5 bridge. In the background are two completed piers. Next an arch ring form has been located upon two piers. These arches have been prefabricated on land and barged in. Finally in the foreground the side forms have been added to the top of the arches. All forms were designed to be reused.
Sketch made from State Archives of Florida photo. floridamemory.com

brochures. It became a trademark for the FEC.

The bridge over channel No. 5 was also an arch bridge. I had not seen the side, as I had been contemplating how to cross it. These two bridges, channel No. 5, almost one mile, the Long Key viaduct, 2.3 miles, plus the land in between, meant that I had lost 6 hiking miles through Long Key.

All-in-all, the Florida East Coast Railway bridges numbered 42 for a total of 18 miles. The Long Key bridge was made with 180 spandrel arches,* each one spanning 50 feet, and was more than 20 feet above mean high tide.

During the construction of the two bridges, Lower Matecumbe, Long, and Craig Keys were the sites for the viaduct construction. This construction started November 1906, and a year later the train crossed Channel No. 5 viaduct, and again a year later in January of 1908 a train crossed the Long Key

Viaduct. It then proceeded down to Knights Key which was to be the shipping terminal and temporary end of the line for regular service from Miami. After the construction was complete, the Long Key work camps were improved and then turned into the Long Key Fishing Camp.* Notorieties such as Zane Grey, Herbert Hoover, Franklin Roosevelt, and William Hearst visited the camp to fish the waters of the Gulf.

This Spandrel Arch bridge construction* is very intriguing, The steps are listed below:
1. The ocean floor is cleaned down to the coral limestone bottom.
2. Wood posts are driven into the coral, and then a cofferdam is lowered down to the bottom.
3. Two feet of concrete are poured in for a seal.
4. The water is pumped out of the cofferdam.
5. Prefabbed final forms are put into the cofferdam and the concrete poured and built up above the water.
6. All throughout tons of reinforcing steel and connecting rods and rebar are used to tie together each new concrete pour.
7. A prefabbed "ring arch" is barged in and set up on two piers using the tide as a lifting device.
8. Side forms and inside forms are made.
9. The concrete is poured into the arch.
10. The final arch is hollow and is filled with gravel.
11. The railroad ties and rails are laid upon the gravel.

I was on Conch Key. I went down from the road to the shore and sat under a large mangrove to draw and look around. This mangrove was more like a small tree. As I was observing my surroundings, I saw it, washing back-and-forth and rolling around in the sand with the movement of the waves, a glass milk bottle. There was something strange about this milk bottle. It had a cork in the top, and inside I could see some kind of folded paper. I picked it up and popped the cork. In it was a yellow piece of notebook paper folded three times

> **HELP**
>
> To Whom it may concern:
> We are stranded on an island of which we think is Conch Key. We cannot, by all obvious methods, determine how long we have been here and of course can not know when we may be departing. Your help is sincerely requested. If this note is possibly found please notify Mr. Roy ███ of Coral Key Village R#1 Box ███ Marathon Fla. of our distress. Should any any expense be incured or otherwise inferred please bill Joe ███ of an address unknown at this time. We respestfully request your indulgence.
>
> The Destressed

Note found in a milk bottle on the shore of Conch Key. It was an interesting experience finding the distress note that afternoon as I was exploring along the shore. Obviously, some visitors having fun.
(I never had the opportunity to stop by, so identifying names obscured)

to allow it to fit into the bottle. I had found a distress note. Some folks obviously were visiting someone in Marathon and desired to have some fun. They stated that they were stranded on Conch Key and needed help.

One never knows just what one will find around the next corner. I would like to have found the person they said to notify. I was sure that he would really have had a laugh over it.

I got back up on the road and crossed the two bridges along that causeway, Tom's Harbor Cut and Tom's Harbor No. 4. This put me on Grassy Key. I got on the old road which cut through the mangroves. It was real hot in there. I came upon a fellow working on his front lawn.

"Hey where you heading?" he hailed.

"From Georgia to Key West," I answered.

"Sounds like fun... Just one question, do you know anything about this tree?" He pointed to a beautiful multi-colored bark tree, orange and light tan.

"No, I stated, "But I'm not using any firewood."

"That helps, but don't even touch it. It's a Poisonwood tree* and it will really do a number on you The poison even comes right through your clothes. It is just like poison sumac and poison oak only much worse!"

"Wow, thanks a lot for the warning. I certainly will not even get close to it."

From Grassy Key all the way to Knight's Key and the Seven Mile Bridge there are a bunch of Keys that were separate until the Railroad filled between them. Developers have since done more of the same. These Keys are Grassy, Crawl, Long Point, and Fat Deer Keys. There is a bridge at Vaca Cut, Vaca and Knights Key. The second largest town in the Keys, Marathon, is mostly on Vaca Key. It has a small airport.

As I approached the Vaca Cut Bridge along the old road on the south (Gulf side), I saw turquoise and emerald green water with small mangrove islands (Keys) in the distance. Some of the larger ones had coconut palms and small Australian pine trees on them, and there were lots of small reef-type harbors

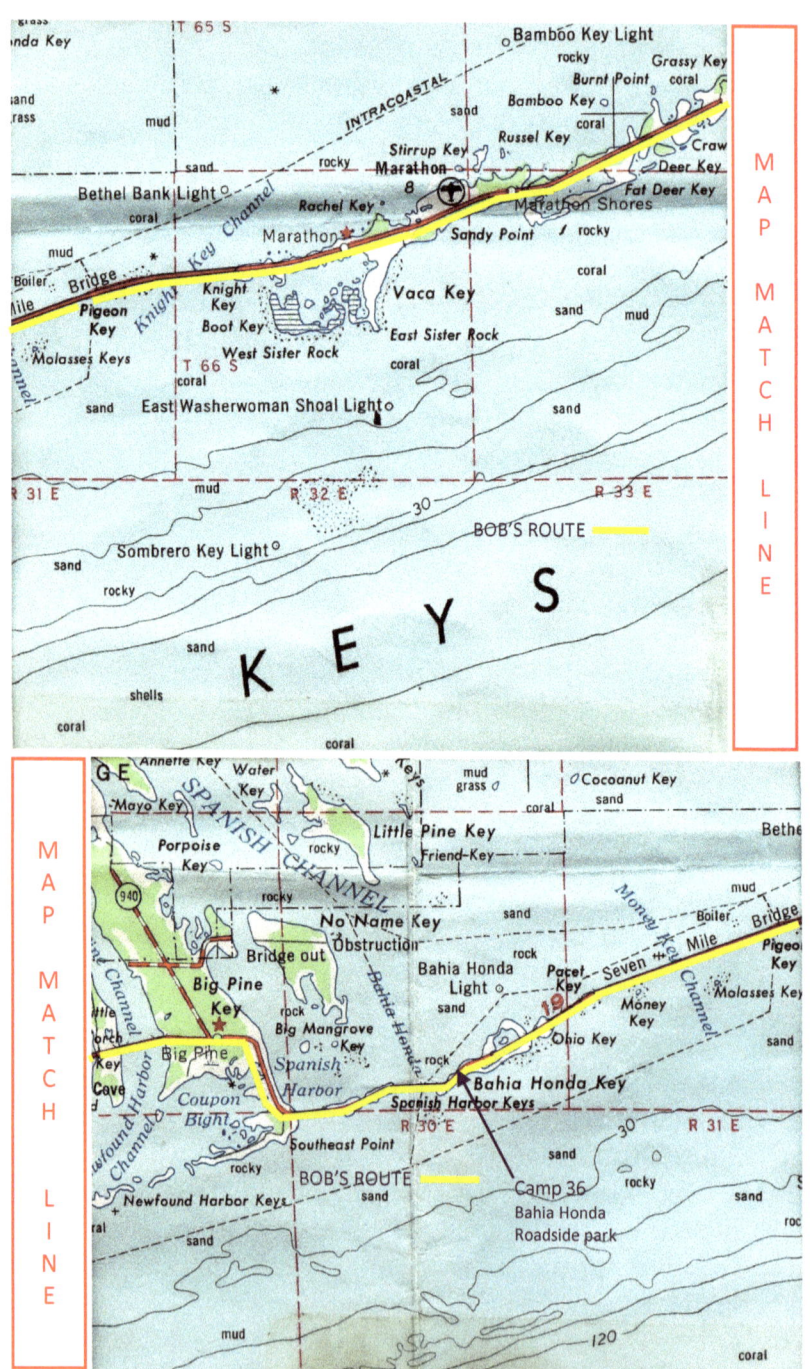

275 A Walk Across Florida

dredged. Some of the closer small Keys had raised coral roads out to them. It appeared that a lot of them were private.

I had to get on the main road to cross the bridge, and to my surprise the man from the Toll Gate Inn went by waving and beeping his horn.

I was now on Vaca Key and in Marathon City proper. This is a town that got its big start from the railroad. It was the main work camp for thousands of men working on the railroad. Many of these men were from the Cayman Islands and others from Philadelphia and New York. It was also one of the stations named by the railroad workers. There was so much pressure to get the job accomplished that they were working night and day around the clock. They started to say, "This is getting to be a real Marathon!"* So the name stuck, and that is what the railroad station was named.

I was walking by a gas station right across from the small airport which was on the north side of Highway No. 1. Three boys in a Camaro called me over. We started talking about hiking. A man who must have just finished getting gas came over and joined the conversation. When he found out that I was also interested in the history of the area he told me that the supposedly small airport across the road originally was a World War II airport.* It's actually 5000 feet long and was built by the Army Air Corps in 1942. It was used for training pilots to fly heavy bombers such as the B-17s and an emergency landing strip. I thanked him for that treasure of information.

Marathon was a fairly busy little town. It was built up then, and I'm sure that today it's full. Street after street of the main road leading to the water had houses lining them. Many of them had docks, piers and boats. As I continued on, I picked up a four-bicycle escort through town. These little boys were really determined. In fact they escorted me all the way to Knights Key, almost to the 7-mile bridge. As they turned to leave, one little boy gave me the *peace sign*. I guessed it was the thing to do in those times.

As I sat my pack down near the road to look around, a VW

Knights Key at the seven mile bridge abutment looking towards Pigeon Key. Three important items can be seen in this photo: the vertical concrete foundation piers, the large steel-girder spans and the one foot in diameter pipe that the U.S. Navy installed in 1941 to bring water to Key West.

van came by with a bunch of *real hippies* in it, hollering,

"Hey need a ride?" I waved them on.

I looked around the bridge abutment. It had the original railroad foundations and railroad track being used for a railing. I was inspecting all this on both sides of the highway, when a man and his boy from Michigan walked up. As usual, I ended up giving them my regular talk on backpacking. Then both of them wanted to try on my pack. I guess I could have paid for my trip if I had been working for one of the backpacking equipment manufacturers!

After they left, I sat there thinking, "In length, this bridge was the big one. Here I am sitting on Knights Key.* In 1908 it was the end of the line, with a dock built far out in the water for ocean steamships to load passengers and freight heading to Key West, Cuba and even the Panama Canal. It took two years to build these facilities and was finished and available for regular service in February of 1908. This dock had a post office, hotel and custom's office. It could handle two complete trains at one time and the Flagler steamships. These facilities were used until the rest of the bridges and line were completed to Key West in January of 1912.

The seven mile bridge* construction was divided into 4 parts. These were Knights Key, Pigeon Key, Moser Channel and Pacet Channel bridges. Knights, Pigeon, and Moser were steel-girder spans on top of vertical concrete foundation piers. Some of the foundations were 28 feet below the waterline. These spans were formally called deck plates and were mostly 80 feet long. In the center of the Moser Channel section was a 253-foot swinging steel truss bridge for Atlantic to the Gulf ship traffic. The Pacet Channel bridge was a series of 210 spandrel arches similar to the Long Key viaduct I had just crossed. The seven-mile bridge took two years to build.

One of the main work camps was Pigeon Key which was about one mile out from Knights Key. Its facilities took care of 400 workers during the bridge construction between 1908 and 1912. Today many of the original work camp buildings are preserved, open to public and administered by the Pigeon Key Foundation and Marine Science Center.* One can go out to them by walking or biking on the old bridge or by boat.

As I sat there looking out, I could see the vertical concrete bridge piers heading out to Pigeon Key. The steel girder spans were on top of these piers, and the water pipe was attached to the side of the girders. It was installed by the U. S. Navy in 1941. The only water in the Keys was from rain. That rain was collected from the metal roofs of houses and buildings and channeled to storage areas. These storage areas were called cisterns and were usually made of reinforced concrete or metal. Even the early Indians stored water in open wells. During and after the railroad was being built, water was hauled to the Keys in tank cars. When the Navy installed the pipeline the Florida Keys Aqueduct Commission paid one-third of the expenses.

Enough of this sitting, I decided. I might as well get on

A house with a system to collect rain water from a metal roof. The tank which is called a cistern is high enough to bring water by gravity flow into the house.

with it, another hitch-hike. After all, if it was too dangerous to walk the one and two mile Long Key bridges, seven miles was out of the question!

I stuck my thumb out and the next vehicle stopped. It was a couple of boys in a VW car, and this time I made sure I said,

"Thanks guys, I only need a ride across this seven-mile bridge."

As we were crossing, three girls in a red sports car convertible came up alongside. That meant they were passing us on this narrow two-lane bridge. The guys and girls started talking and they said something about pulling off on the other side of the bridge. That was good for my request, and before I knew it we were on the other side. They pulled up right behind the girls' convert', got out, and sprinted right over. I pulled my pack out of the back, hollered thanks to a couple of guys who were obviously distracted, and went on my way.

The southern end of the seven-mile bridge and about three miles, three Keys, and three short bridges later.....Missouri, Ohio and Bahia Honda... and I had arrived at the Bahia Honda Park. I was thinking about a nice swim, shower, meal, and camp. It wasn't to be, the park ranger told me. They were closed. Not to be discouraged, I crossed the road. On the other side were roadside picnic tables, with concrete roofs and an entire beautiful sand and windswept beach....all to myself! Not only that, I had the fantastic and awesome view of the Bahia Honda railroad bridge heading across to the Spanish Harbor Key with U. S. Highway No. 1 hanging precariously on top.

This is the life! I placed my pack down next to one of the picnic tables.

That night I put my plastic tarp down right on the sand of the beach and slept on top of my sleeping bag. There was a delightful wind all night and no mosquitoes.

In the morning I walked along the newly washed beach. There were shells of all colors, a Portuguese-man-of-war lying in the damp sand, and a mystery: *Footprints in the sand*. I never did see or hear anyone. I went for a great swim and as luck would have it, I found a shower stand at one end of the parking area. A little breakfast and I was off back to the road- side in front of the huge bridge. As I waiting for a car to take me over my last hitch-hike, I pondered my previous days total mileage, 22 miles hiking, plus 16 additional miles that were hitchhiking.

This Bahia Honda Bridge* over Bahia Honda Channel is the really big one, as far as height is concerned. The water here is the deepest, 24 to 35 feet. The piers were built the same way

The Bahia Honda bridge heading out across the Bahia Honda Channel towards Scout Key in the distance. This is right where I slept that glorious night on the beach in the sand at the Bahia Honda rest stop. Some of the picnic table shelters can be seen at the extreme left.

This is on Little Duck Key (first Key south of the seven mile bridge). The beaches were definitely improving since I slept on the coral at Long Key. It must have been from the deeper water. You can see my pack upper right.

and looked similar to the seven-mile bridge piers, but they were larger and taller. By using Pratt and Parker Camelback trusses the engineers were able to reduce the number of concrete pilings from 64 to 34. This bridge was one of the last items to be completed in 1912, just in time for Flagler to ride his railroad from Miami to Key West. After the 1935 hurricane, the highway was completed in 1938. In the case of the Bahia Honda Bridge, it was too much trouble to widen the actual trusses so they built the highway on top of them. As a tribute to Flagler's engineering team and workers, not one of the F.E.C. Railway bridges was ever damaged by hurricanes.

Back in the 1900's this railroad was a tremendous engineering feat built by steam engines, intensive man-labor and unsophisticated tools by today's standards. In fact it was even called the 8th wonder of the world. Today the bridges and road have been replaced by projects that dwarf the original railroad and later highway.

A Department of Environment Protections Office of Greenways and Trails is working together with the Florida Department of Transportation and Monroe County to build a 106 mile Hiker-Biker trail from Key Largo to Key West. They are hoping to use the old bridges and roads where possible. People will be able to travel the route that I did with ease; however, there will be a much greater population surrounding them.

I put my thumb out and immediately a car slowed down and stopped. It was an elderly man and his wife in a station wagon. They were going to Key West to spend a couple of days. I told them what I was doing in the brief time I had, only one mile. We went out on that narrow bridge built on the top of the railroad bridge trusses. I figured that we were approximately 40 feet above the water, and then we went up again another 10 feet at the longest truss which was in the middle of the crossing. It may not seem a lot at today's standards but on that narrow road it was impressive. They dropped me off as soon as we got across. I thanked them and they continued on.

Full grown Key Deer recovering from injuries possibly from automobiles kept in a pen at the Key Deer Wildlife Refuge in Big Pine Key. The does weighed 45 to 65 pounds, the bucks weighed 55 to 75 pounds and they stood less than 3 feet high.

23
Key West On My Horizon

I now found myself on Scout Key. There seems to be some disagreement or confusion on this and the next two Keys' names. Wikipedia has a very helpful Key bridge and mile marker listing that calls this Key, Scout Key, formerly known as West Summerland Key. Google maps says Spanish Harbor Key and West Summerland Key. Nevertheless I was on the Key West side of Bahia Honda Bridge, and the next three keys were all filled in by the railroad and were one piece of land!

The bridge over Spanish Harbor channel was one-half mile long and composed of 77 spandrel arches. I took a deep breath and went on across. Every time a car came I would jump up on the curb and hold on for dear life. I walked about six miles to the center of this Big Pine Key. There was a small store at the intersection of U.S. No. 1 and State Road 940. During my discussion with the store owner it seemed that he had hiked a lot in the Smoky Mountains of North Carolina.

I asked him about the history of Big Pine Key and why it seemed to not be as built up as some of the other keys. He said that there had been little development for so many years because there was no public electricity and water, even though Big Pine Key is the second largest key in the total Florida Keys. Also the schools were non-existent until the late 1920's.

He said that the railroad did have a large camp of about 400 men on the Key in 1906-07, but it moved on as soon as the construction was completed. There were a few homesteaders who tried in some ways to make a living such as charcoal, glass blowing, and shark oil processing, but they didn't last long. I told him that I was very interested in the Key Deer preserve. Just then a local man in the store who I'm sure was listening in on our conversation said that he would drive me the three miles back to the Key Deer Refuge.

It would be a side trip north from my route, so I didn't mind the helpful ride. This fellow said his name was Jeff and that he had lived on Big Pine Key all of his life. In fact he used to farm pineapples mostly for his own, friends' and neighbors' use. When he had a good crop he would sell some to local stores. He told me that there was also a fresh water lake on Big Pine Key. That is because the Key is made of something called oolitic limestone* and fresh water can be found in that kind of formation.

This fresh water lake was called Blue Hole.* It is thought by some that it was dug at first for fill for the first road or by the railroad construction workers. Today it is located in the National Key Deer Refuge. It is filled with both fresh and salt water. The salt water filters in from the ocean through the limestone of the Key, but it is denser and settles on the bottom. This allows a treasure trove of fishes, animals and birds to live in and around the quarry. Because of hurricane storm surges many salt water fish have been dumped into this preserve. I didn't get a chance to hike this side trip, but today there is a hiking trail and observation platform.

Jeff dropped me off at the refuge. I thanked him and went on into the small ranger office there. I talked to the ranger on duty and asked him about the Key deer and the refuge. He showed me where there was a pen out back which had three Key deer recuperating from auto injuries. He said that these were not hurt badly and were going to be released into the refuge some time soon. I took a photo and watched the little deer for some time.

It is thought that the Key deer* are related to the Virginia white-tail deer. They are unique because the Keys is their only habitat. Scientists also speculate that the deer migrated to the Keys across a land bridge from the mainland between 6,000 and 12,000 years ago. This migration would have taken place before the Wisconsin Glacier melted. These deer are less than 3 feet high, and shoulder height is 24 to 28 inches. Does weigh 45 to 65 pounds and bucks 55 to 75 pounds.

Because of hunting throughout the years and the danger from cars, the population of the Key deer in the 1940's was less than 50 deer.

To save the Key Deer the National Key Deer Refuge was established in 1957. Speed limits were reduced on Big Pine Key. Today there are more than 300 deer, and they mainly live on both Big Pine and a Key next to it, No Name Key.

On my way back along State Route 940 I saw some Key Deer in the wild grazing along the highway. Not only that, it seemed that both the pine trees and the palms were both very small compared to the trees I had hiked through on the mainland. That together with the very small Key Deer made me feel that I was hiking through the land of Lilliputians.

I finished the three miles back to U.S. Highway No. 1 and headed west towards Key West. In a little more than a mile I crossed the bridge over North Pine Channel and then a half mile later the bridge over South Pine Channel. These bridges were only about one-tenth and one-fifth of a mile long respectively. I was now on Little Torch Key which was only about one-half mile long. Then I crossed two bridges to get to Ramrod Key, and they were one-tenth of a mile each. Ramrod Key was only about a mile long but to get to Summerland Key I had to walk a bridge over Niles Channel, almost a mile long. Actually eight-tenths of a mile!

I said to myself, let's get it over!

I did as before, took a deep breath, picked up the pace and every time a car came, stepped up on the curb and waited until the car had gone.

I was now on Summerland Key and I was about to be really surprised. I was nearing a gas station with a fairly large gravel drive. A big Greyhound bus pulled off from behind me and pulled into the drive parallel to the highway.

As I came along side, the door opened.

"Hey, where you going? What are you doing?" the bus driver asked.

"I'm hiking to Key West," I said as I went over to him and

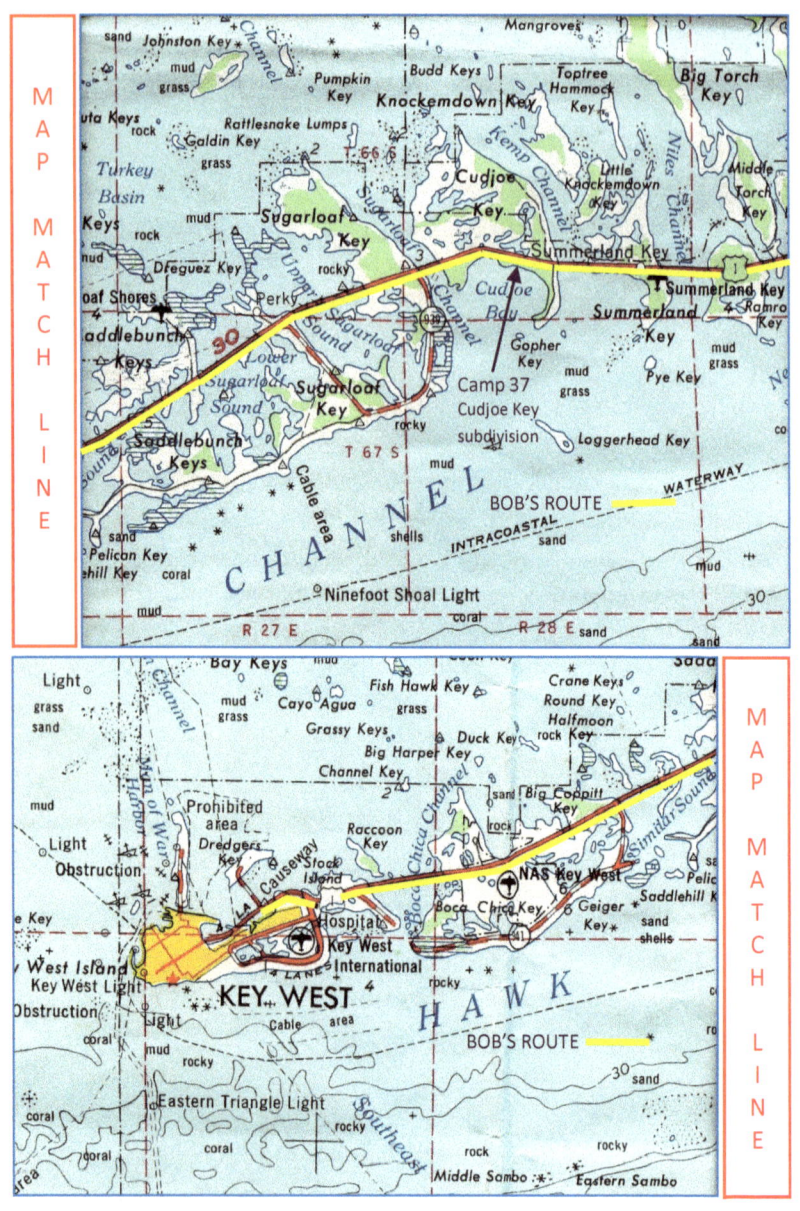

looked up into the bus.

"I've been seeing you at least two times every day, when I come down from Miami in the afternoon on my way to Key West, and then when I go back in the morning. Get on and I'll give you a ride to Key West, no charge!"

By this time the bus passengers and even people at the gas station were looking, in fact staring.

"Sir, I'm really grateful for the offer. In fact I don't know what to say. It's just that I'm hiking from Georgia to Key West, and I have to keep on walking it."

"Wow that is really something else!" he exclaimed, "I'll be a wild man! Well, good luck and take care."

He closed the door, fired up the bus and pulled out, hesitated slightly, crossed the highway and shot off in a blast of black diesel smoke and a roar!

I was really taken back, What a nice offer!

I noticed a lonely phone booth standing like a sentinel along the road by a telephone pole. It gave me the idea to phone my Uncle Norman and Aunt Dolores. I had talked to them before I left and by now they were probably wondering if I was still heading their way.

"Hello, Aunt Dolores, It's me, Bob."

"Yes Bobby, is that you?"

" It sure is."

"We knew you were in the Keys. Yesterday one of the men Uncle Norman works with had been out for a drive and saw a guy with a red pack walking along the road. By his description, we knew it was you!"

"Well I should be along tomorrow afternoon if everything goes ok. So take care and tell Uncle Norman I said hello."

I hung up and got back into my pack straps. This was the first realization that my adventure was fast drawing to a close.

Summerland Key couldn't have been any more than a mile or two long…..because from where I was now walking I could see the next bridge I would cross. The blue-green waters of Kemp Channel captured my interest as I crossed to Cudjoe

Three Brown Pelicans* glide across the ocean looking like long extinct Pterodactyls. Strangely fossil records* show that the relatives of the pelican may have existed for some 30 million years. In fact the fossil beak is almost identical to pelicans of the present. The Brown Pelican weighs between 6 to 12 pounds. Its wingspan is 6 to 8 feet. Because of its long beak, 28 to 34 inches, it is between 40 to 54 inches long. A nice size bird, it needs 4 pounds of fish a day to survive. They sometimes will fly at heights of 60 to 70 feet and can still spot a small fish. They usually fly in single file low over the water and when they spot a fish will dive into the water to catch it in their beaks.

Key. It would be dark in a couple of hours; I was being followed by the long shadow the sun was casting.

The billboard proclaimed:

CUDJOE KEY LOTS

The mangroves had been bulldozed, fill pumped in and some nice asphalt drives run about. Only a couple of houses at the far side were visible. I crossed the side road and ducked under the billboard. I chose a nice lot on the water near the beach. It felt good to drop my pack, sit down and just rest there. This, the tropic part of the Atlantic Ocean was so dramatic.

In quiet reflection I watched three pelicans fly in single file along the water's surface in search of their evening meal. They resembled the long extinct Pterodactyls. It took pangs of hunger to break the spell. I needed to find some fresh water. I got out my familiar aluminum cooking pot and glanced around. The houses were far off and there weren't any businesses along the highway where I came into this subdivision.

I decided to try the sand road dropping off the highway on the other side of U. S. No 1 that was cut into the jungle-like mangroves and brush. I crossed over and followed it, only a wide trail cut into the dense thicket. It turned off to the right. As soon as I got around the curve, I could see that there was a fishing shack that looked inhabited. I could see the channel's blue water over which I had minutes ago crossed peaking through the vegetation. I approached the shack cautiously. A resounding knock brought no one to the door. No one was in sight.

I spoke loudly, "Hello, anybody home?"

On the side of the house was a water spigot from which I filled my pot to the brim. I left the way I'd come, feeling like a successful thief. Soon I had my supper boiling, for the sun was setting across the island in all its majesty, red-orange reflecting on the clouds above and waves below.

Without a single bush or tree for shelter, I spread my ground cloth out here near the shore. Since the night promised no rain I felt safe from the elements. I washed my pot and spoon in the salt water all the while enjoying the sea breeze.

It was slightly cool. I climbed into my sleeping bag. Then the mosquitoes reminded me to put on the head net. The stars were peeking out all over the sky as I lay back and looked up. I thought back to all the experiences I had the last five weeks and couldn't help giving thanks for being on such a great earth………..

Light was visible in the East as I opened my eyes. I was rested and raring to go. I had slept straight through and was getting used to sleeping outdoors, in hammock or on the ground. Thank goodness for the gift of sleep. I had 23 miles to go and I felt like I could make them today without any trouble. By now my pack didn't bother me a bit. In fact, I could say it had been part of my body for the last 3 to 4 weeks. The first week had been a little tough!

I was back on the road, and before I knew it I was crossing the Sugarloaf Channel to Sugarloaf Key. At this point the still used old road followed the major part of the islands and then turned off to the left. However, I would have to stay on the new part which was mostly causeway and about nine bridges. Each of them were about one-tenth of a mile long for the next ten miles until I got to Big Coppitt and Boca Chica Keys. This road was heading straight for Key West.

In a couple of miles a man and his wife, who must have felt sorry for me walking all by myself on this causeway, pulled up along side and offered me a ride. I naturally had to decline the ride with thanks. They then said that when I got to Key West to come by and visit.

After they left I was in an area on the causeways with mangroves growing up high on each side, no breeze, and here came a ferocious daytime attack of saltwater mosquitoes. I swatted them and walked faster. The bridges up ahead which would have ocean breezes were a welcome sight.

I came alongside a parked car with Illinois license plates and no one in sight. This seemed to me a bit unusual for there weren't houses, businesses or habitation of any sort nearby. This part of the key was deserted and it didn't appear to be a good fishing spot.

Four miles later, and guess what, two boys come walking towards me. They wanted to know if I had seen their car with the Illinois license plates, and just how far it was to it. They were carrying a gas can and said that it had been a long way to a gas station from their car. I told them that they had about 4 miles to go, and good luck.

My next conversation was with an electric pole construction crew. The causeway was so narrow that a person couldn't help but bump into them. They had lots of questions and were all ears to hear my story of starting from Georgia.

Big Coppitt Key, and about a mile further, I crossed a two-fifths of a mile bridge over Rockland Channel and I was on Boca Chica Key. I could already see the Navy planes taking off and landing from the big naval air station.* I could also see three blimps in the background. The Hawkeye aircraft* carrier radar planes with large disks on the top were coming and going. To a novice like me, it appeared that they were practicing takeoffs and landings. These aircraft provided all-weather airborne early warning. They also had many advanced capabilities that supported aircraft carrier groups .

This particular naval base was started in 1940 when Monroe County gave the U. S. Army Air Corps a county airport on Boca Chica Key for fixed-wing aircraft. It was later transferred to the U. S. Navy and became part of Naval Air Station (NAS) Key West. Today it is a training facility with the latest and best equipment and facilities. It is used for training by air-to-air combat fighter aircraft of all the military services. The weather here is almost perfect for flying year round. Since it is in the Atlantic and Gulf, aircrews can begin training as soon as they get airborne.

I came to a "Share The Ride" location where some Navy guys were waiting for a ride into Key West. I stopped and joked with them, that they could share the ride with me, but it was a long walk. I kidded them about going AWOL (absent without leave). When they learned that I had been in the United States Army just a year and one half ago, we got along real fine. They all said that they would rather "Fly Navy" than walk. I wished the guys good luck.

I was way ahead of schedule, and the weather was perfect. I crossed the bridge over Boca Chica Channel and now was on Stock Island. This was the Key next to Key West where historically livestock were raised for the market on Key West. The highway here was busy. The last bridge over Cow Key Channel was a real milestone for me. I had counted a total of 40 bridges that I had crossed, including the 4 bridges I had to ride because they were too dangerous to walk. I was now on Key West. This last bridge connecting Stock Island and Key West was a divided highway with a sidewalk.

That is when I came upon a Navy man and his girlfriend taking a picture at the Key West city sign. I told them that I would take their picture with their camera if they would take mine. It was a deal!

Now there was lots of traffic. People waved out of their cars to me. The tourist rubber tire Conch Tour Train went by, and all of the tourists riding on it waved and hollered. I noticed a couple of motorcycle policemen watching me. A boy on a bicycle came up as U. S. Highway 1 ended and I turned onto North Roosevelt Boulevard. He talked to me about my trip as we walked along. He stayed with me until I crossed over North Roosevelt to First Street to look for my relative'-s house which was on Fogarty.

A man walking on the sidewalk coming towards me said, "From Homestead?"

I say, "Even longer…from Georgia." He looked stupefied.

I walked past a shopping center, crossed up two blocks, and went past some Cuban-American boys playing baseball.

"Aqui!" they shouted to one another.

I turned left onto Fogarty Street and continued on. I was now in my Uncle Normand and Aunt Dolores' neighborhood.

That is when I heard someone calling from behind, "Uncle Bob, Uncle Bob." I looked around and to my surprise, my uncle and aunt's daughter's children were running up to me.

Sandy and Robin said, "We just got off from our piano lessons, and we saw you walk by. We were looking for you because one of our girlfriends said that she had seen a beatnik walking down the road carrying a big red pack!"

" A beatnik!" I said.

They started laughing and so did I. We later looked up the definition of beatnik.

"A person who rejects or avoids conventional behavior or dress."

I guessed at that moment I was a bit unconventional, but more exhilarated than beat! I had just completed my walk across Florida...700+ miles in 5 1/2 weeks!

At Last!
700+ miles, 5 1/2 weeks and 15 pounds lighter.

Editors Notes of Definitions and References

P 8   Fletcher, Colin.
The Thousand Mile Summer.
Berkeley, Calif.:
Howell-North, 1964.

P 20   Levings Forest Products Inc
386-752-2908
Al "Gator" Levings Jr.
Lake City, Florida 32056

P 22   Bow Chainsaws
aborististsite.com/chainsaw
Story by Tom Hawkins
& Sons

P 25   "Sustained yield management" foresthistory.org
Lands In National Forests
Florida National Forests
(page 7)

P 25   Rayonier Inc.
wikipedia.org
answers.com
jaxdailyrecord.com

P 28   10 wheeler
A straight flat-bed truck
(no tractor-trailer) with 8
tandem wheels n the rear
and two in the front.

P 30   Heinrich, Bernd.
A year in the Maine Woods.
Reading, Massachusetts:
Perseus, 1994. (page 95,99)

P 35   Osceola National Forest
Florida National Forests
foresthistory.org

P 35   *naval stores*
Lands In National Forests
Florida National Forests
(page 3, 4, 5)
foresthistory.org

P 38   Florida Panther
bigcatrescue.org

P 39   Animal prints
(Panther and Black Bear)
Virginia's Wildlife
Richmond, Virginia
Virginia Commission of
Game and Inland Fisheries
1984

P 42   Florida black bear
wikipedia.org
kidsplanet.org

P 48   Olustee Battlefield Historic
State Park
Unit Management Plan
exploresouthernhistory.com
floridastateparks.org
wikipedia.org

P 60   collect pine resin
Lands In National Forests
Florida National Forests
(page 4-6)
foresthistory.org

P 62   Trail Ridge Deposit
Rogers, Michelle.
*Stark Mines. (*paper)
valdosta.edu
kingsleylake.org

P 66   Camp Blanding
Frisbee, Sayer, Col.Ret'd
*Camp Blanding Florida
"In War and Peace"* 1979
30thinfantry.org
kingsleylake.org

P 66   Natural Resources
Camp Blanding
Wildlife Management Plan
kingsleylake.org
30thinfantry.org

P 68	Mike Roess Gold Head Branch State Park floridastateparks.org ccpl.lib.fl.us/historical/keystone floridaramblings.com	P 98	Sabal Palmetto wikipedia.org
		P100	Hessian soldier Kelley, C. Brian. *Best Little Stories from the American Revolution.* Nashvile, Tennessee: Cumberland House, 1999. (page 141)
P 70	Martin John Roess *The National Cyclopaedia of American Biography* Volume 41, page 320, 321		
P 72	American Alligator npca.org	P 100	Saw Palmetto homeguides.sfgate.com voices.yahoo.com/
P 78	Cross Florida Barge Canal wikipedia.org fladefenders .org sptimes.com floridatrend.com	P108	surplus of lakes Florida Fish and Wildlife myfwc.com (Natural Lakes) paper, (page 265, 266
		P 112	Orlando frommers.com city-data.com travel.aol.com
P 80	crusher-crawler floridamemory.com practicalmachinist.com Ring Power CAT, photo		
		P122	introduction of cattle freshfromflorida.com edis.ifas.ufl.edu floridamemory.com manatee.ifas.ufl.edu
P 85	Oklawaha River wikipedia.org outpostresort.com		
P 85	steam boat transportation wikipedia.org	P125	Florida Cracker cattle freshfromflorida.com manatee.ifas.ufl.edu livestockconservancy.org
P 86	Ocala National Forest forest history.org wikipedia.org		
		P 125	*Crooked Trails* Remington, Frederic. Facsimile of the 1898-Edition. New York: Bonanza Books. (page 116-126)
P 92	Pinecastle Bombing Range wikipedia.org		
P 92	Vought A-7 Corsair Combataircraft.com wikipedia.org		
		P 125	*Frederick Remington* Hodge, Jessica. New York: Barnes & Noble Books Saturn Books Ltd. 1997.
P 94	Florida Trail, Association floridatrail.org fs.usda.gov wikipedia.org		

P125   Brahman cattle
          freshfromflorida.com
          edis.ifas.ufl.edu
          floridamemory.com
          manatee.ifas.ufl.edu

P 126   Florida Turnpike
          wikipedia.org

P 128   Bald Eagle
          foridabirding trail.com
          earthtimes.org
          wildflorida.com
          orlandosentinel.com
          floridanature.com
          myfwc.com
          wikipedia.org

P 130   Kissimmee Cooperative
          Bald Eagle Sanctuary
          audubon.org

P 130   Everglades Headwaters
          National Wildlife Refuge
          and Conservation Area
          audubon.org
          nature.org

P 136   Spanish Moss
          ufl.edu
          beaufortcountylibrary.org
          southernliving.com
          homeguides.sfgate.com
          wikipedia.org

P 138   Gopher Tortoise
          fws,gov
          myfwc.com
          wikilpedia.org

P 149   Florida wading birds
          National Geographic Society.
          Field Guide to the Birds of North America.
          Washington, DC:
          Nat. Geo. Soc., 2001.

P 150   Florida East Coast Railway
          Bramson, Seth H.
          Florida East Coast Railway
          Charleston, SC:
          Arcadia, 2006.
          wickipedia.org
          floridahistory.org
          oocities.org
          okeechobeerea.com
          tommymarkham.com

P 153   Okeechobee city
          Gregware, Bill & Carol.
          Guide to the Lake Okeechobee Area.
          Sarasota, Florida
          Pineapple Press, 1997.

P 155   Kissimmee River
          Gregware, Bill & Carol.
          Guide to the Lake Okeechobee Area.

P 155   Hoover Dike
          Gregware, Bill & Carol.
          Guide to the Lake Okeechobee Area.
          saj.usace.army.mil(H H Dike)
          pcbgov.com(scenic trails)

P 162   Hammock
          edis.ifas.ufl.edu

P 164   Seminole Indians
          flheritage.com
          seminolewars.us/history.html
          semtribe.com
          lamartin.com
          wikipedia.org
          medbib.com

P 165 runaway slaves
       Stoneman, Marjory
       Douglas.
       The Everglades:
       River of Grass
       Sarasota, Florida:
       Pineapple Press,1997.
       (Page 192, 193)

P 166 forts,
       Kimball, Chris.
       Fort List.
       southernhistory.usfortlist.htm

P 166 bounty system
       History of Okeechobee
       County, chapter 1
       lamartin.com

P 167 journal,
       Hitchcock, Major
       Ethan Allen
       Fifty Years In Camp &
       Field, Diary of Major-
       General Ethan Allen
       Hitchcock
       Ed. W. A. Croffut PHD.
       G Putman Sons, 1909.
       okstate.edu
       wikipedia.org

P 168 Brown, Dee.
       Bury My Heart At
       Wounded Knee.
       New York:
       Henry Holt,1991.
       1st Owl Book Edition

P 168 *Last Of The Dogmen*
       1995 VCR,
       HBO ,Savoy Pictures

P 168 Brighton Reservation
       Covington, James W.
       Brighton Reservation,
       Florida 1935-1938

P 172 Melaleuca trees
       usgs.gov
       duke.edu
       National Park Service-
       Melaleuca

P 174 Fort Center, mounds
       and archaeological digs
       wikipedia.org
       myfwc.com
       lost worlds.org

P 176 hiking and nature trail,
       (Fort Center)
       floridahikes.com

P 176 Caloosahatchee River
       wikipedia.org
       sugarrealty.com
       timohr.com
       earthjustice.org

P 178 Disston
       Stoneman, Marjory
       Douglas.
       The Everglades:
       River of Grass
       Sarasota, Florida:
       Pineapple Press,1997.
       (Page 282-283)

P 178 Moore Haven
       Gregware, Bill and Carol.
       Guide to the Lake
       Okeechobee Area.
       Sarasota, Florida:
       Pineapple Press, 1997.

P 182   scorpion species in-
        Florida
        floridiainnature.com

P 184   Gold Coast Railroad
        Museum
        (Florida East Coast's
        steam locomotives no's
        113 & 153)
        gcrm.org

P 184   U. S. Sugar's South
        Central Florida
        Express Railroad
        rr-roadtrip.com
        ussugar,com
        *Modeling Sugar
        Production on Your
        Model Railroad*
        Scale Models, Arts &
        Technologies, Inc.
        smarttinc.com

P 184   sugar cane
        edis.ifs.ufl.edu
        assct.org

P 184   U.S. Sugar Corp.
        (Company History)
        wikipedia.org
        ussugar.com.

P 195   Florida Black Bass
        justsportfishing.com

P 195   Devils Garden
        State of Florida-
        (study & update)

P 196   Big Cypress Seminole
        Indian Reservation
        wikipedia.org
        floridaseminoletour-
        ism.com

P 200   *The Everglades,
        River of Grass*
        Douglas,Marjory
        Stoneman.
        Sarasota, Florida:
        Pineapple Press,1997.
        50th Anniversary Edition

P 201   *Marjory Stoneman
        Douglas, Voice of the
        Everglades.*
        Bryant, Jennifer.
        Frederick, MD.:
        Twenty-First Century
        Books, 1992.

P 204   nine-banded Armadillo
        myfwc.com
        ugaurbang.com
        wikipedia.org

P 204   Miami Limestone
        Douglas, Marjory
        Stonman.
        *The Everglades
        River of Grass.*
        Page 27

P 206   Everglades Parkway-
        (Alligator Alley)
        gator.naples.net
        princeton.edu

P 208   Big Cypress National-
        Preserve
        wikipedia.org
        nps.gov

P 214   Tamiami Trail
        wikepedia.org
        naplesnewscom
        floridamemory.com
        sun-sentinel.com

P 214   "Trailblazers"
floridamemory.com
naplesnews.com

P 214   town of Everglades
colliermuseums.com

216   Bay City Walking-
Dredge
asme.org
mybaycity.com
sun-sentinel.com
groundspeak.com

P 218   Cottonmouth Moccasin
ufl.edu

P 218   Cottonmouth bites-
(snake venom)
cottonmouthsnake.org

P 220   Coot
allaboutbirds.org
floridasnature.com
wikipedia.org

P 220   Monroe Station
National Park Service-
Historic American-
Building Survey
bigcypressswamp.com
jacksbromeliads.com
keysnews.com
nps.gov

P 222   Everglades Society for
Historic Preservation
evergladeshistorial.org
eshp@hotmail.com

P 222   Miccosukee Indians
floridamemory.com
(Tamiami Trail)

P 228   Jet Port, Miami-Dade
Port-Authority
paving paradise.org
sptmes.com

P 228   Screech Owls
floridanature.com
wikipedia.org

P 229   calls, Screech Owl
*Field Guide to the
Birds of North America*
Washington, DC.:
National Geographic,
2001.

P 234   HM-69, Nike Missile
wikepedia,org
nps.gov

P 236   Homestead-
vegetable farms
gardenguides.com
voices.yahoo.com
artofeating.com
villageprofile.com

P 236   Bulldozers with specially
designed blades
artofeating.com

P 236   a perfect growing -
environment
gardenguides.com

P 236   Royal Palm
florida-palm-trees.com
wikipedia.org

P 237   Florida Pioneer Museum
wikepedia.org
cityprofile.com

P 238 open to homesteading
homestead.fly
wikepedia.org

P 238 "Gentlemen the railroad
will go to sea"
(Henry Flagler)
Bramson, Seth H.
*Florida East
Coast Railway*
Charleston, SC.:
Arcadia Publishing, 2001.

P 242 Flagler's two dredges
keyshistory.org
Bramson, Seth H.
*Florida East
Coast Railway*
Charleston, SC.:
Arcadia Publishing, 2001.

P 242 Why build a railroad-
To Key West
Overseasrairoad.-
railfan.net
Standiford, Les.
Last Train to Paradise.
New York:
Broadway Books, 2002.

P 248 Keys
wikepedia.org

P 248 cayo
floridakeysnews.info

P 248 plants and animals
floridakeysnews.info
wikepedia.org

P 248 John Pennekamp Coral-
Reef State Park
flkeysgc.com/Info-
historyKeyLargo

P 250 Marvin Adams-
Waterway (the Cut)
keyshistory.org

P 258 *Harpers Monthly-
Magazine*
(Plantation Key)
keyshistory.org

P 258 David Monroe
ufdc.jfl.edu

P 258 DCT Vocational Teacher
markndivdadeschools.net

P 260 FEC Railway bridges
wikiepeia.org

P 262 Florida Keys Memorial
(Hurricane Monument)
keyhistory.org

P 262 1935 hurricane
Standiford, Les.
Last Train to Paradise.
New York:
Broadway Books, 2002.
Chapt. 1
keyhistory.org

P 262 Old timer hurricane signs
Williams, Joy.
The Florida Keys.
New York:
Random House, 2003.P 38

P 264 Red Mangrove
n-the-florida-keys.com
wikipedia.org

P 271 spandrel arches
webworldwonders.firm.edu
florida memory.com

P 272   Long Key Fishing Camp
        keyhistory.org
        keysrambler.blogspot.com

P 272   Spandrel Arch bridge-
        construction
        webworldwonders.firn.edu

P 274   Poisonwood Tree
        shoestringweekends.-
        wordpress.com

P 276   A real Marathon
        wikipedia.org

P 276   World War II Airport,
        (Marathon)
        keyshistory.org

P 277   Knights Key (dock)
        mysite.verizon.net
        flaglerkeys100.com

P 278   seven mile bridge
        mysite.verizon.net
        friends of old seven.org
        n-the-florida-keys.com
        Standiford, Les.
        Last Train to Paradise.
        New York:
        Broadway Books, 2002.

P 278   Pigeon Key Foundation
        pigeonkey.net

P 280   Bahia Honda Bridge
        wikipledia.org
        keysnet.com
        n-the-florida-keys.com

P 285   oolitic Limestone
        keyshistory.org

P 285   Blue Hole
        florida-keys-vacation.com
        wikipedia.org
        keyshistory.org

P 285   Key Deer
        floridakeys.com
        discoveringfloridskeys.com
        gorp.com
        Keith, June
        *Key West &
        the Florida* Keys.
        Key West, Florida:
        Palm Island Press, 2005.

P 289   Brown Pelicans &
        fossil records
        wikepedia.org
        forida-outdoors.com

P 292   naval air station
        (Boca Chica)
        wikepedia.org

P 292   Hawkeye aircraft
        wikepedia.org

About the author:

In 1967, while serving in the U.S. Army in Korea, Bob spent much of his spare time walking mountain trails. After being discharged from the U.S. Army in January 1968 Bob became interested in serious hiking. He completed his first solo hike in the Smokey Mountains National Park from the lower elevations to the very top on the Appalachian Trail.

In 1969, Bob read a book by the "bard of hiking and hiking stories", Colin Fletcher who hiked across California, north to south. From this great story he gets the idea to be the first one to hike across his own state of Florida.

Hence this book, *A Walk Across Florida*.

In 1971 he took a three month, around the west trip in his especially prepared 1957/58 self-contained Ford Ranchero visiting: Texas, Colorado, Wyoming, Montana, Idaho, Washington, Oregon, California, Arizona, New Mexico and back to Texas. All solo hiking trips:

State	Major Hiking Areas	Days
1. Colorado	Chicago Basin, San Juan National forest, high country.	7
2. Colorado	Rocky Mountain National Park, high country.	5
3. Washington	Around Mount Rainier at 8-10,000ft. Elevation.	7
4. Oregon	Crater Lake National Park, around entire lake.	1
5. California	Mount Whitney area, John Muir trail, lower elevation.	3
6. Arizona	Grand Canyon National Park, South Rim to North Rim and return.	5
7. Texas	Big Bend National Park, Chisos Mountain down onto the desert below and then up through the window trail.	5

In 1972 Bob decided that the United States needed a backpacking magazine. He started the "American Hiker" publication in mid-June of that year with a part-time volunteer staff of seven persons. He did all of the layout and design. First bi-monthly issue in October, fourth and last issue in June of 1973 after the depletion of his funds.

In 1974 Bob built and started a country inn, (B & B) Folkstone Lodge, in the Smokey Mountains, one mile from the National Park, Deep Creek Campground near Bryson City, North Carolina. Besides building and running the inn, Bob outfitted and guided visitors to his inn on backpacking trips in the Park.

Today Bob lives 10 miles north of the Shenandoah National Park, works in a mechanical engineering field, writes his books and builds wood projects in his shop. He is happily married to his wife, Joanne, has five children, two by birth and three by marriage, and five grandchildren two by birth and three by marriage. That is enough to keep one busy!

Happy hiking,
Bob
bobkranich.com

www.ingramcontent.com/pod-product-compliance
Lightning Source LLC
Chambersburg PA
CBHW040320300426
44112CB00020B/2821